# Complete English as a Foreign Language

## Sandra Stevens

Assistant author
Bismarck Vallecillo

Language consultant
John Shepheard

For UK order enquiries: please contact Bookpoint Ltd,
130 Milton Park, Abingdon, Oxon OX14 4SB.
*Telephone:* +44 (0) 1235 827720. *Fax:* +44 (0) 1235 400454.
Lines are open 09.00–17.00, Monday to Saturday, with a 24-hour
message answering service. Details about our titles and how to
order are available at www.teachyourself.com

For USA order enquiries: please contact McGraw-Hill Customer
Services, PO Box 545, Blacklick, OH 43004-0545, USA.
*Telephone:* 1-800-722-4726. *Fax:* 1-614-755-5645.

For Canada order enquiries: please contact McGraw-Hill
Ryerson Ltd, 300 Water St, Whitby, Ontario L1N 9B6, Canada.
*Telephone:* 905 430 5000. *Fax:* 905 430 5020.

Long renowned as the authoritative source for self-guided
learning – with more than 50 million copies sold worldwide –
the *Teach Yourself* series includes over 500 titles in the fields of
languages, crafts, hobbies, business, computing and education.

British Library Cataloguing in Publication Data: a catalogue record
for this title is available from the British Library.

Library of Congress Catalog Card Number: on file.

First published in UK 2001 as Teach Yourself English as a Foreign
Language by Hodder Education, part of Hachette UK,
338 Euston Road, London NW1 3BH.

First published in US 2001 by The McGraw-Hill Companies, Inc.

This edition published 2010.

The *Teach Yourself* name is a registered trade mark of Hachette UK.

Typeset by MPS Limited, A Macmillan Company.

Printed in Great Britain for Hodder Education, an Hachette UK
Company, 338 Euston Road, London NW1 3BH.

The publisher has used its best endeavours to ensure that the URLs
for external websites referred to in this book are correct and active
at the time of going to press. However, the publisher and the
author have no responsibility for the websites and can make no
guarantee that a site will remain live or that the content will remain
relevant, decent or appropriate.

Hachette UK's policy is to use papers that are natural, renewable
and recyclable products and made from wood grown in sustainable
forests. The logging and manufacturing processes are expected to
conform to the environmental regulations of the country of origin.

Impression number     10 9 8 7 6 5 4 3 2 1
Year                  2014 2013 2012 2011 2010

# Acknowledgements

The author and publisher would like to thank the following for their kind permission to use their copyrighted material in this book:

The Royal Scot is now a Travelodge (p. 365)

London Underground (p. 245)

# Credits

**Front cover:** © RTimages/Alamy

**Back cover and pack:** © Jakub Semeniuk/iStockphoto.com, © Royalty-Free/Corbis, © agencyby/iStockphoto.com, © Andy Cook/iStockphoto.com, © Christopher Ewing/iStockphoto.com, © zebicho – Fotolia.com, © Geoffrey Holman/iStockphoto.com, © Photodisc/Getty Images, © James C. Pruitt/iStockphoto.com, © Mohamed Saber – Fotolia.com

**Pack:** © Stockbyte/Getty Images

# Meet the author

I have worked in English as a foreign language for many years, as a teacher, teacher trainer, trainer of trainers, materials writer and consultant. Places of work have included the UK, France, Spain and Nicaragua with the British Council, Ministries of Education and private language schools. I have also made working trips to other countries, including Argentina, Hong Kong, Italy, Kuwait, Mexico, Poland and Uruguay.

Before becoming a teacher of English as a foreign language, I was an interpreter/translator (English/French) and a teacher of French. I have taught myself Spanish and have an understanding of German.

My current work includes specialist 1:1 teaching, e.g. pronunciation, communicative grammar and writing skills, together with design, materials development and management of projects for both learners and teachers of English.

Having lived and worked in a number of countries and taught students from many parts of the world, I have developed a practical knowledge of ways in which culture (the unwritten rules, beliefs and behaviours of a society) can influence international communication. As a result of this, linguistic and cultural mentoring have become a part of my current professional activities.

*Sandra Stevens*

# Contents

understanding travel information –
the time, timetables, itineraries
**Vocabulary**: public transport; the time
**Pronunciation**: stress – place names

**Grammar and communication**: impersonal *it*;
asking for opinions – *how was?*; adjectives +
*-ed* and *-ing*; saying *thank you*; obligation
and necessity – *have to*; the imperative;
offering, rejecting, insisting, accepting;
introducing something negative politely
**Vocabulary**: public signs; large numbers
**Pronunciation**: intonation – expressing
strong feelings

**Grammar and communication**: asking *Who?*
+ short answers; talking about the number
of people; talking about the same thing –
*one*, *ones*; asking for an alternative;
negative comparisons; decisions – buying
things; verb *hope*; talking about the past –
past simple; past experience – present perfect
**Vocabulary**: hotel language; ordinal numbers
**Pronunciation**: *schwa /ə/*

# *Only got a minute?*

Do you want to learn more English? English has been the language of international communication for many years now. This trend to use English for business, science, sport, home entertainment, tourism and many other purposes has grown and grown. More recently, the development of technology has led to English being used internationally even more. There is a lot of talk about globalization, at least partly driven by modern technology. This global sharing and constant exchange between individuals and countries often happens in English when there isn't a common language. This means that learning English has become an important tool, in order to be more employable, to have access to up-to-date information, to travel with ease, to have access to modern technology and to have the opportunity to share ourselves with the rest of the world for whatever purpose, as an individual, a member of an organization, or as a country.

Many years ago English used to be taught with what we now call 'old fashioned methods'. This meant learning a lot of grammar and words. The only model, in terms of experience of the language, was the teacher. The listening facilities in the classroom were very poor or simply non-existent and there was little or no speaking practice. Some people say it was laborious, tedious and even boring. Learning English, like modern technology, has developed, in some ways, beyond recognition. Modern methods are based on communication so developing language skills, e.g. listening and speaking, is just as important as learning grammar and vocabulary. In addition, wherever you live, you can have much more access to English in your everyday life through television, radio and the Internet – this can help you learn.

Whether you are a 'false beginner' or know quite a lot of the language already, *Complete English as a Foreign Language* will help you feel confident to use your English in everyday situations. We hope you enjoy your learning journey.

# 5 Only got five minutes?

The English language has developed into what we call Modern English over many centuries. It is known that English together with Dutch, German, Norwegian, Danish, Swedish, and Icelandic, etc., belongs to a group of languages called Germanic. As expected, therefore, speakers of these languages find it relatively easy to learn another language of the same family. In addition to this Germanic base, over the centuries the English language has had a number of other contributions. One of the earliest, well-known important influences is from the Romans, even before the Anglo-Saxons arrived. English was also greatly influenced by the Norman Conquest of 1066, which was followed by a number of significant changes in the various spheres of life in the British Isles, including French becoming the language of the ruling classes. Other influences have included Greek, which was mainly used to introduce scientific ideas. Modern English is consequently a big mixture of languages in terms of its grammar, vocabulary and pronunciation.

The teaching and learning of English have also had their own developments through the decades. As the need to communicate has grown so has the need to have a reliable tool to do this. The English language has become the international means of communication, so nowadays there are millions of people of all ages all over the world learning English.

As far as how to learn English is concerned, one of the earlier approaches used was the Grammar/Translation method. This was based on developing the skills of translating in and out of the target language, alongside the grammar component, consisting of grammar rules which learners applied to collections of unconnected sentences. Books consisted of grammar explanations and written grammar transformation exercises. The realization that speaking skills weren't developed with this method led to a new way of teaching called 'the audio-lingual approach'. This was based on behaviourism and consisted of oral stimulus/response between learners and teachers. It was at this point that reel to reel recordings were introduced in some classrooms as an aid to the teacher, thus giving students the opportunity to hear conversations in English for the first time.

The above method also gave rise to the use of pictures. This was in response to the realization that language does not happen in isolation but that it is influenced by the context – in other words, the place, the gender, age and relationship between the speakers and the purpose of or reason for the conversation. At this point, it was felt that knowledge of grammar and vocabulary in themselves did not enable a learner to participate in a wide range of situations. In other words, it became clear that grammar and vocabulary alone were not enough to communicate well. This realization, together with the analysis of the language used in these situations, led to the introduction of a different type of learning syllabus, based on the communication needs of the speaker e.g. inviting, suggesting, offering. These reasons for speaking are called 'communicative functions'. In modern teaching, the aim is to combine the grammar syllabus and the functional syllabus.

Alongside the development of teaching approaches came both the birth of exams to certify the level of learners' English and the professionalization of qualifications for teachers. The main examination boards offering English as a Foreign Language Examinations are the University of Cambridge and Trinity. The Cambridge Proficiency (top level) exam was the first level offered. This reflected a previous belief that in order to be able to use a language competently, the learner had to reach a very high level. As ideas began to change and it became clear that learners were increasingly wanting to acquire English as an extra tool to their profession, job or other area of interest in their lives, the First Certificate in English, an exam at upper intermediate level, was introduced. As the popularity of English continued to spread and learners needed a wider range of exams to certify their level, the number of boards offering exams in English and the number of exams available grew rapidly. Once the testing of general English was fully established, exams in specific areas of the language began to be introduced. Currently there are exams in Business English, Financial and Legal English but by far the most popular of the specialist exams is IELTS (the International English Language Testing System). This exam tests the English level of students wishing to apply for university courses taught in the medium of English and is currently taken by approximately 1 million people worldwide per year.

As we have seen, students' English language learning needs have steadily grown in scope and complexity. These days, reasons for learning the language range, for example, from doctors who need to keep up to date with the latest medical developments through reading in English, to taxi drivers working in an international setting to a tourist coming on a short visit to the UK wanting to learn just a few phrases for the trip. These diverse learning needs have led, in more recent years, to an explosion in the amount of materials available to learners of English, both in the form of books and also on TV, radio and from the Internet.

Where do you go to find the type of English that you want to learn? If you want to learn social English *Complete English as a Foreign Language* is the right course for you. So what makes *Complete English as a Foreign Language* special? This course is based on verbal communication – you will learn the English you need to feel comfortable and confident in your understanding and speaking in everyday situations. We hope you will enjoy learning with this course, will make good progress and that it will help you be where you want to be with your English.

Welcome to *Complete English as a Foreign Language*!

# Introduction

***What is 'Complete English as a Foreign Language'?***

A complete self-access course to learn English without a teacher.

***Who is 'Complete English as a Foreign Language' for?***

This course is for adult learners who want to understand and speak English with confidence.

***How much English do I need to use this book?***

You can follow this course with very basic English.

If you know a lot of English, this book teaches you how to use the language in real, everyday situations.

***What is different about this book?***

It is a real self-access course. We use a new method, devised especially for learners without a teacher.

***How does this new method work?***

The 'learn alone method' is carefully organized, step by step to help you *understand* and *use* new language.

- ▶ First, you listen to a conversation. The course follows a story, so you know the characters and the situation. Questions help you understand the conversation.
- ▶ Then you listen for some of the words and expressions they use in the conversation.

▶ Next we look at this new language (grammar, functions, vocabulary and pronunciation). The explanations are in clear, simple English.

▶ Finally, you practise the new language in lots of different situations.

### What is special about this course?

▶ You learn English in English.

▶ The course is flexible. You decide where, when and how long you study. Each exercise has a complete title, so you can stop and start at any time. We recommend that you study little and often. Some people find it fun and helpful to work with a friend.

▶ The focus of the course is communication. You learn some grammar and you also learn how to do things in English, for example, *ask for information, offer to do something, accept or reject an invitation, make a suggestion* etc. This book also teaches 'the little things', for example how to attract attention. These 'little things' help learners feel more confident with their English.

▶ It teaches you how British people communicate their feelings and attitudes through language, stress and intonation.

▶ It teaches you about British life, habits and customs.

▶ It prepares you to talk about yourself, your life, your family, your work or studies and your country.

▶ After every practice exercise, we give you the answers. You can check your progress immediately.

### What is the structure of this course?

The complete course consists of this course book and two CDs with all the listening and pronunciation material.

It is important to have the CDs, if possible:

▶ They give you practice in listening and understanding.

▶ They are also a model for pronunciation.

▶ They include the guided pronunciation exercises.

All the material on the CDs is in grey ▓▓▓▓.

## *What is in this book?*

This course book contains ten topic areas and a reference section.

Each topic area starts with a list of the important new language points in that topic. There are four main sections in each topic:

### 1 Understanding new language

**Understanding the important information** Listening to a conversation and understanding the key points.

**Understanding more** Listening again and understanding more details.

**What do they say?** Listening for some of the words and phrases they use. These are the important grammar points.

**Find the words and phrases** Listening/reading for useful words and expressions.

**How do you pronounce it?** Listening (for pronunciation) and practice.

**What's the right word?** Vocabulary and dictionary exercises on the topic.

### 2 Using the new language

**Using these words and phrases** Practising some words and expressions from 'Find the words and phrases' above.

**Grammar and communication** Explanations and lots of practice from 'What do they say?' above. These are the main language points in the topic.

## Insights

These are the most important learning points in the course.

This information is often with *, sometimes it is in the form of Q and A, (questions that learners of English often ask, with answers). It can also be part of a 'Common Mistake' section (advice on problem spots for learners) or extra information in 'Check your answers' after an exercise.

**British culture**
Information about British life, customs and habits.

**About you, your family and your country** You talk about the topic in relation to you, your life and your country.

**What would you say?** We give you some practice in unusual situations.

### 3 Revision

**Join the conversation** Another look at the first conversation in the topic. This time you participate.

**Translation** You translate into your language some examples of the main language points.

### 4 Test

There is a test at the end of each topic for you to check your progress.

Each test has two parts. In the first part, each question asks you to choose the correct or better option of two possibilities and in the second part you write one side of a guided dialogue.

## 5 Reference section

The reference section at the back of the book has four sections:

**1** A **glossary** The first time we use a grammar term it is in *italics*, with a short definition in brackets ( ). In the glossary we give full definitions, with more examples, of these grammar terms.

**2** A **quick reference section of phrases** for communication. This is in alphabetical order, to help you find words and expressions quickly.

**3** A quick reference section of English grammar. This gives clear explanations and examples of the main points of English grammar.

**4** A complete **index** With the help of the index, you can find a specific exercise quickly. This is particularly useful for teachers.

*I study English in a school. Is this book useful for me?*

Yes, you can use this course at the same time as other books, for extra practice. The Insights can be used for revision.

*I'm a business person. Can this book help me?*

Yes. This book emphasizes social competence in English in a variety of situations.

*I want to travel. Is this book useful?*

Yes. This book gives lots of practice in the language you need, for example, to order food and drink, find a hotel and use public transport.

*I'm an English teacher. How can I use this book?*

▶ For reference
▶ As a course book

▶ As supplementary material
▶ The recorded material as a listening course
▶ For homework
▶ The grammar
    functions
    pronunciation ⎫ syllabus and exercises can be used alone
    vocabulary ⎭ or in the combination you choose
▶ The **Common mistake** exercises can help with persistent problem areas
▶ The **You, your family and your country** sections can be used for personalization
▶ The **British culture** sections can be starting points for comparisons with customs and habits in students' own countries/fluency work
▶ The **tests** can be used independently

# 1

# Saying 'hello'

Grammar and communication
- **Starting a conversation – question tags**
- **Continuing a conversation – short answers**
- **Continuing a conversation – saying more**
- **Invitations and offers –** *would you like…?*
- **A/some – countables and uncountables**
- **Offering more – food and drink**
- **Saying** yes and no **to offers**

Vocabulary
- **Food and drink**

Pronunciation
- **Introduction to intonation**

*Our story begins on a plane...*

## The first conversation

→ If you have the CD, cover the text of Recording 1, *The Story*.
→ Read the sentences below.
→ Listen to the conversation 1, 2 or 3 times.
→ If you don't have the CD, read the text of the recording.
→ Choose the correct answer a, b or c.

**1** It's $\left.\begin{array}{l}\textbf{a} \text{ cold} \\ \textbf{b} \text{ sunny} \\ \textbf{c} \text{ hot}\end{array}\right\}$ in the plane.

**2** The conversation is about
    **a** London.
    **b** a drink.
    **c** dinner.

**3** The woman would like
    **a** some Coke.
    **b** to sleep.
    **c** to eat.

### Recording 1 (and 8) – The Story

🔊 **CD1 TR 1, 00:28**

| | |
|---|---|
| **Man** | It's hot, isn't it? |
| **Woman** | Yes, it is – very hot. |
| **Man** | Would you like a drink? |
| **Woman** | M'm, yes, please. |
| **Man** | What would you like? |
| **Woman** | Some Coke, please. |

**Check your answers**
**1** c  **2** b  **3** a

## What do they say?

→ Cover the text of Recording 1 again.
→ Read the sentences below.
→ First listen and complete the words.
→ Then read the text of the recording to help you.

**1 a** The man starts the conversation.
He says, 'I _'s / h _ _ /, i _ n' _ / i _ ?'
**b** The woman answers,
'Y _ _, i _ / i _ / – / v _ _ _ / h _ _ .'

**2 a** The man offers a drink.
He says, 'W _ _ _ d / y _ _ / l _ k _ / a / d _ _ _ k?'
**b** The woman accepts.
She says, 'Y _ _ / p _ _ _ s _.'

**3 a** The man asks what drinks she wants.
He says, 'W _ _ _ / w _ _ _ _ / you / l _ _ _ ?'
**b** The woman answers,
'So _ e / C _ k _ /, p _ _ _ _ e.'

**Check your answers**

**1 a** It's hot, isn't it? **b** Yes, it is – very hot.
**2 a** Would you like a drink? **b** Yes, please.
**3 a** What would you like? **b** Some Coke, please.

## English pronunciation

### Insight 1

**Intonation**

★ Intonation is very important in English. What is intonation? The *music* or movement of our voice. Sometimes our voice goes up ➚ (a rise) – sometimes our voice goes down ➘ (a fall). This is **intonation**.

*(Contd)*

★ Different languages express things in different ways. English uses intonation a lot for communication. A different intonation gives a different message. Is intonation important in your language? This book explains and gives practice in understanding and using intonation in English.

## Intonation and grammar – questions

Listen to Recording 2, part 1 and repeat the words. (a rises and b falls)

### Recording 2, part 1

🔊 **CD1 TR 1, 00:50**

| | | | |
|---|---|---|---|
| **1 a** Yes? | **b** Yes. | **4 a** OK? | **b** OK. |
| **2 a** This? | **b** This | **5 a** Alright? | **b** Alright. |
| **3 a** No? | **b** No. | **6 a** Sorry? | **b** Sorry. |

*Q Is there a pattern here?*
*A* Yes. In general, a rise is a question. (Some questions go down. See Topic 3.)

*Q Where exactly is this rise or fall?*
*A* On the syllable with stress or emphasis. (A syllable is a word or part of a word with a vowel sound.)

## Intonation and feelings – voice movement

★ In English we use intonation to express **attitude**
(our feelings).
★ In general, big voice movements express strong feelings.
★ Flat intonation expresses that you are not interested or that your attitude is **negative**.

→ Listen to Recording 2, part 2, and repeat the words. (**a** big movements = positive and interested, **b** small movements = not very positive, not interested, negative.)

**Recording 2, part 2**

🔊 **CD1 TR 1, 02:01**

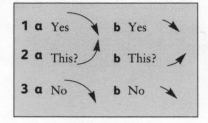

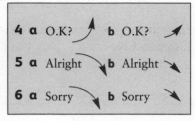

---

## Find the right word

### Drinks

→ Find seven drinks in this word search. The words go across →
and down ↓.

→ Use the pictures and your dictionary if necessary.

| o | w | r | m | c | s | z |
|---|---|---|---|---|---|---|
| s | i | j | b | o | g | w |
| v | n | e | n | f | o | a |
| y | e | m | w | f | a | t |
| j | u | i | c | e | t | e |
| l | a | l | b | e | e | r |
| c | o | k | e | r | a | p |

| o | w | r | m | c | s | z |
|---|---|---|---|---|---|---|
| s | i | j | b | o | g | w |
| v | n | e | n | f | o | a |
| y | e | m | w | f | a | t |
| j | u | i | c | e | t | e |
| l | a | l | b | e | e | r |
| c | o | k | e | r | a | p |

---

## Grammar and communication 1

### Starting a conversation – question tags

**Example from *The Story*:**

The man starts the conversation. He says, 'It's hot, **isn't it?**'

## Insight 2

*Q What is 'isn't it?'*
*A* It's a question tag.

★ Question tags are very common in English.

*Q What are question tags?*
*A* Question tags are short questions at the end of a sentence.

### Meaning
*Q Is this a real question?*
*A* No. The man knows it's hot. The falling intonation also tells us it's not a real question. Here, the question tag starts a conversation.

### Form
★ We use the same tense in the main verb and the question tag.
★ With a **positive main verb**, we use a **negative question tag**.
  With a **negative main verb**, we use a **positive question tag**.

## Grammar summary – Question tags with verb *be*

| Positive verb + negative tag | | | Negative verb + positive tag | | |
|---|---|---|---|---|---|
| I am right, | aren't I? | | I'm not wrong, | am I? | |
| He<br>She is } English,<br>It | isn't | { he?<br>she?<br>it? | He<br>She } isn't English,<br>It | is | { he?<br>she?<br>it? |
| We<br>You } are happy,<br>They | aren't | { we?<br>you?<br>they? | We<br>You } aren't happy,<br>They | are | { we?<br>you?<br>they? |

## Insight 3

*Q And if there isn't a verb?*

*A* That depends. Here are some examples.

| Positive | Negative |
|---|---|
| 'It's good, isn't it? | It's not very good, is it? |
| or | or |
| 'Good, isn't it? (Informal) | Not very good, is it? (Informal) |

With an **adjective** we use a **negative question tag**. With '*not*' + adjective, we use a **positive question tag**.

★ In informal spoken English, it is possible to start with the adjective. For example, 'It's interesting, isn't it?' is correct and always appropriate. 'Interesting, isn't it?' is correct and informal.

## British culture – the weather

▶ In Britain it is very common to talk about the weather. Why? Because the weather can change a lot.
▶ People often use the weather to start a conversation.

### Question tags with falling intonation

→ Complete with the correct question tag.

1 It's really cold today, _____/_____?
2 Nice and warm this morning, _____/_____?
3 The weather's not bad today, _____/_____?
4 Lovely day, _____/_____?

**Check your answers** (*Recording 3*)
◆ **CD1 TR 1, 3:54**

> 1 It's really cold today, <u>isn't it?</u>
> 2 Nice and warm this morning, <u>isn't it?</u>
> 3 The weather's not bad today, <u>is it?</u>
> 4 Lovely day, <u>isn't it?</u>

## How do you pronounce it?

### Starting a conversation

→ Listen to Recording 3 above and start these conversations. Pay special attention to the falling intonation on the question tag.

### Question tags with falling intonation

→ Match the pictures (1–9) below with the correct sentence **a–i** and complete the question tags.

a  It's a very good film, _____ ?
b  You're David, _____ ? My name's Sam.
c  This food's very nice, _____ ?
d  This programme's not very interesting, _____ ?
e  She's beautiful, _____ ?
f  This isn't right, _____ ?
g  It's not very warm in here, _____ ?
h  They're lovely, _____ ?
i  He's a good singer, _____ ?

**Check your answers** (*Recording 4*)
◄) **CD1 TR 1, 04:57**

| | | |
|---|---|---|
| 1 | d | This programme's not very interesting, is it? |
| 2 | g | It's not very warm in here, is it? |
| 3 | a | It's a very good film, isn't it? |
| 4 | b | You're David, aren't you? My name's Sam. |
| 5 | h | They're lovely, aren't they? |
| 6 | i | He's a good singer, isn't he? |
| 7 | e | She's beautiful, isn't she? |
| 8 | c | The food's very nice, isn't it? |
| 9 | f | This isn't right, is it? |

**More pronunciation practice**

→ Listen to Recording 4 above and start these conversations. Pay special attention to the falling intonation on the question tags.

---

## Grammar and communication 2

### Continuing a conversation – short answers

**Example from *The Story*:**

Man: 'It's hot, isn't it?'   Woman: 'Yes, it is – very hot.'
*Yes, it is* is a short answer.

**Meaning**

The woman wants to continue the conversation.

**Form**

Man: 'It's hot, isn't it?'    Woman: 'Yes, it is – very hot.'
Here's a different example:

Man: 'It's not very nice, is it?'    Woman: 'No, it isn't.'

## Insight 4
### Short answers

*Q Can I just say 'Yes'?*
*A* Yes and No alone can sound impolite. ☹

It can mean you are not interested in the conversation.

*Q The negative has two forms 'No, it isn't' and 'No, it's not'.*
*Are they different?*
*A* No, they are the same.

## Insight 5
### Common mistake – short answers

'It's hot, isn't it?'

**'Yes, it is.'** (Not: 'Yes, it's')

'It's' is the **contraction** (short form) of 'it is'. It is not possible
to end a sentence with a positive contraction.

And in the negative?

'It isn't very hot, is it?'

**'No, it isn't.'**

This is correct. It is possible to end a sentence with a negative contraction.

### Short answers

→ Complete the short answers with expressions from the box below.

**Example:** They aren't here, are they?     *No, they aren't.*
**1** He's not there, is he?          No, _____
**2** She's pretty, isn't she?        Yes, _____
**3** This isn't difficult, is it?    No, _____
**4** We're ready, aren't we?         Yes, _____
**5** You're Paul, aren't you?        Yes, _____
**6** They're in France, aren't they? No, _____

*I am    he isn't    it isn't    they aren't    she is    we are*

---

## Grammar and communication 3

## Insight 6
### Continuing a conversation – saying more

★ It is very common to say more after short answers.

→ Look at these responses:

**A** Nice weather, isn't it?
**B** Yes it is,     OR    Yes, lovely.
              OR    Yes, it's lovely.
              OR    Yes, it is. It's lovely.
              OR    Yes, it is, isn't it?

→ Here are the sentences from Recording 4 (page 9) again.
→ This time match sentences 1–9 with responses a–i and complete the responses.

**Response**

**1** It's a very good film, isn't it? **f**   **a**   Yes _____. They're beautiful.

**2** You're David, aren't you? ☐   **b**   Yes,_____. It's delicious.

**3** The food's very nice, isn't it? ☐   **c**   No,_____. Not at all.

**4** This programme's not very interesting, is it? ☐   **d**   Yes,_____. I like him a lot.

**5** She's beautiful, isn't she? ☐   **e**   Yes, _____. She's wonderful.

**6** This isn't right, is it? ☐   **f**   Yes, *it is*. It's excellent.

**7** It's not very warm in here, is it? ☐   **g**   No,_____. You're not too good at maths, are you?

**8** They're lovely, aren't they? ☐   **h**   Yes, that's right_____. And your name is …?

**9** He's a good singer, isn't he? ☐   **i**   No, _____. The window's open.

**Check your answers**

**1** f Yes, it is. **2** h I am. **3** b Yes, it is. **4** c No, it isn't. **5** e Yes, she is.
**6** g No, it isn't. or No, it's not. **7** i No, it isn't. or No, it's not.
**8** a Yes, they are. **9** d Yes he is.

---

## Grammar and communication 4

### Invitations and offers – food and drink

**Example from *The Story*:**

The man suggests a drink.
He says, 'Would you like a drink?'

→ Listen to Recording 5 and practise your pronunciation and intonation.

### Recording 5

🔊 **CD1 TR 1, 06:36**

> Would you like a drink?
>
> W...
>
> Would...
>
> Would you...
>
> Would you like...
>
> Would you like a...
>
> Would you like a <u>drink</u>?

## What's the right word?

**Food**

→ Label these pictures. Use your dictionary if necessary.

**Check your answers**

rice     crisps     sandwich     bread

biscuits     grapes     soup     hamburger

---

## Grammar and communication 5

### 'A'/'Some'

The man offers a drink. He says, 'Would you like a drink?'

The woman wants Coke. She says, 'Yes, **some** Coke please.'

→ Look at these examples:

| | | |
|---|---|---|
| Would you like **a** sandwich? | **a** sandwich | *singular* (one) |
| Would you like **some** crisps? | **some** crisps | *plural* (more than one) |
| Would you like **some** bread? | **some** bread | *uncountable* (can't count it) |

> ## Insight 7
> ★ '*A*' is for singular things, for example, a hamburger, a biscuit.
> ★ '*Some*' is for plural things, for example, some grapes, some biscuits, and things we can't count, for example, some soup, some rice.

## A or some?

→ Write 1–10 next to the correct picture.

**1** an ice cream
**2** some ice cream
**3** some ice creams
**4** a cake
**5** some cake
**6** some cakes
**7** a chocolate
**8** some chocolate
**9** some chocolates
**10** a pizza
**11** some pizza
**12** a Coke
**13** some Coke

## Check your answers

a chocolate

some cakes

some Coke

some cake

some ice creams

some chocolates

some pizza

some chocolate

a pizza

some ice cream

an ice cream

a Coke

a cake

→ Now write invitations for these pictures.

**1 Example:** *Would you like a hamburger?*

2

4 3

5

6

7

8

_____
_____
_____
_____
_____
_____

**Check your answers** (*Recording 6*)
◄) **CD1 TR 1, 07:09**

| | |
|---|---|
| **1** | Would you like a hamburger? |
| **2** | Would you like some bread? |
| **3** | Would you like some soup? |
| **4** | Would you like a sandwich? |
| **5** | Would you like some grapes? |
| **6** | Would you like a biscuit? |
| **7** | Would you like some crisps? |
| **8** | Would you like some rice? |

→ Listen to the exercise above on Recording 6 and repeat the questions.

**Invitations and offers – food and drink**

## Insight 8

*Q Can I say, 'Do you want a drink?'*
A Do you want...?
★ The grammar is correct.
★ It is very informal.
★ You can sound rude. ☹

Use: Would you like…?
Say: Do you want…? only with people you know very well.

*Q Can I say 'Do you like…' for offers and invitations?*
*A* No.

*Do you like…?* is a general question about likes.

For example: **'Do you like** ice cream?' – **a general question.**
                **'Would you like** an ice cream?' – **an invitation**
                **or offer.**

---

## Grammar and communication 6

### Offering more – food and drink

→ Look at the table below.

| *First offer* | *Second offer* | |
|---|---|---|
| **A** sandwich? | **Another** sandwich? | *singular* |
| **Some** crisps ? | **(Some) more** crisps? | *plural* |
| **Some** water? | **(Some) more** water? | *uncountable* |

→ Complete these offers with '*another*' or '*more*' or '*some more*'.

**1** _____ drink?
**2** Would you like _____/_____ crisps?
**3** _____ wine?
**4** Would you like _____ biscuit?
**5** _____/_____ milk?

**Check your answers**

**1** Another drink? **2** Would you like some more crisps? **3** More wine? **4** Would you like another biscuit? **5** Some more milk?

## British culture – saying *yes* and *no* to offers

- ▶ People say *please* and *thank you* a lot in English.
- ▶ It is the norm to say *Yes, please* or *No, thank you* (or *thanks*) to offers.
- ▶ *Yes* or *no* alone can sound rude.
- ▶ *Thanks* is a little more informal than *thank you*.

## Grammar and communication 7

### Saying *yes* and *no* to offers

→ Look at these examples.

**Saying** *yes*

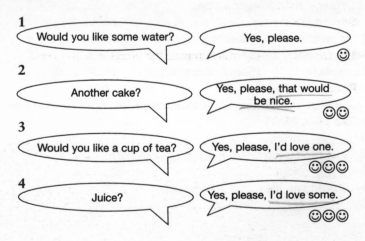

## Saying *no*

1
Would you like some ice cream? — No, thank you.

2
Some more coffee? — No, thanks. I'm fine.

## Insight 9

*Q* In an offer, for example, 'Would you like some tea?' can I answer, 'Yes, I would' or 'No, I wouldn't'?

*A* The grammar is correct but they are not appropriate answers to offers. ☹ Say, 'Yes, please' and 'No, thank you' with offers.

## How do you pronounce it?

**Offers – rising intonation**
**Saying** *yes* **and** *no*

→ Listen to Recording 7 and repeat the offers and answers.

**Recording 7**

◀ CD1 TR 1, 08:50

1    **A**    Coffee?

     **B**    Yes, please.

2    **A**    Some more tea?

     **B**    No, thanks.

*(Contd)*

**3**  **A**  Would you like another drink?

    **B**  Yes, please.

**4**  **A**  More orange-juice?

    **B**  No, no more thank you. I'm fine.

**5**  **A**  Would you like some more bread?

    **B**  Yes, please, I'd love some.

*About you – food and drink. Answer these questions.*

Are you hungry? Would you like something to eat?_____
What would you like?_____
Are you thirsty? Would you like something to drink?_____
What would you like?_____

*What would you say?*

**Situation 1**  You are in the street.
              A person says to you, 'Hello Chris.' You are not
              Chris.
              You say: _____
**Situation 2**  You are in a coffee shop.
              You want tea, your friend wants coffee.
              The waiter says to you: 'Here's your coffee and tea for
              your friend.
              You say: _____

**Possible answers**
**1** Sorry, I'm not Chris.  **2** Thanks, but the coffee's for my friend
and the tea's for me.

## Revision

### What is it in your language?

→ Here are some examples of the important points in this topic.
→ Translate the sentences below into your language in the spaces.
→ Remember – translate the idea, not the words.

**1** It's hot, isn't it?

_____

**2** Yes, it is – very hot.

_____

**3** Would you like a drink?

_____

**4** Yes, please.

_____

**5** What would you like?

_____

**6** Some Coke, please.

_____

### Join the conversation

🔊 **CD1 TR 1, 09:48**

→ Look at Recording 1 on page 2 again.
→ Listen to Recording 8.
→ Say the man's words in the spaces.

*That's the end of Topic 1.*
*Well done!*
*Now try the test.*
*There's one at the end of each topic.*

# Test yourself 1

## Which one is right?

→ Choose the correct sentence, a or b.

**1 Starting a conversation**
  **a** Nice day, is it?
  **b** Nice day, isn't it?

**2 Offering**
  **a** Would you like a drink?
  **b** Do you like a drink?

  **Saying** *yes*
  **a** Yes, I do.
  **b** Yes, please.

**3 Starting a conversation**
  **a** This food's not very hot, isn't it?
  **b** This food's not very hot, is it?

**4 Starting a conversation**
  **a** This soup are delicious.
  **b** This soup's delicious.

  **Responding**
  **a** Yes, it is, isn't it?
  **b** Yes, it's.

**5 Offering more**
  **a** Another bread?
  **b** Some more bread?

  **Saying** *no*
  **a** No thanks, I'm fine.
  **b** No.

### Write a dialogue

**Situation** You are in the street with a friend. It's cold.

| You | Your friend |
|---|---|

**1** Start the conversation

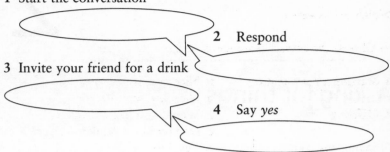

**2** Respond

**3** Invite your friend for a drink

**4** Say *yes*

*OK Let's go then*

## Check your answers
### Which one is right?

| | |
|---|---|
| **1** Starting a conversation | **b** Nice day, isn't it? |
| **2** Offering | **a** Would you like a drink? |
| Saying *yes* | **b** Yes, please. |
| **3** Starting a conversation | **b** This food's not very hot, is it? |
| **4** Starting a Conversation | **b** This soup's delicious. |
| Responding | **a** Yes, it is, isn't it? |
| **5** Offering more | **b** Some more bread? |
| Saying *no* | **a** No, thanks. I'm fine. |

### Dialogue: model answers

| | | |
|---|---|---|
| **1** | You | Cold, isn't it? |
| **2** | Your friend | Yes, it is – very cold. |
| **3** | You | Would you like a hot drink? |
| **4** | Your friend | Yes, please. |
| | | Yes please, that would be nice! |
| | | Yes please, I'd love one. |

# 2

## Asking for things

Grammar and communication
- **Responding to offers**
- **Making decisions – I'll**
- **Asking for things,** Could I have…?
- **Ordering drinks**
- **Talking about availability –** have got, there is + some/any, any
- **Opinions and comparisons,** What's … like, smaller, **etc.**
- **Asking for permission,** Is it alright if I…?

Vocabulary
- **Food and drink (2)**

Pronunciation
- **Introduction to stress**
- **Intonation and communication**

*The two passengers would like a drink…*

## Understanding the important information

→ Cover the text of Recording 1.
→ Read the sentences below.
→ Listen and answer 'Yes' or 'No'.

**1** The woman wants Coke     Yes/No
**2** The man wants water     Yes/No
**3** The woman wants ice     Yes/No
**4** The woman wants lemon     Yes/No
**5** The man wants ice     Yes/No
**6** The man wants lemon     Yes/No

### Recording 1 (and 11) – The Story

◀ CD1 TR 2, 00:13

| | |
|---|---|
| **Man** | Excuse me. |
| **Flight attendant** | Yes, sir? |
| **Man** | Could I have a Coke and some orange juice, please? |
| **Flight attendant** | Of course. Would you like the Coke with ice and lemon? |
| **Woman** | Yes please. |
| **Flight attendant** | Ice for you, sir? |
| **Man** | No thanks. |
| **Flight attendant** | Here you are. One Coke with ice and lemon and one orange juice. |
| **Man and woman** | Thank you/Thanks. |

**Check your answers**
**1** Yes **2** No. He wants orange juice **3** Yes **4** Yes **5** No **6** No

## What do they say?

→ Read the sentences below.
→ First, listen to Recording 1 and try to complete the words.
→ Then read the text to help you if necessary.

**1** The man wants the attention of the flight attendant.
He says, 'E_x_ _c_ _u_ _s_ _e_ / m _e_.'

**2** The man asks for the drinks.
He says, 'C_o_ _u_ _l_ _d_ / I / h _a_ _v_ _e_ / _a_ / Coke and / s _o_ _m_ _e_ /o _r_ a _n_ _g_
_e_ j _u_ i c _e_ /, please?'

**3** The flight attendant gives them the drinks.
He says, 'H _e_ _r_ / y _o_ _u_ / a _r_ _e_ /. O _n_ _e_ / Coke with ice and
lemon and / _o_ _n_ _e_ / orange juice.'

### Check your answers
**1** Excuse me. **2** Could I have a Coke and some orange juice,
please? **3** Here you are. One Coke with ice and lemon and one
orange juice.

### British culture – attracting attention
▸ In English, we say, *Excuse me* to attract attention.
▸ Other ways, for example, a sound like 'ts,ts,ts', are impolite.

## English pronunciation

### Insight 10
*Stress*

*Q* **What is stress?**
*A* Emphasis or accent. English has no written accents. It has
stress on some words and syllables. This book explains
and gives practice in stress.

## Word stress

*Q Where's the stress in words?*
A In words with two syllables or more, one syllable has stress.
   (*Q* What's a syllable? *A* Part of a word with a vowel sound.)

Examples from the conversation above are, 'ex<u>cuse</u>', '<u>o</u>range',
'<u>le</u>mon'.

→ Listen to the words below and <u>underline</u> the syllable with stress.

**Recording 2, part 1**

◄» **CD1 TR 2, 01:54**

> **1** syllables
> **2** examples
> **3** conversation
> **4** above
> **5** important
> **6** information

**Check your answers**
**1** <u>syl</u>lables **2** ex<u>am</u>ples **3** conver<u>sa</u>tion **4** a<u>bove</u> **5** im<u>por</u>tant
**6** infor<u>ma</u>tion

*Q Where's the stress on a word? How do I know?*
A In some dictionaries, they show stress (ˈ) at the beginning of the
   syllable. For example, *above* / əˈbʌv / v /

## Insight 11
Stress in phrases and sentences

*Q Where's the stress in phrases and sentences?*
A On the important or new information.
   For example, in *My name's Tom*, the stress is on <u>Tom</u>.

→ Listen to the phrases below and <u>underline</u> the syllable with stress.

**Recording 2, part 2**

◀) **CD1 TR 2, 01:56**

> **1** Some Coke
> **2** To London
> **3** From David
> **4** Are they here?
> **5** Does it change?
> **6** Ask them

**Check your answers**
**1** Some <u>Coke</u>. **2** To <u>Lon</u>don. **3** From <u>Da</u>vid. **4** Are they <u>here</u>?
**5** Does it <u>change</u>? **6** <u>Ask</u> them.

## Insight 12
Unstressed syllables

*Q  **What about the other syllables – the syllables without stress?***
*A*  In these little words (for example, *some*, *to*, *from*, *are*, *does*, *them*), sometimes the vowel sound changes to the first sound in the word *above*. It's the only sound with a name. It's called *schwa*. We write it like this / ə /. *Schwa* means 'weak'.

→ Listen to Recording 2, part 2 again.

How many / ə / sounds are there: 4, 5, 6, 7 or 8? Where are they?

**Check your answer**
      /ə/         /ə/    /ə/    /ə/
Seven. **1** Some Coke. **2** To London. **3** From David.
  /ə/           /ə/       /ə/
**4** Are they here? **5** Does it change? **6** Ask them.

# Insight 13
Weak forms

*Q* *Is the pronunciation of the words above, for example 'some' 'to', always the same?*

*A* No. Without stress the vowel sound is weak (*schwa*).
When the word is important, the vowel sound is strong.

*Q* *So, one word has two different pronunciations?*

*A* Yes, that's right.

→ Listen to Recording 2, part 3 and repeat the phrases with these words. In **a** the vowel is weak, in **b** the vowel is strong.

**Recording 2, part 3**

◄⬤ **CD1 TR 2, 03:00**

| | | | |
|---|---|---|---|
| **1** Some | weak | **a** | /ə/ Some <u>Coke</u> |
| | strong | **b** | Would you <u>like</u> some? |
| **2** To | weak | **a** | /ə/ to <u>London</u> |
| | strong | **b** | Where <u>to</u>? |
| **3** From | weak | **a** | /ə/ from <u>David</u> |
| | strong | **b** | Who <u>from</u>? |
| **4** Are | weak | **a** | /ə/ Are they <u>here</u>? |
| | strong | **b** | Yes, they <u>are</u>. |
| **5** Does | weak | **a** | /ə/ Does it <u>change</u>? |
| | strong | **b** | Yes, it <u>does</u>. |
| **6** Them | weak | **a** | /ə/ <u>Ask</u> them. |
| | strong | **b** | Ask <u>them</u>, not <u>me</u>. |

*Q  Is there a name for this, when one vowel has two different pronunciations?*

*A*  Yes, the weak pronunciation, / ə /, is called a weak form.

*Q  Why are weak forms important for learners of English?*

*A*  Learners often say 'I can't understand English people – they speak very fast and swallow their words'. One reason for this is weak forms. This book explains and gives practice in understanding and using weak forms.

---

## What's the right word?

**Food**

fish

chicken

beef

lamb

vegetarian

pork

→ Label the pictures with the food names.
→ Use your dictionary if necessary.

**Check your answers**
**a** beef **b** pork **c** chicken **d** fish **e** lamb **f** vegetarian

*Our story continues... the flight attendant serves dinner*

## Understanding the important information

→ On Recording 3 the flight attendant serves eight passengers.
→ Listen and tick the right answer.

| Passenger **1** | **a** chicken | **b** beef | |
|---|---|---|---|
| Passenger **2** | **a** beef | **b** vegetarian | |
| Passenger **3** | **a** fish | **b** pork | |
| Passenger **4** | **a** lamb | **b** fish | |
| Passenger **5** | **a** fish | **b** beef | |
| Passenger **6** | **a** fish | **b** beef | |
| Passenger **7** | **a** vegetarian | **b** chicken | |
| Passenger **8** | **a** fish | **b** chicken | **c** a sandwich |

### Recording 3 – The Story

◄)) **CD1 TR 2, 04:20**

| **1 Attendant** | Chicken or beef, sir? |
|---|---|
| **Passenger** | Chicken, please. |
| **2 Attendant** | Beef or vegetarian, madam? |
| **Passenger** | Beef for me, please. |
| **3 Attendant** | Would you like fish or pork, sir? |
| **Passenger** | I'd like fish, please. |

*(Contd)*

| | | |
|---|---|---|
| **4 Attendant** | What would you like to eat, madam, fish or lamb? | |
| **Passenger** | Could I have the lamb, please? | |
| **5 Attendant** | Is it fish or beef for you, madam? | |
| **Passenger** | I'll have beef, please. | |
| **6 Attendant** | And for you, sir? | |
| **Passenger** | The same for me too, please. | |
| **7 Attendant** | Would you like vegetarian or chicken, sir? | |
| **Passenger** | I don't mind. I like both. | |
| **8 Attendant** | Would you like fish or chicken, madam? | |
| **Passenger** | Nothing for me thanks. I'm not very hungry. Could I have a sandwich instead? | |
| **Attendant** | Of course. | |

**Check your answers**

**1** a chicken **2** a beef **3** a fish **4** a lamb **5** b beef **6** b beef
**7** a or b we don't know **8** c a sandwich

---

## What do they say?

### Responding to offers – food and drink

→ Cover the text of Recording 3, *The Story* again.
→ Read the questions and responses below.
→ Listen and try to complete the responses.
→ Then read the text of Recording 3 to help you if necessary.

| | | |
|---|---|---|
| **1 Attendant** | Chicken or beef, sir? | |
| **Passenger** | Chicken, / p _ _ _ _ _/. | |
| **2 Attendant** | Beef or vegetarian, madam? | |
| **Passenger** | Beef / f _ _ / m _,/ please. | |
| **3 Attendant** | Would you like fish or pork, sir? | |
| **Passenger** | I' _ / l _ _ _ / fish, please. | |
| **4 Attendant** | What would you like to eat, madam, fish or lamb? | |
| **Passenger** | C _ _ _ _ / I / h _ _ _ / the lamb, please? | |
| **5 Attendant** | Is it fish or beef for you, madam? | |
| **Passenger** | I' _ _ / h _ _ _ / beef, please. | |

**Check your answers**

**1** Chicken, please. **2** Beef for me, please. **3** I'd like fish please.
**4** Could I have the lamb, please? **5** I'll have beef, please.

→ Now listen to Recording 3, Passengers 1–5, and repeat the responses.

---

# Grammar and communication 1

### Responding to offers

→ Look at the text of Recording 3 on pages 31–2.
→ Complete the sentences below and answer the questions.

**1 Asking for the same**
In the mini-dialogues on page 32, Passenger 5 wants beef.
Passenger 6 wants beef, too.
Passenger 5 says 'I'll have beef, please.'
Passenger 6 says, 'The / same / for / me / too, please.'

**2 Verb** *mind*
The flight attendant asks Passenger 7, 'Would you like vegetarian or chicken, sir?'
He says, 'I don't mind...'

→ Choose the correct meaning below, **a**, **b** or **c**.

  **a** He wants vegetarian.
  **b** He wants chicken.
  **c** It isn't important. He likes vegetarian and chicken.

**3 Saying** *no*; **talking about alternatives**
The flight attendant asks Passenger 8, 'Would you like fish or chicken, madam?' She isn't hungry. She says, 'Nothing / for / me, thanks. I'm not very hungry. Could I have a sandwich instead?'

**Check your answers**

**1 Passenger 6** The same for me too, please. **2 c 3** Nothing for me, thanks. I'm not very hungry. Could I have a sandwich instead?

---

## Grammar and communication 2

### Making decisions – *I'll*

Example from the listening exercise on page 32:

The flight attendant asks Passenger 5, 'Is it fish or beef for you, madam? The passenger says, 'I'll have beef, please.'

..........................................................................
**Tip:** When you decide and speak, say *I'll*...
..........................................................................

→ Make decisions in these situations.

**1** Would you like Coke or fruit juice?
   I'll have fruit juice, please.

**2** Which cake would you like, fruit or chocolate?
   I'll have a slice of the chocolate one, please.

**3** It's lunch time... I think I'll have some bread and cheese.

**4** Are you tired?
   Yes, I think I'll go to bed.

**5** The supermarket is closed now. I'll / ~~go~~ tomorrow.

**Check your answers**
**1** I'll have fruit juice, please. **2** I'll have a slice of the chocolate one, please. **3** I think I'll have some bread and cheese. **4** I think I'll go to bed. **5** I'll go tomorrow.

## Insight 14
Common mistake – negative decisions

It's time to go to work but you feel terrible. You decide to stay at home.

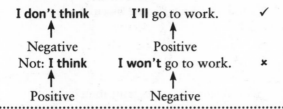

**Tip:** Put the negative with *think*, not with *I'll*.

## Grammar and communication 3

### Asking for things (requests)

**Example from *The Story*:**

Oliver asks for the drinks. He says, 'Could I have a Coke and some orange juice, please?'

In Topic 1 we look at *a/an* and *some* with offers.

For example, 'Would you like some coffee?'

## Insight 15
★ *Please* is very common when you ask for something.

→ Look at the examples below:

**Singular**

| | |
|---|---|
| Offer | Would you like **a cup** of coffee? |
| Request | Could ⎫ I have **a cup** of coffee, please? |
| | Can ⎭ |

**Plural**

| | |
|---|---|
| Offer | Would you like **some biscuits**? |
| Request | Could ⎫ I have **some biscuits**, please? |
| | Can ⎭ |

**Uncountables**

| | |
|---|---|
| Offer | Would you like **some fruit juice**? |
| Request | Could ⎫ I have **some fruit juice**, please? |
| | Can ⎭ |

## Insight 16

The use of *a/an* and *some* is the same in offers and requests.

→ Complete the requests below. Put the words in the right order.

**1 A** Would you like a drink?
  **B** Yes, _____, please?
    have/I/coffee/some/could

**2 A** Would you like something to eat?
  **B** Yes, _____, please?
    sandwich/have/can/I/a

**3 A** What would you like to drink?
  **B** _____, please?
    have/something/we/can/cold

**4 A** Would you like some pizza?
  **B** Yes, _____, please?
    slice/have/I/could/small/a

**5** Excuse me, _____, please?
   a/water/I/glass/could/have/of
**6 A** Would you like some grapes or some strawberries?
   **B** _____, please?
   grapes/could/have/I/some

**Check your answers**
**1** Could I have some coffee, please? **2** Yes, can I have a sandwich,
please? **3** Can we have something cold, please? **4** Could I have
a small slice, please? **5** Excuse me, could I have a glass of water,
please? **6** Could I have some grapes, please?

# Insight 17

Flight attendants and other people who work with food and
drink don't always say *some*. They say 'Tea?', 'Chicken?',
'Fish or beef?', etc. for offers. This is practical and short.

---

## How do you pronounce it?

# Insight 18

### Requests – intonation

★ Intonation is important with requests.
★ A big fall sounds polite.
★ Flat intonation can sound rude.

→ Listen to the requests on Recording 4. You will hear each one
  twice.
→ Listen to the fall on the syllable with stress. One is rude (flat
  intonation) and one is polite (big fall).
→ Circle 'R' for rude (flat intonation) ➘ or 'P' for polite (big
  fall). ➘

### Recording 4

◀)) **CD1 TR 2, 05:39**

> **A** Could I have some <u>cof</u>fee, please?
>    1 R/P                    2 R/P
> **B** Yes, can I have a <u>sand</u>wich, please?
>    1 R/P                    2 R/P
> **C** Can we have something <u>cold</u>, please?
>    1 R/P                    2 R/P
> **D** Could I have a <u>small</u> piece, please?
>    1 R/P                    2 R/P
> **E** Excuse me, could I have a glass of <u>water</u>, please?
>    1 R/P                    2 R/P
> **F** Could I have some <u>grapes</u>, please?
>    1 R/P                    2 R/P

### Check your answers

| | | |
|---|---|---|
| **A** | 1 Polite | 2 Rude |
| **B** | 1 Rude | 2 Polite |
| **C** | 1 Rude | 2 Polite |
| **D** | 1 Polite | 2 Rude |
| **E** | 1 Rude | 2 Polite |
| **F** | 1 Polite | 2 Rude |

→ Now listen to Recording 5 and repeat the request.
→ Pay special attention to the big fall on **Coke**.

### Recording 5

◀)) **CD1 TR 2, 11:23**

> Could...
> Could I...
> Could I have...
> Could I have some...
> Could I have some <u>Coke</u>...
> Could I have some <u>Coke</u>, please?

## More requests

→ Ask for the things in the pictures.

**1** Could _____, please?

**2** _____

**3** _____

**4** _____

**5** _____

**Check your answers** (*Recording 6*)
◄ CD1 TR 2, 07:24

**1** Could I have some <u>wa</u>ter, please?     (uncountable)
**2** Could I have some <u>bread</u>, please?     (uncountable)
**3** Could I have an ice <u>cream</u>, please?     (countable)
**4** Could I have another <u>sand</u>wich, please?     (countable)
**5** Could I have some more <u>cof</u>fee, please?     (uncountable)

**OR**

Could I have another cup of <u>cof</u>fee, please? (countable)

→ Now listen to Recording 6 and repeat the requests.
→ Pay special attention to the big fall on the syllables with stress.

## Grammar and communication 4

### Ordering drinks

**Situation** You work in a coffee shop.

→ On Recording 7 below, three customers are ordering drinks.
  What would they like?
→ Listen and write their orders.

Customer 1          Customer 2          Customer 3
_____          _____          _____
_____          _____          _____
                    _____

**Check your answers** (*Recording 7*)
🔊 **CD1 TR 2, 08:08**

> **1** Three coffees and one tea, please.
> **2** Could I have four Cokes, two orange juices and one hot chocolate?
> **3** We'd like two lemon teas, please.

.....................................................................
**Insight 19**
It is common to omit *cup* and *glass* when you order drinks.
.....................................................................

.....................................................................
**Insight 20**
**Asking for things**

*Q* *What's the difference between 'Could I have...?' and 'Can I have...?'*
*A* ★ The grammar in both is correct.
   ★ *Could I...?* is always appropriate.
   ★ *Can I...?* is a little informal.

'*Give me...*' The imperative can be impolite. Use it only in informal situations and with people you know well. (See Topic 9.)

*Our story continues... the flight attendant serves drinks*

## Understanding the important information

What drinks would these three passengers like?

→ Cover the text of Recording 8.
→ Listen and write the drink they would like.
→ Is it possible? Choose *Yes* or *No*.

Passenger **1** _____ Yes/No
Passenger **2** _____ Yes/No
Passenger **3** _____ Yes/No

**Recording 8**

◆) **CD1 TR 2, 08:38**

**Passenger 1**
Would you like a drink with your dinner? I've got some apple juice.
Yes, please.

**Passenger 2**
What would you like to drink with your dinner, sir?
Have you got any cold beer?
Of course... Here you are.

**Passenger 3**
Could I have some white wine, please?
I'm sorry, madam. I haven't got any more white wine. Would you like red instead?

**Check your answers**
**1** Apple juice – possible. **2** Beer – possible. **3** White wine –
impossible.

---

## Grammar and communication 5

### Talking about availability – *have got*

→ Cover the text of Recording 8 again.
→ Listen and try to complete the words below.
→ Then read the text of the recording to help you if necessary.

Passenger **1**
Flight attendant: I'_ve_ / g _ot_ / some apple juice.
Passenger **2**
H _ave_ / y _ou_ / g _ot_ / any cold beer?
Passenger **3**
Flight attendant: I h _aven'_ t / g _ot_ / any more white wine.

**Check your answers**
**1** I've got some apple juice. **2** Have you got any cold beer?
**3** I haven't got any more white wine.

### Insight 21
**Meaning**

★ *Have got* is about availability.

**Form**

| Grammar summary – *have got* | | | |
|---|---|---|---|
| **Affirmative** | | | |
| I/you/ we/they | have 've | got | a drink. |
| He/she/it | has 's | | |

**Grammar summary – *have got***

**Negative**

| I/you/ we/they | haven't | got | a drink? |
|---|---|---|---|
| He/she/it | hasn't | | |

**Question**

| Have | I/you/ we/they | got | a drink? |
|---|---|---|---|
| Has | he/she/it | | |

**Question tags** — **Short answers**

| I you we they | 've got… | haven't | I? we? you? They? | Yes, | I? you we they | Have |
|---|---|---|---|---|---|---|
| he she it | 's got … | hasn't | he? she? it? | yes, | he she it | Has |
| I you we they | haven't got… | have | I? you? we? they? | No, | I you we they | haven't |
| he she it | hasn't got… | has | he? she? it? | No, | he she it | hasn't |

→ Complete the sentences below with the correct parts of *have got*.
→ Use the table above to help you.

**1 A** What sort of drinks ***have you got?***
  **B** I' ̲v̲e̲ / g ̲o̲t̲ / water, juice, beer or wine.
**2 A** Could I have chicken, please?
  **B** I'm sorry, we h̲a̲v̲e̲n̲'̲t̲ / g̲e̲t̲ / any more chicken.
**3 A** If you're hungry, I' ̲v̲e̲ / g ̲o̲t̲ / a pizza.
  **B** H ̲a̲v̲e̲ / y ̲o̲u̲? Could I have some now, please?

**4 A** Has he got any milk for the coffee?
  **B** Yes, he has. Here it is.
**5 A** We haven't / got any bread.
  **B** Haven't / we? OK I'll go and buy some.
**6 A** I _ _ _ _ _ 't / _ _ _ chicken but I' _ _ / _ _ _ lamb.
  **B** No, thanks. Can I have a sandwich, instead, please?
**7 A** They've / got / Coke, haven't / they?
  **B** Yes, I'll ask for some.
**8 A** Why _ _ _ _ ' _ he / _ _ _ / any rice?
  **B** I don't know.

## Check your answers

  **1** I've got water, juice, beer or wine.
  **2** We haven't got any more chicken.
  **3 A** If you're hungry, I've got a pizza.
   **B** Have you? Could I have some now, please?
  **4 A** Has he got any milk for the coffee?
   **B** Yes, he has. Here it is.
  **5 A** We haven't got any bread.
   **B** Haven't we? OK I'll go and buy some.
  **6 A** I haven't got chicken but I've got lamb.
  **7 A** They've got Coke, haven't they?
  **8** Why hasn't he got any rice?

### Talking about availability – *there is/there are*

What food or drink is it – tea, lemonade, etc.?
Have they got it?

→ Listen to these six mini-dialogues on Recording 9.
→ **a** Write the food or drink, and **b** choose Yes/No/We don't know.

|   | Name of food/drink | Have they got it? |
|---|---|---|
| **1** | _____ | Yes/No/We don't know |
| **2** | _____ | Yes/No/We don't know |
| **3** | _____ | Yes/No/We don't know |
| **4** | _____ | Yes/No/We don't know |
| **5** | _____ | Yes/No/We don't know |
| **6** | _____ | Yes/No/We don't know |

**Recording 9**

**1 A** What is there to drink?
   **B** There's some beer, if you like.
**2 A** Is there any bread?
   **B** Yes, it's in the cupboard.
**3 A** There isn't any cheese!
   **B** Yes, I know. I'll get some later.
**4 A** There are some biscuits in the tin, aren't there?
   **B** I'm not sure.
**5 A** Are there any crisps?
   **B** Sorry.
**6 A** There aren't any grapes.
   **B** Yes, there are. They're in the fridge.

**Check your answers**
**1** Beer – yes. **2** Bread – yes. **3** Cheese – no. **4** Biscuits – we don't know. **5** Crisps – no. **6** Grapes – yes.

| Grammar summary – Availability – *there is, there are* | |
|---|---|
| **Affirmative**<br>There is + *singular/uncountables*<br>    's | There are + *plurals* |
| **Negative**<br>There isn't + *singular/uncountables* | There aren't + *plurals* |
| **Questions**<br>Is there? + *singular/uncountables* | Are there? + *plurals* |
| **Question tags**<br>There's…, isn't there?<br>There isn't…, is there? | **Short answers**<br>Is there…? Yes, there is<br>    No, there isn't<br>Are there…? Yes, there are<br>    No, there aren't |

# Insight 22

## 'Some'/'any' **with plurals and uncountables**

→ Look at these examples with *there is* and *have got*.
→ Pay special attention to the words *some* and *any*.

| | | |
|---|---|---|
| **Yes** | There's **some** beer | I've got **some** apple juice |
| **No** | There isn't **any** cheese | I haven't got **any** wine |
| **Question** | Is there **any** bread? | Have you got **any** cold beer? |

★ We use *some* to say yes.
★ We use *any* to say no.
★ We use *any* to ask questions.

→ Complete these sentences with *some* or *any*.

**1** I've got _____ wine but there isn't _____ beer.
**2 A** Is there _____ more pizza?
 **B** No, but there's _____ bread.
**3 A** Are there _____ hamburgers?
 **B** No, but there are _____ sandwiches.
**4 A** Have you got _____ biscuits?
 **B** No, and there isn't _____ chocolate either.
**5 A** Is there _____ soup?
 **B** Sorry, I haven't got _____ more.

**Check your answers**
**1** I've got some wine but there isn't any beer. **2 A** Is there any
more pizza? **B** No, but there's some bread. **3 A** Are there any
hamburgers? **B** No, but there are some sandwiches. **4 A** Have you
got any biscuits? **B** No, and there isn't any chocolate either.
**5 A** Is there any soup? **B** Sorry, I haven't got any more.

### Summary – offering, choosing and asking for an alternative

**Situation** You're at home with a friend. It's time to eat.

→ Put this dialogue in the correct order.
→ Use your dictionary if necessary.


_____ **A** Actually, I don't drink alcohol, so could I have some
Coke, fruit juice or something like that instead, please?

_____ **B** I really don't mind. I like all vegetables.

_I_ **C** What would you like to eat? There's chicken or I've got
some beef, too.

_____ **D** We've got some apple juice in the fridge. Could you get
it for me?

_____ **E** And would you like something to drink? I've got some
wine if you'd like some.

_____ **F** I'd like some chicken, please.

_____ **G** Of course. Here you are.

_____ **H** With peas or carrots?


## Check your answers

**1 C** What would you like to eat? There's chicken or I've got some
beef too.

**2 F** I'd like some chicken, please.

**3 H** With peas or carrots?

**4 B** I really don't mind. I like all vegetables.

**5 E** And would you like something to drink? I've got some wine if
you'd like some.

**6 A** Actually, I don't drink alcohol, so could I have some Coke,
fruit juice or something like that instead, please?

**7 D** We've got some apple juice in the fridge. Could you get it
for me?

**8 G** Of course. Here you are.


*... and the story continues... the passengers have dinner. The flight
attendant talks to a passenger*

→ Cover the text of Recording 10.
→ Read the questions on the next page.
→ Listen and choose True or False.

| | | |
|---|---|---|
| **1** | The chicken isn't good. | True/False |
| **2** | More passengers eat beef. | True/False |
| **3** | More passengers eat chicken. | True/False |
| **4** | The passenger wants to try the beef. | True/False |
| **5** | The passenger wants to try the chicken. | True/False |

### Recording 10 – The Story

**CD1 TR 2, 10:13**

| | |
|---|---|
| **Passenger** | This fish isn't very nice at all. What's the chicken like? |
| **Attendant** | I think it's very good. |
| **Passenger** | Nicer than the beef? |
| **Attendant** | I think so, but the beef is more popular. In fact, beef is always the most popular dish on the plane. |
| **Passenger** | Could I change this fish then, please? Is it alright if I have a different dinner? |
| **Attendant** | Of course. What would you like instead? |
| **Passenger** | Can I try the chicken, please, if that's OK? |

**Check your answers**

**1** False **2** True **3** False **4** False **5** True

## What do they say?

→ Cover the text of Recording 10 again.

→ Read the sentences below.

→ Listen and try to complete the words.

→ Then read the text to help you, if necessary.

**1** The passenger isn't happy with the fish.
She says, 'This fish / i _ _ ' _ / very nice/ a _ / a _ _ .'

**2** She wants an opinion about the chicken.
She says 'W _ _ _ ' s / the chicken / l _ _ _ ?'

**3** The flight attendant thinks it's very good.

The passenger asks for a comparison with the beef.
She says, 'N i _ce_r / t h a _ n / the beef?'
**4** The flight attendant thinks yes.
She says, 'I think / s o .'
**5** But the passengers eat more beef.
'Beef is m o r e / p o p u l a r than chicken. In fact beef is
t h e / m o s t / p o p u l a r dish on the plane.'
**6 a** The passenger wants to change the fish.
He says, 'C o u l d / I / change this fish then, please?'
**b** He wants to have another dinner.
He says, 'I s / i t / a l r i g h t / i f / I have a different
dinner?'
**c** He would like to try the chicken.
He says, 'C a n / I / try the chicken, please, if that's OK?'

## Check your answers
**1** This fish isn't very nice at all.
**2** What's the chicken like?
**3** Nicer than the beef?
**4** I think so.
**5** Beef is more popular than chicken. In fact beef is the most
popular dish on the plane.
**6 a** Could I change this fish then, please?
**b** Is it alright if I have a different dinner?
**c** Can I try the chicken, please, if that's OK?

---

# Grammar and communication 6

### Opinions and comparisons

**Example from *The Story* above:**

The passenger asks for an opinion about the chicken.

She says, 'What's the chicken like?'

The attendant thinks the chicken is **nicer than** the beef, but beef is **more popular** than chicken. In fact, beef is **the most popular** dish on the plane.

| **Grammar summary –** *comparisons* |
| --- |
| **Comparing two** <br> Short adjectives → *adjective* + er + than → nicer than <br> Long adjectives → more + *adjective* + than → more popular than |
| **Comparing three or more** <br> Short adjective → the + *adjective* + 'est' → the nicest <br> Long adjectives → the + most + *adjective* → the most popular |

→ Complete these sentences.
→ Use the table above to help you, if necessary.

**1 A** How big is London?
   **B** Well, it's b i gge r / t h a n New York.
**2 A** Which is the t a ll e s t building in the world?
   **B** That's the Burj Khalifa Tower in Dubai, isn't it?
**3** Which is m o r e / difficult, understanding English or speaking it?
**4** He's t h e / m o s t / interesting person I know!

**Check your answers**
**1** It's bigger than New York. **2** Which is the tallest building in the world? **3** Which is more difficult, understanding English or speaking it? **4** He's the most interesting person I know.

## Insight 23
### Common mistake

'Tea is the most popular drink in Britain.'
Not, 'Tea is the ~~more~~ popular drink in Britain.'
*To compare three or more, say *the most* or *the ...est*.

## British culture – food

▶ The most popular drinks in Britain are tea and coffee. There are lots of coffee shops.

▶ Traditional English food is meat, potatoes and vegetables, but nowadays there's a lot of international food from all over the world in the supermarkets and markets.

▶ There are normally two courses, a meat dish and a dessert.

▶ People usually eat a light lunch and a big meal in the evening.

▶ The most traditional dish is roast beef with roast potatoes (cooked in the oven) and vegetables. One of the most traditional desserts is called trifle.

▶ Beer is very popular. People often go to pubs for a drink and to talk. Pubs are typical British bars. Many pubs also have restaurants.

*About your country: Food and drink*

→ Write answers to the questions below or prepare to tell a friend.
→ Use the text above and your dictionary to help you.

**1** What is the most common drink in your country?

_____

**2** What is the most common food? Is it with rice, potatoes, pasta, etc.?

_____

**3** Talk/write about the traditional drinks and dishes in your country.

_____

**4** When is the biggest meal of the day – in the middle of the day or in the evening?

_____

# Grammar and communication 7

## Asking for permission

**Examples from *The Story*:**

The passenger wants to change the fish, have a different dinner and try the chicken.

He says, '**Could I** change this fish then, please?'
　　　'**Is it alright if I** have a different dinner?'
　　　'**Can I** try the chicken instead?'

The flight attendant responds: '**Of course.**'

Ask for permission in these situations. You are in a friend's house.

**1** You want to use the phone _____
**2** You want to use the toilet _____
**3** You want to smoke _____
**4** You want to have some more bread _____
**5** You want to watch TV _____

## Check your answers

| | | |
|---|---|---|
| **1** | | use the phone? |
| **2** | Can I | use the toilet? |
| **3** | Could I | smoke? |
| **4** | Is it alright if I | have some more bread? |
| **5** | | watch TV? |

## Saying *yes* and *no* to requests

The attendant says: 'Of course.'
Another response: 'Yes, go ahead.'

Negative responses: *I'm sorry but* + reason, for example,
'I'm sorry but my mother's on the phone at the moment.'

→ Complete these mini-dialogues.

**1 A** Is it alright if we go later?
  **B** Yes, o _ / c _ _ _ _ _ .
**2 A** Can I invite my friend?
  **B** I'm s _ _ _ _ . We've only got three tickets.
**3 A** Could I read your magazine?
  **B** Yes, g _ / a _ _ _ _.
**4 A** Is it alright if I borrow your car?
  **B** I'_ / _ _ _ _ _ . I don't think that's possible.

## Check your answers

**1** Yes, of course. **2** I'm sorry. We've only got three tickets.
**3** Yes, go ahead. **4** I'm sorry, I don't think that's possible.

### What would you say?

**Situation 1 You are a customer in a coffee shop**
  Another customer says to you, 'Excuse me, could I have two teas, please?'

**Situation 2 In a restaurant**
  You ask the waiter for chicken. Then your friend says, 'Oh the chicken here isn't very nice at all but the beef's wonderful'. Now you want beef. Talk to the waiter.

## Possible answers

**1** 'I'm sorry, I'm a customer here too.'
  Advanced alternative: 'I'm sorry but I don't work here.'
**2** 'Excuse me, could I have beef and not chicken, please?'
  Advanced alternative: 'Excuse me, would it be possible for me to have beef instead of chicken, please?'

## Revision

### What is it in your language?

→ Here are some examples of the important points in this topic.
→ Translate the sentences below into your language.
→ Remember – translate the idea, not the words.

**1 A** Excuse me, could I have some bread, please?
  **B** Of course, here you are.

_____

**2 A** Beer or wine?
  **B** I don't mind. I like both.

_____

**3 A** I've got some coffee but I haven't got any milk.
  **B** There's some milk in the fridge, isn't there?

_____

**4 A** Is it alright if I use your toilet, please?
  **B** Yes, go ahead.

_____

**5** One tea and two coffees, please.

_____

### Join the conversation

→ Look at Recording 1 (page 25) again.
→ Listen to Recording 11.

**◄) CD1 TR 2, 10:36**

→ Say the **man's** words in the spaces.

# Test yourself 2

## Which one is right?

→ Choose **a** or **b**.

**1** In a restaurant
  **a** Please, please, a Coke.
  **b** Excuse me, could I have a Coke, please?

**2** I'll make you a cup of tea
  **a** Is it alright if I have water instead, please?
  **b** Is it possible I have water in the place of tea?

**3** Would you like some white wine or red?
  **a** Red for me, please.
  **b** Red to me, please.

**4** Fruit juice or lemonade?
  **a** I don't mind.
  **b** I'm not mind.

**5 a** I think I go to the supermarket later.
  **b** I think I'll go to the supermarket later.

**6 a** Could I have some biscuits, please?
  **b** Could I have any biscuits, please?

**7 a** I haven't got some beer.
  **b** I haven't got any beer.

**8 a** There isn't any more cake, is there?
  **b** There isn't any more cake, isn't it?

**9 a** Would you like something for drink?
  **b** Would you like something to drink?

**10 a** Which test is the more difficult in the book?
  **b** Which test is the most difficult in the book?

## Write a dialogue

**Situation** You are in a restaurant with a friend. It is the end of the meal.

**1** You
Offer your friend tea or coffee

**2** Your friend wants coffee

**3** You would like coffee too.
Call the waiter and order.
You'd like some ice cream
but it's not on the menu. Ask

**4** The waiter hasn't got any
ice cream

**5** He gives you the coffee

[10 minutes later]

**6** Offer your friend more coffee

**7** Your friend says no

**8** Call the waiter and ask for the bill

[The waiter brings the bill]

**9** Check if it's possible to pay by card

**10** The waiter says yes

**Check your answers**
**Which one is right?**
**1** b **2** a **3** a **4** a **5** b **6** a **7** b **8** a **9** b **10** b

**Dialogue: model answers**

| | | |
|---|---|---|
| **1** | You | Would you like tea or coffee? |
| **2** | Friend | <u>Coffee for me, please.</u> |
| **3** | You | Excuse me, (Can/Could I have) two coffees, please? |
| | | Have you got any ice cream? |
| **4** | Waiter | No, I'm sorry, we haven't. |
| **5** | Waiter | Two coffees. |
| **6** | You | Would you like some more coffee? |
| **7** | Friend | No thanks, I'm fine. |
| **8** | You | Excuse me, can/could I have the bill, please? |
| **9** | You | <u>Is it alright if I pay by card?</u> |
| **10** | Waiter | Yes, of course. |

# 3

## Making conversation

Grammar and communication
- *Everyday activities – present simple*
- *Ability – can*
- *Expressing interest – echo questions*

Vocabulary
- *Countries, nationalities, languages*

Pronunciation
- *Intonation – 'wh' questions – expressing interest with echo questions*
- *Plurals with an extra syllable*
- *Stress and weak forms – can/can't*

*The conversation on the plane continues...*

## Understanding the important information

→ Cover the text of Recording 1, *The Story*.
→ Read the sentence below.
→ Listen to the recording and circle ⬭ ALL the correct answers.

They talk about  **a** countries
              **b** their families
              **c** nationalities
              **d** their names
              **e** languages

### Recording 1 (and 10) – The Story

◀) **CD1 TR 3, 00:16**

| | |
|---|---|
| **Woman** | Where are you from? |
| **Man** | I'm English. And you? |
| **Woman** | I'm from England too. |
| **Man** | Oh, really? But your book isn't in English. |
| **Woman** | Well, actually, I live in South America, in Uruguay and so I speak Spanish. |
| **Man** | Do you? That's interesting! |
| **Woman** | Yes, I like it there. How about you? Do you speak any foreign languages? |
| **Man** | I can speak a bit of French. |
| **Woman** | Can you? |
| **Man** | Yes, I use it in my job sometimes – but I'm not really very good at it. |
| **Woman** | Oh, aren't you? I really like languages. |

**Check your answers**
**a** countries **c** nationalities **e** languages

## Understanding more

→ Cover the text of Recording 1 again.
→ Read the sentences below.
→ Listen to the recording and choose the correct answer.

| | | |
|---|---|---|
| **1** | The woman's English. | Yes/No/We don't know |
| **2** | The man's English. | Yes/No/We don't know |
| **3** | She speaks Spanish. | Yes/No/We don't know |
| **4** | She uses her foreign language in her job. | Yes/No/We don't know |
| **5** | She lives in London. | Yes/No/We don't know |
| **6** | He lives in London. | Yes/No/We don't know |
| **7** | He can speak a little French. | Yes/No/We don't know |
| **8** | He uses his foreign language in his job. | Yes/No/We don't know |
| **9** | Languages are easy for him. | Yes/No/We don't know |
| **10** | She's interested in languages. | Yes/No/We don't know |

**Check your answers**
**1** Yes **2** Yes **3** Yes **4** We don't know. **5** No – she lives in South America. **6** We don't know. **7** Yes **8** Yes **9** No **10** Yes

## What do they say?

→ Read the sentences below.
→ Listen to Recording 1 again and try to complete the words.
→ Read the text of the recording to help you, if necessary.

**1** **Nationalities**
 **a** The woman asks, 'W_here_ / a_re_ / yo_u_ / f_rom_?'
 **b** The man answers, 'I_m_ / E_nglish_.'
 **c** The woman says 'I_m_ / f_rom_ / E_ngland_ / t_oo_.'

## 2 Asking questions; expressing interest

**a** The woman says, 'I'm from England.'
The man is interested. He says, 'Oh, really?'

**b** The woman says, 'Actually, I live in South America, in Uruguay.'
The man is interested. He says, 'Do you?'

**c** The woman asks about languages.
She says, 'Do you speak any foreign languages?'
The man answers.
'I can speak a bit of French.'
The woman is interested. She says, 'Can you?'

**1 a** Where are you from?
**b** I'm English.
**c** I'm from England too.

**2 a** Oh! Really?
**b** Actually, I live in South America, in Uruguay. Do you?
**c** Do you speak any foreign languages? I can speak a bit of French. Can you?

---

## Find the words and phrases

→ Read the questions below.
→ Read the text of Recording 1 (page 59) and find the answers.

**1 Asking the same question**
**a** The woman asks: 'Where are you from?'
The man doesn't ask, 'Where are you from?' He asks,
'A _ _ / y _ _ ?'
**b** The woman says, 'I speak Spanish.'
She doesn't ask the man, 'Do you speak Spanish?' She asks, 'How / about / you?'

**2 Making conversation**
The woman says, 'I speak Spanish.'
Then she says, 'A c t u a l l y, I live in South America.'

**3** The man doesn't speak French very well.
He says, 'I speak a bit of French … but I'm not very good /ət/ it.'

**Check your answers**
1 **a** And you?
  **b** How about you?

**Insight 24**
★ These two questions mean the same.
★ You can use both questions with all tenses.
★ The structure of the questions is always the same.

**2** Actually, I live in South America.
**3** I speak a bit of French … but I'm not very good at it.

## Using these words and phrases

**1 Asking about the same topic** – *And you? How about you?*

→ Complete these dialogues.

**1 A** What's your name?
  **B** I'm Sam. And you ?
  **A** My name's…

**2 A** I'm cold. How about you?
  **B** I'm alright, actually.

**3 A** Here's the coffee bar. I'd like something cold to drink.
  How about you ?
  **B** I think I'll have the same.

**Check your answers**
**1, 2, 3** 'And you?' or 'How about you?'.

### 2 Making conversation – *actually*

## Insight 25
★ *Actually* makes the sentence less direct.

→ Make mini-dialogues. Match 1–5 below with a–e.

**1** Terrible weather, isn't it?    **a** Yes, actually the food here is always good.

**2** Are you Japanese?    **b** I don't mind, actually. I like both.

**3** Tea or coffee?    **c** Yes, I'm from Tokyo, actually.

**4** Where is he?    **d** Yes, it is actually, isn't it?

**5** This is really delicious!    **e** Actually, I'm not sure.

**Check your answers**
**1** d **2** c **3** b **4** e **5** a

## Insight 26
Common mistake – *actually*

**Situation** A tourist in Europe.
'~~Actually, I'm in Paris.~~ Tomorrow it's Madrid.'

★ In some languages *actually* means *now, at the moment*.
★ In English *actually* does not refer to time.

---

## Grammar and communication 1

### Everyday activities – present simple

Examples from *The Story*:

**1** The woman says, '**I live** in South America.'
**2** The man says, '**I use** my French in my job sometimes.'

## Insight 27
### Meanings

★ In sentence **1** above the present simple is for <u>permanent situations</u>.
★ In sentence **2** the present simple is for <u>repeated actions</u>.

## Form – present simple

### Affirmative *(yes)*

| I<br>You<br>We<br>They | live | He/she/it | lives |
|---|---|---|---|

### Questions

| Do | I<br>you<br>we<br>they | live? | Does he/she/it live? |
|---|---|---|---|

### Negatives *(no)*

| I<br>You<br>We<br>They | don't live<br>(do not) | He/she/it | doesn't live |
|---|---|---|---|

### Short answers

| | Positive | | | Negative | |
|---|---|---|---|---|---|---|
| Yes, | I<br>you<br>we<br>they | do | No, | I<br>you<br>we<br>they | don't | |
| | he/she/it | does | | he/she/it | doesn't | |

## Question tags

| I | | I? | He | lives, doesn't | he? |
|---|---|---|---|---|---|
| You | live, don't | you? | She | doesn't live, does | she? |
| We | don't live, do we? | we? | It | | it? |
| They | | they? | | | |

→ Complete the sentences about the two passengers.
→ Use the grammar summary to help you, if necessary.

She says

Talking about the woman:

1 'I speak Spanish.' — She _____ Spanish.
2 'I live in South America.' — She _____ in South America.
3 'I like it there.' — She _____ it there.

He says

Talking about the man:

4 'I use French in my job sometimes.' — He _____ French in his job sometimes.

## Check your answers

**1** She speaks Spanish. **2** She lives in South America. **3** She likes it there. **4** He uses French in his job sometimes.

### Present simple – questions and answers

→ Look at the table above and complete the questions and answers about the two passengers. Use the information from *The Story* on page 59.

**Example:** Does she speak Spanish?   *Yes, she does.*

1  _Does_ she live in South America?   _____
2  _Does_ she like it there?   _____
3  _Does_ the man speak Spanish?   _____
4  _Does_ he speak French?   _____
5  _Does_ he live in South America?   _____
6  _Do_ they work together?   _____

**7** Do you speak Spanish?      No, I don't

**8** Do you speak French?      No, I don't

## Check your answers

**1** Does she live in South America?      Yes, she does.

**2** Does she like it there?      Yes, she does.

**3** Does the man speak Spanish?      No, he doesn't.

**4** Does he speak French?      Yes, he does.

**5** Does he live in South America?      No, he doesn't.

**6** Do they work together?      No, they don't.

**7** and **8** Yes, I do, or No, I don't.

---

## How do you pronounce it?

**Intonation of questions with** *what?, where?* **etc.**

**Example from** *The Story*:

The woman asks 'Where are you <u>from</u>?'

→ Read the questions below.

→ Listen to these mini-dialogues on Recording 2, part 1. Pay special attention to the important word in the question – the syllable with stress.

In questions with *what? where?* etc. the voice:

**a** goes up on the syllable with stress or  ➞

**b** goes down on the syllable with stress. ➘

→ Choose **a** or **b**. The answer is the same for all the questions.

**Recording 2, part 1**

| | | |
|---|---|---|
| **1** | What's your <u>name</u>? | Monica. |
| **2** | Where are you <u>from</u>? | New York. |
| **3** | Where does he <u>work</u>? | In a school. |
| **4** | When do they arr<u>ive</u>? | At 5 o'clock. |
| **5** | Who can <u>drive</u>? | I can. |
| **6** | Which one's <u>yours</u>? | That one. |
| **7** | Why aren't they <u>here</u>? | Their train's late. |
| **8** | How's your <u>Mother</u>? | She's fine. |
| **9** | Whose is <u>this</u>? | I don't know. It's not mine. |

**Check your answer**

**b** The voice goes down. ➘

## Insight 28

★ Many learners of English go up with questions.

★ Questions with question words (*what*, *when*, etc.) go down. ➘

→ Now listen again and repeat the questions.

→ Pay special attention to the fall on the syllable with stress.

### Plurals with an extra syllable – languages

**Example from *The Story*:**

The woman says 'Do you speak any foreign languages?' And
'I really like languages.'

## Insight 29

★ Sometimes plural nouns have an extra syllable.

For example, *language* has two syllables (lang-uage) and
*languages* has three syllables (lang-uag-es). (A syllable is part
of a word with a vowel sound.)

★ The pronunciation of the extra syllable is 'is' / iz /.

→ Look at the pictures below and listen to Recording 2, part 2.

→ Write the number of syllables you hear in the boxes.

**Recording 2, part 2**

◄ CD1 TR 3, 02:09

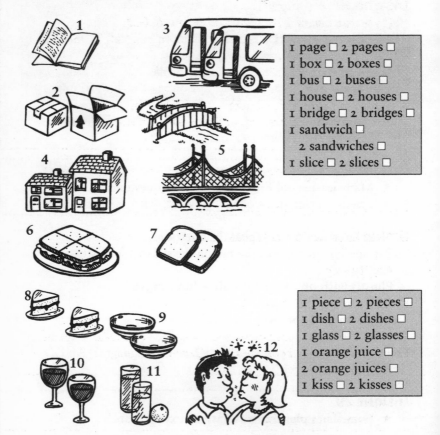

1 page □ 2 pages □
1 box □ 2 boxes □
1 bus □ 2 buses □
1 house □ 2 houses □
1 bridge □ 2 bridges □
1 sandwich □
 2 sandwiches □
1 slice □ 2 slices □

1 piece □ 2 pieces □
1 dish □ 2 dishes □
1 glass □ 2 glasses □
1 orange juice □
2 orange juices □
1 kiss □ 2 kisses □

**Check your answers**

**1** page (1) pages (2) **2** box (1) boxes (2) **3** bus (1) buses (2) **4** house (1) houses (2) **5** bridge (1) bridges (2) **6** sandwich (2) sandwiches (3) **7** slice (1) slices (2) **8** piece (1) pieces (2) **9** dish (1) dishes (2) **10** glass (1) glasses (2) **11** orange juice (3) orange juices (4) **12** kiss (1) kisses (2)

## Insight 30

*Q* *How do I know when there's an extra syllable?*
*A* After the letters 's', 'ss', 'sh', 'ch', 'ge', 'se', 'ce', 'x' there's an extra syllable.

*Q* *Why these letters?*
*A* Because after these letters it's difficult to pronounce the 's' without an extra vowel in the middle. An extra vowel = an extra syllable.

→ Now listen to Recording 2, part 2 again and repeat the words.

## Grammar and communication 2

**Ability –** *can*

**Examples from** *The Story*:

The woman asks about languages. He says, 'I can speak a bit of French.' She's interested. She says, 'Can you?'

## Insight 31

**Meaning**
★ Here, *can* is for ability.

**Form – *can***

<table>
<tr><td colspan="3">Affirmative</td></tr>
<tr><td>I<br>You<br>He/she/it<br>We<br>They</td><td>can</td><td>eat fish</td></tr>
</table>

<table>
<tr><td colspan="3">Negative</td></tr>
<tr><td>I<br>You<br>He/she/it<br>We<br>they</td><td>can't</td><td>eat fish</td></tr>
</table>

<table>
<tr><td colspan="7">Questions, short answers and question tags</td></tr>
<tr><td>Can</td><td>I<br>you<br>he/she/it<br>we<br>they</td><td>eat fish?</td><td>Yes,<br>No,</td><td>I<br>you<br>he/she/it<br>we<br>they</td><td>can, can't<br>can't, can</td><td>I?<br>you?<br>he/she/it?<br>we?<br>they?</td></tr>
</table>

## Insight 32
**Common mistakes – *can***

'He can speak French.'
➤ Not 'He can to speak French.'

'Can you speak English?'
Not 'Can you to speak English?'
Or 'Do you can speak English?'

**Ability,** *can*

→ Complete the questions and short answers.

1 The man _can_ / _speak_ French but he _can't_ ~~not~~ speak Spanish.
2 _Can_ the woman _speak_ Spanish? Yes, _she_ / _can_.
3 _Can_ they both _speak_ English? Yes, they're English.
4 About you: I _can_ / _speak_ some English.

**Check your answers** (*Recording 3*)
◄) **CD1 TR 3, 03:20**

> 1 The man can speak French but he can't speak Spanish.
> 2 Can the woman speak Spanish? Yes, she can.
> 3 Can they both speak English? Yes, they're English.
> 4 I can speak some English.

## How do you pronounce it?

## Insight 33
*Can*

★ The vowel 'a' in *can* has two different pronunciations, one strong / æ / and one weak / ə /.
★ The vowel 'a' in *can't* / a: / is different from the two pronunciations of 'a' in *can*.

→ Listen to Recording 3 above. Can you hear three different vowel sounds?
→ Then read 1, 2, 3 below to check your answers.

1 weak *can* / ə / (*can* is not the important word in the sentence):
  **a** The man can speak <u>French</u>.
  **b** Can the woman speak <u>Spa</u>nish?

**c** Can they both speak <u>English</u>?

**d** I can speak some <u>English</u>.

**2** strong *can* / æ / (*can* is the important word):

**a** Yes, she <u>can</u>.

**3** Negative *can't* / a: / (The negative doesn't change. The vowel is the same as in 'car'):

**a** He can't speak Spanish.

*Q Why is this pronunciation important?*

*A* Because if you say strong 'can' instead of weak *can*, sometimes people hear *can't*.

→ Now listen to Recording 3 again and repeat the sentences.
→ Pay special attention to *can/can't*.

---

## Grammar and communication 3

### Expressing interest – echo questions

→ Look at these examples from *The Story* and answer the questions.

**1** The woman says,          'I'm from England too.'
The man is interested. He says,          'Really?'
**2** The woman says,          'I live in South America.'
The man is interested. He says,          'Oh, <u>do you</u>?'
**3** The man says,          'I can speak a bit of French.'
The woman is interested. She says,          'Oh, <u>can you</u>?'

          'I live in South America.'
          'Oh, really?'

Another possibility for **2** and **3** above:          'I can speak a bit of French.'
          'Oh, <u>really</u>?'

→ Answer these questions.

**1** It is always possible to use *really*.  Yes/No
**2** We use short question forms to express interest.  Yes/No

**Check your answers**
**1** Yes.
**2** Yes.

## Insight 34

You can use *really* with all tenses. It doesn't change.

Use **auxiliary** (*do*, *can* etc.) + subject. These are **echo questions.**

---

## How do you pronounce it?

## Insight 35

### Intonation – expressing interest, echo questions

★ To express interest, intonation is important.
★ A big fall and a little rise in the voice expresses interest.
★ A small fall and no rise in the voice expresses little or no interest.

**a** very interested    **b** not interested

→ Listen to Recording 4.
→ Write 'I' for 'interested or 'NI' for 'not interested' in the boxes.

**Recording 4**

◀ CD1 TR 3, 04:00

Examples:
| | | | |
|---|---|---|---|
| **1** | a Really? ☑ | b | Really? ☐ |
| **2** | a Do you? ☐ | b | Do you? ☐ |
| **3** | a Can't she? ☐ | b | Can't she? ☐ |
| **4** | a Is it? ☐ | b | Is it? ☐ |
| **5** | a Does he? ☐ | b | Does he? ☐ |
| **6** | a Aren't you? ☐ | b | Aren't you? ☐ |

**Check your answers**

| | | | |
|---|---|---|---|
| **2** | a Interested | b | Not interested |
| **3** | a Interested | b | Not interested |
| **4** | a Not interested | b | Interested |
| **5** | a Interested | b | Not interested |
| **6** | a Not interested | b | Interested |

**Expressing interest, making conversation – echo questions**

→ Express interest. Choose the correct question from box 1 on page 75.

→ Continue the conversation. Choose from box 2.

**Example:** His new song is really good. *Is it? What's it called?*

**1** I can play the guitar.
**2** My brother's new job's very interesting.
**3** My father lives in the States.
**4** My children don't like ice cream.
**5** I'm thirsty.
**6** Sue's not here today.
**7** I like this cold weather.
**8** Jessica can't drive.
**9** I don't drink tea.
**10** I'm not very well.

## Box 1

<table>
<tr><td>Are you?</td><td>Oh, can you?</td></tr>
<tr><td>Don't you?</td><td>Isn't she?</td></tr>
<tr><td>Do you?</td><td>Does he?</td></tr>
<tr><td>Can't she?</td><td>Aren't you?</td></tr>
<tr><td>Don't they?</td><td>Is it?</td></tr>
</table>

## Box 2

What's the matter?
So, how does she get to work?
What does he do?
I prefer the summer myself.
What sort of music do you play?
Isn't that her, over there?
I have about five cups a day.
Whereabouts?
Would you like something to drink?
It's very popular in my house.

**Check your answers** (*Recording 5*)

◀)) **CD1 TR 3, 05:09**

**1  A**  I can play the guitar.
  **B**  Oh, can you? What sort of music do you play?
**2  A**  My brother's new job's very interesting.
  **B**  Is it? What does he do?
**3  A**  My father lives in the States.
  **B**  Does he? Whereabouts?
**4  A**  My children don't like ice cream.
  **B**  Don't they? It's very popular in my house.
**5  A**  I'm thirsty.
  **B**  Are you? Would you like something to drink?
**6  A**  Sue's not here today.
  **B**  Isn't she? Look, isn't that her over there?
**7  A**  I like this cold weather.
  **B**  Do you? I prefer the summer myself.
**8  A**  Jessica can't drive.
  **B**  Can't she? So, how does she get to work?
**9  A**  I don't drink tea.
  **B**  Don't you? I have about five cups a day.
**10  A**  I'm not very well.
  **B**  Aren't you? What's the matter?

→ Now listen to these mini-dialogues on Recording 5 and respond. Remember to show your interest with your intonation.

_____⌐⌐→ Very interested _____↘ Not very interested

**Example:** Can you?          Can you?

_____

## How do you pronounce it?

### Countries – stress

→ Look at the names of the countries in the box.
→ Look at the stress patterns below the box, for example, (●o).
→ Listen to Recording 6.
→ Write the countries under the correct stress pattern.

**Recording 6**

◄) **CD1 TR 3, 07:00**

| the United States | | Italy | Portugal | Egypt |
|---|---|---|---|---|
| China | Australia | Mexico | England | Poland |
| Brazil | Germany | Japan | | |

**a** ●o
Example: *Egypt*
_____
_____
_____

**b** o●
_____
_____
_____

**c** ●oo
_____
_____
_____

**d** o●oo
_____

**e** ooooo●
_____

76

## Check your answers

**a** ●○
Egypt
China
England
Poland

**b** ○●
Brazil
Japan

**c** ●○○
Mexico
Italy
Portugal
Germany

**d** ○●○○
Australia

**e** ○○○○●
The United States

---

## What's the right word?

### Countries, nationalities and languages

→ Match these countries, nationalities and languages.
→ Write your answers in the spaces below.
→ Use your dictionary to help you, if necessary.

**Example: a**  Country    **a**   Spain
         Nationality   **2**   Spanish
         Language   **B**   Spanish

| Country | | Nationality | | Language | |
|---|---|---|---|---|---|
| **a** | Spain | **1** | Polish | **A** | English |
| **b** | Japan | **2** | Spanish | **B** | Spanish |
| **c** | the United States | **3** | Mexican | **C** | Polish |
| **d** | Italy | **4** | Portuguese | **D** | German |
| **e** | Portugal | **5** | Australian | **E** | Chinese |
| **f** | Egypt | **6** | Brazilian | **F** | Portuguese |
| **g** | China | **7** | American | **G** | Japanese |
| **h** | Australia | **8** | English | **H** | Arabic |
| **i** | Mexico | **9** | Italian | **I** | French |
| **j** | England | **10** | Egyptian | **J** | Italian |
| **k** | Poland | **11** | Japanese | | |
| **l** | Brazil | **12** | Chinese | | |
| **m** | Germany | **13** | French | | |
| **n** | France | **14** | German | | |

a _2B____    b ____    c ____    d ____    e ____
f ____    g ____    h ____    i ____    j ____
k ____    l ____    m ____    n ____

**Check your answers**
**a** 2 B  **b** 11 G  **c** 7 A  **d** 9 J  **e** 4 F  **f** 10 H  **g** 12 E  **h** 5 A  **i** 3 B
**j** 8 A  **k** 1 C  **l** 6 F  **m** 14 D  **n** 13 I

---

## How do you pronounce it?

### Languages – stress

→ Look at the groups of languages in Recording 7 below.
→ Listen to the recording.
→ <u>Underline</u> the syllable with stress.

### Recording 7

🔊 **CD1 TR 3, 08:40**

| | | | |
|---|---|---|---|
| English | Japanese | Italian | Arabic |
| Spanish | Chinese | | |
| Polish | Portuguese | | |
| German | | | |

**Check your answers**

| | | | |
|---|---|---|---|
| <u>Eng</u>lish | Japa<u>nese</u> | I<u>tal</u>ian | <u>Ar</u>abic |
| <u>Span</u>ish | Chin<u>ese</u> | | |
| <u>Pol</u>ish | Portugu<u>ese</u> | | |
| <u>Ger</u>man | | | |

### Nationalities and languages

→ Write the name of your country and three more – not those on the list above.
→ Write the nationality and language for each one.

→ <u>Underline</u> the stress on all the words.
→ Use your dictionary if necessary.

| | Country | Nationality | Language |
|---|---------|-------------|----------|
| **1** | | | |
| **2** | | | |
| **3** | | | |
| **4** | | | |

→ Check your answers in a dictionary.

Stress is marked (ˈ) at the beginning of the stressed syllable in the phonetics in dictionaries. For example, *Swedish* in the dictionary is

Swedish / ˈswiːdɪʃ/.

## Insight 36
Countries and languages

*Q  In Recording 1 the woman says, 'Where are you from?' Can I
say 'Where do you come from?'*
A  Yes, both are correct and common. The meaning is the same.

*Q  Can I say 'Do you speak English?'
and 'Can you speak English?'*
A  Yes, both are correct and common.

## British culture – ability, responses
The British don't usually say *I can... very well.*

More common expressions are:
*I can... but not very well* and *I can... not too badly.*

→ Look at the symbols in Recording 8, for example (+) and the expressions below.
→ Listen and repeat the answers.

**Recording 8**

🔊 **CD1 TR 3, 09:12**

| | | | | | |
|---|---|---|---|---|---|
| **1** | **A** | Do you speak Polish? | (−) | **B** | No, not at all. |
| **2** | **A** | Do you speak Japanese? | (+) | **B** | Yes, but not very well. |
| **3** | **A** | Can you speak Russian? | (++) | **B** | Yes, not too badly. |
| **4** | **A** | Do you speak Italian? | (+++) | **B** | Yes, actually it's my native language. |

**Ability, can, responses**

**Situation** You can speak two foreign languages.

→ Read the questions below and look at the response symbols.
→ Copy the right response phrase from the exercise above.
→ Listen to Recording 9.
→ **a** Write the language you hear.
   **b** Read your response.

**1** Can you speak _Arabic_ ?   You (−) _No, not at all_
**2** And do you speak _Italian_ ?   You (++) _Yes, not too badly_
**3** How about _Jap_ ?   You (+) _Yes, but not very well_
**4** And what is your native language?   You _My native language is Italian_ .

**Check your answers** (*Recording 9*)
🔊 **CD1 TR 3, 09:51**

*What can you do? How well? A little? Not too badly?*

| | | |
|---|---|---|
| **1** | Can you speak Arabic? | No, not at all. |
| **2** | And do you speak Italian? | Yes, not too badly. |
| **3** | How about Japanese? | Yes, but not very well. |
| **4** | And what's your native language? | Yours _____ |

→ Write about the topics below or prepare to tell a friend.
→ Use your dictionary to help you if necessary.

**1** Transport – for example, can you ride a bike, drive a car, drive a bus...?

_____

**2** In the house – for example, cook

_____

**3** Sport – for example, swim

_____

**4** Hobbies – for example, play chess

_____

**5** Music – for example, play the guitar, sing

_____

**6** Languages

_____

## What would you say?

**Situation 1 In the street**
Someone speaks to you in a language you can't speak.

_____

**Situation 2 You are in a language class**
At the end of the class another student takes your dictionary by mistake.

_____

**Possible answers**
**1** I'm sorry but I don't understand. **2** Excuse me, that's my dictionary. Advanced alternative: Excuse me, I think that dictionary's mine.

_____

## Revision

### How do you say it in your language?

→ Here are some examples of the important points in this topic.

→ Translate the sentences into your language.
→ Remember – translate the idea, not the words.

**1** Where are you from?

_____

**2** I'm from…

_____

**3** Oh, really?

_____

**4** How about you?

_____

**5** A Can you speak German?   **B** Yes, but not very well.

_____

**6** A Do you like it here?   **B** Not very much, actually.

_____

**7** He lives in Paris.   **B** Does he? That's interesting.

_____

### Join the conversation

→ Look at the text of Recording 1 on page 59, *The Story*, again.
→ Listen to Recording 10.

◀ **CD1 TR 3, 10:51**

→ Say the **woman's** words in the spaces.

_____

# Test yourself 3

### Which one is right?

→ Choose the correct sentence **a** or **b**.

**1** Ability
  **a** He can swim.
  **b** He can to swim.

**2 a** I'm not very good in maths.
  **b** I'm not very good (at) maths.

**3** Present simple – everyday activities.
  **a** Do he drive to work?
  **b** Does he drive to work?

**4** Echo questions – making conversation.
  I'm not an English student.   **a** Are you?
                                **b** Aren't you?

**5** He lives next door.   **a** Does he?
                            **b** Is he?

### Write a dialogue

**Situation** You are at a friend's house. You meet Claudia there. She isn't from your country.

**You**

**1** Ask Claudia where she's from

> *Where are you from*

**Claudia**

**2** Respond. Ask the same question

> *I'm from UK. How about you?*

**3** Reply

> *I'm from Italy*

**4** Express interest and make conversation

> *Are you?*

**5** Ask about languages – which?

> *Which language do you speak*

**6** Respond

> *I can speak English and Spanish not too badly*

**7** Express interest and make conversation.

> *Can you.*

**Which one is right?**
**1** a **2** b **3** b **4** b **5** a

**Dialogue: model answers**

| | | |
|---|---|---|
| **1** | **You** | Where are you from? |
| **2** | **Claudia** | I'm from Italy. And you? |
| **3** | **You** | I'm [your nationality] |
| **4** | **Claudia** | Are you? That's interesting. |
| **5** | **You** | Which languages do you speak? |
| **6** | **Claudia** | Italian, of course, some English and a little Chinese. |
| **7** | **You** | Chinese? Really? Isn't it difficult? Can you write it too? |

# Talking about your daily life

Grammar and communication
- **Jobs and** a/an **– the article**
- **Using prepositions** in, for, to
- **Asking** Do you like it? **– saying** yes **and** no
- **Likes and dislikes – verbs +** ing **– the gerund**

Vocabulary
- **Jobs and work**

Pronunciation
- **Stress and weak forms –** do/don't, does/doesn't
- **Stress for emphasis**
- **Intonation – single words/short phrases**

*The two passengers continue their conversation. They talk about their work...*

# Understanding the important information

→ Cover the text of Recording 1, *The Story*.
→ Read the questions below.
→ Listen to the recording and answer the questions.

**1** What's the man's job?

_____

**2** What does the woman do?

_____

### Recording 1 (and 6) – The Story

🔊 **CD1 TR 4, 00:15**

| | |
|---|---|
| **Woman** | What do you do? |
| **Man** | I work in computers. And you? – what's your job? |
| **Woman** | I'm a teacher. |
| **Man** | You're not an English teacher by any chance, are you? |
| **Woman** | Yes, I am, actually. I teach in a school in Uruguay. |
| **Man** | Really? Whereabouts? |
| **Woman** | In a town about 75 miles from the capital. I teach in an International School. |
| **Man** | Do you? Do you like your job? |
| **Woman** | Yes, I really enjoy teaching and the students are lovely. What about you? What sort of work do you do in computers? |
| **Man** | Well, I'm in marketing. I work for a big company, so I travel a lot for my job. In fact, I'm on my way home now from a Computer Fair in Argentina. |
| **Woman** | And do you enjoy working in marketing? |
| **Man** | It's OK, but I'm not very keen on all the travelling. |

**Check your answers**
**1** He works in marketing computers. **2** She teaches English.

86

## Understanding more

→ Cover the text of Recording 1 again.
→ Read the sentences below.
→ Listen to the recording and tick ✓ all the correct answers.

**1** The woman
- ☐ **a** lives in London.
- ☐ **b** works in South America.
- ☐ **c** teaches in an International School.
- ☐ **d** doesn't like her job.

**2** The man
- ☐ **a** lives in Argentina.
- ☐ **b** is on a business trip.
- ☐ **c** works for a small company.
- ☐ **d** likes his job.
- ☐ **e** really enjoys the travelling.

### Check your answers

**1** The woman
**b** works in South America
**c** teaches in an International School.

**2** The man
**b** is on a business trip.
**d** likes his job.

## What do they say?

→ Read the sentences below.
→ Listen to Recording 1 again and try to complete the words.
→ Then read the text of the recording to help you, if necessary.

### 1 Talking about jobs
**a** The woman asks, 'What /do / you /do?'
The man answers, 'I / w o r k i n/ computers.'
**b** The man asks, 'W h a t' s / y e u r / j o b?'
The woman answers, 'I'm / a/ teacher.'

**c** The woman asks for more information. She says,
'Wh<u>o</u>t / s<u>or</u>t / of / w<u>ork</u> / do you do in computers?'
The man answers,
'I'<u>w</u> / <u>in</u> / m<u>arketin</u>g.'

**d** The man talks about his company.
He says, 'I work / <u>for</u> / a big company.'

## 2 Likes and dislikes

**a** The man asks, 'D<u>o</u> / y<u>ou</u> / like / your / <u>job</u>?'
She answers, 'Yes, I / really/ e<u>n</u><u>oy</u> / t<u>e</u>ch<u>in</u>g.

**b** She asks,
'D<u>o</u> / you / e<u>n</u><u>o</u>y / w<u>or</u>k<u>in</u>g / <u>in</u> / marketing?
He answers, '<u>It</u>'<u>s</u> / OK'

**c** He doesn't like the travelling very much. He says,
I'm n<u>ot</u> / v<u>er</u><u>y</u> / k<u>ee</u>n / <u>o</u>n / all the travelling.'

## Check your answers

**1** Talking about jobs
  **a** 'What do you do?'
    'I work in computers.'
  **b** 'What's your job?'
    'I'm a teacher.'
  **c** 'What sort of work do
    you do in computers?'
    'I'm in marketing.'
  **d** 'I work for a big company.'

**2** Likes and dislikes
  **a** 'Do you like your job?'
    'Yes, I really enjoy teaching.'
  **b** 'Do you enjoy working in
    marketing?'
    'It's OK'
  **c** 'I'm not very keen on all the
    travelling'.

## Find the words and phrases

→ Read the questions below.
→ Read the text of Recording 1 again and find the answers.

**1** The man thinks the woman is an English teacher. He wants to
check and make conversation.
He says, 'You're / <u>not</u> / an English teacher, b<u>y</u> / <u>any</u>/ ch<u>an</u>
<u>ce</u> /, / <u>Are</u> / you?

**2** The woman says she teaches in an International School.
He asks where. He says 'W~~hereabouts~~?'
**3** The woman talks about her job. Then she asks the man about his job.
She doesn't ask, 'How about you?'
Instead she asks, '~~What~~ about you?'
**4** It's the end of the computer fair in Argentina. Where is the man going?
He says, 'I~~n~~/ f~~act~~, / I'm / o~~n~~/ m~~y~~/ w~~ay~~/ h~~ome~~/ now/ f~~rom~~ a fair in Argentina.'

**Check your answers**
**1** You're not an English teacher, by any chance, are you?
★ The phrase 'by any chance' makes the question less direct.
**2** Whereabouts?
**3** What about you?
★ 'What about you?' and 'How about you?' mean the same.
**4** In fact, I'm on my way home now from a fair in Argentina.
★ 'In fact' is very similar to 'actually'. (See Topic 3.) 'In fact' can be more formal.

---

## Using these words and phrases

**1** *Where?* **and** *whereabouts?*

........................................................................................
# Insight 37
*Q What's the difference between 'where?' and 'whereabouts?'*
*A* The meaning is the same.
*Where* is more direct and specific.
**Example:** 'I can't find my keys? Where are they?'

_Whereabouts_ is common because it is less _direct_.

It is especially common when it is the only word in the question.
**Example: A** 'Paul works in the States.'
          **B** 'Does he? Whereabouts?'
........................................................................................

### Whereabouts

→ Complete these conversations.
→ Choose a–f from the box below.

**1** A I live in London.
   B _Do you? Whereabouts?_

**2** A We go to Italy for our holidays.
   B _That's nice, whereabouts do you go?_

**3** A My parents are in Australia.
   B _Really? Whereabouts are they?_

**4** A I travel to Cadaques a lot.
   B _That's interesting but whereabouts is it?_

**5** A This is the name of the hotel.
   B _I know what it's called but whereabouts is it_

**6** A Whereabouts do you work?
   B _In the centre of town actually_

---

**a** Really? Whereabouts are they?
**b** Do you? Whereabouts?
**c** I know what it's called but whereabouts is it?
**d** In the centre of town, actually.
**e** That's nice. Whereabouts do you go?
**f** That's interesting but whereabouts is it?

## Check your answers
**1** b  **2** e  **3** a  **4** f  **5** c  **6** d

**2** *On the way…*

→ Look at the pictures below and complete the sentences.

## Check your answers

**1** No, I'm on my way back. **2** They're on their way to school.
**3** She's on her way home. **4** He's on his way to work. **5** We're on
our way to the airport. **6** I'm on my way there right now.

| On the way | there<br>back | No *to* with these words |
|---|---|---|
| | to school<br>to work | No *the* with these places |
| | to the airport | |

## How do you pronounce it?

### Do/don't

**Insight 38**

★ The vowel in *do* has two pronunciations, one strong / u: / and one weak / ə /.

★ The vowel 'o' in *don't* / əʊ / is different from the two pronunciations of 'o' in *do*.

→ Listen to Recording 2, part 1. Can you hear three different vowel sounds?

**Recording 2, part 1,** *do/don't*

◄)) **CD1 TR 4, 01:22**

| | |
|---|---|
| **A** Do you <u>drive</u>? | Weak *do* / ə / (*do* is not the important word) |
| **B** Yes, I <u>do</u>. | Strong *do* / u: / (*do* is the important word) |
| **C** Oh! I <u>don't</u>. | Negative *don't* / əʊ / (the negative doesn't change) |

## Insight 39

★ The vowel in *does* has two pronunciations, one strong / ʌ /, one weak / ə /.

★ The vowel in *doesn't* / ʌ / is the same as in strong *does* / ʌ /.

→ Listen to Recording 2, part 2. Can you hear two different vowel sounds?

**Recording 2, part 2,** *does/doesn't*

◄◙ **CD1 TR 4, 01:48**

| | |
|---|---|
| **A** Does David <u>drive</u>? | Weak *does* / ə / (*does* is not the important word) |
| **B** Yes, he <u>does</u>. | Strong *does* / ʌ / (*does* is the important word) |
| **C** No, David <u>doesn't</u> <u>drive</u>. | Negative *doesn't* / ʌ / (the same vowel as strong *does*) |

→ Listen to Recording 2, part 3 below and repeat.
→ Pay special attention to the vowels in *do, don't, does, doesn't*.

**Recording 2, part 3, do/don't,** *does/doesn't*

◄◙ **CD1 TR 4, 02:18**

| | |
|---|---|
| **1** <u>What</u> do you <u>do</u>? | weak / ə / strong / u: / |
| **2** <u>Where</u> do you <u>live</u>? | weak / ə / |
| **3** <u>How</u> do you <u>know</u>? | weak / ə / |
| **4** I <u>don't know</u>. | negative / əʊ / |
| **5** <u>Yes</u>, you <u>do</u>. | strong / u: / |
| **6** A Does your <u>father</u> like <u>golf</u>? | weak / ə / |
| **7** B <u>Yes</u>, he <u>does</u> C <u>No</u>, he <u>doesn't</u>. | strong and negative / ʌ / |

**Stress for emphasis**

In *The Story*, the woman asks the man about his job.
She says, 'What do you do?'
The man answers. Then he asks 'What's <u>your</u> job?'

→ Read the seven half-dialogues below. The person answers a
  question and then asks the same question. <u>Underline</u> the stressed
  word in the questions.

**1** I'm <u>fine</u> thanks. How are you?
**2** I'm <u>Carol</u>. And you? What's your name?
**3** I live in <u>Lon</u>don. Where do you live?
**4** My birthday's in <u>April</u>. When's yours?
**5** I <u>don't smoke</u>. Do you?
**6** I'd like some <u>coffee</u>. How about you? Would you like a drink?
**7** I <u>live</u> with my <u>parents</u>. Do you live with yours?

> **1** I'm fine, thanks. How are <u>you</u>?
> **2** I'm Carol. And <u>you</u>? What's <u>your</u> name?
> **3** I live in London. Where do <u>you</u> live?
> **4** My birthday's in April. When's <u>yours</u>?
> **5** I don't smoke. Do <u>you</u>?
> **6** I'd like some coffee. Would <u>you</u> like a drink?
> **7** I live with my parents. Do you live with <u>yours</u>?

→ Listen again and repeat the answers and questions.
→ Pay special attention to the stress in the questions.

### Intonation and meaning – single words and short phrases

## Insight 42

★ One way to express feelings in English is through intonation.

**Example from** *The Story*:

'It's **OK**' is positive. 'It's OK' is not very positive.

★ To sound positive, start high and finish low.
★ Flat intonation expresses that you are not very happy or interested.

## Intonation summary

| | | |
|---|---|---|
| positive | = high start | + big fall |
| not very positive | = low start | + small fall |

→ Listen to Recording 2, part 5 below.
→ For each question, one response is positive and one response is not very positive.
→ Write 'P' for 'positive' or 'NP' for 'not very positive' in the boxes.

### Recording 2, part 5

◄» CD1 TR 4, 03:58

| | | | |
|---|---|---|---|
| **1** Can you help me? | | **5** Is this alright? | |
| **a** OK ☐ | | **a** Yes, it's fine. ☐ | |
| **b** OK ☐ | | **b** Yes, it's fine. ☐ | |
| **2** How are things? | | **6** Do you agree? | |
| **a** Alright. ☐ | | **a** Of course. ☐ | |
| **b** Alright. ☐ | | **b** Of course. ☐ | |
| **3** Is that nice? | | **7** Do you like it? | |
| **a** It's not bad. ☐ | | **a** Yes. ☐ | |
| **b** It's not bad. ☐ | | **b** Yes. ☐ | |
| **4** Are you happy about it? | | | |
| **a** Yeah. ☐ | | | |
| **b** Yeah. ☐ | | | |

### Check your answers

**1 a** P
  **b** NP
**2 a** P
  **b** NP
**3 a** NP
  **b** P
**4 a** NP
  **b** P

**5 a** P
  **b** NP
**6 a** NP
  **b** P
**7 a** NP
  **b** P

→ This time listen and repeat the responses. Can you hear the difference? Can you use intonation to sound positive?

## What's the right word?

**Jobs**

**1** ITAX VREDIR

**2** TAWREI

**3** ROTCOD

**4** TPSIERECONTI

**5** CIMECAHN

**6** STEDNIT

**7** TACRO

**8** OPSH SSTANISAT

**9** UROT DUEGI

**10** REDSSREAIHR

**11** AVRTEL GTAEN

**12** EIRSHCA

**13** TDUSENT

→ Look at the pictures and the letters.
→ Write the correct word for each job.
→ Use your dictionary if necessary.

**Check your answers**
**1** Taxi driver **2** Waiter **3** Doctor **4** Receptionist **5** Mechanic
**6** Dentist **7** Actor **8** Shop assistant **9** Tour guide **10** Hairdresser
**11** Travel agent **12** Cashier **13** Student

---

## Grammar and communication 1

**Jobs** – *a, an*

**Example from *The Story*:**
The man asks, 'What's your job?'
The woman says, 'I'm a teacher.'

## Insight 44

**Common mistake**

'She's a teacher.' ✓

(Not 'She's teacher.')

| Grammar summary – *Jobs* | | |
|---|---|---|
| She's | a | travel agent |
| He's | an | actor |

| Subject + verb *be* | indefinite article | job |
|---|---|---|
| **Plurals** | | |
| Compare He's | a | doctor (+ article *a*) |
| They're | X | doctors (no article) |

## Jobs

→ Look again at the pictures on pages 97 and 98. Some people have name labels, for example, the waiter is Dan.

→ Complete the answers and questions below.

Example: 'What does Dan do?' You *'He's a waiter.'*

**1** What does Dan do? _____

**2** What's Pat's job? _____

**3** What does Carl do? _____

**4** What's Kate's job? _____

**5** Now you ask: Jo?_____ She's a tour guide.

**6** You ask again: Jim? _____ He's a travel agent.

---

**1** What does Dan do? He's a waiter.
**2** What's Pat's job? He's a hotel receptionist.
**3** What does Carl do? He's a mechanic.
**4** What's Kate's job? She's a shop assistant.
**5** What does Jo do? OR What's Jo's job? She's a tour guide.
**6** What's Jim's job? OR What does Jim do? He's a travel agent.

---

→ Listen to Recording 3 and repeat the questions and answers.

---

## Grammar and communication 2

**Using prepositions – work in**

**Example from *The Story*:** 'I'm in marketing.'

→ Correct A in the conversations below. Use the words in the box at the end.
→ Use your dictionary if necessary.

**Example:** David makes planes.
   **A** You're a dentist, aren't you, David?
   **B** No, *I'm in engineering,* actually.
**1** Jack is a Member of Parliament.
   **A** Jack works in publishing.
   **B** No, he's _in politics_
**2** Brenda works for Barclay's Bank.
   **A** Brenda's in education.
   **B** No, she's _in banking_
**3** Paul is the director of a language school.
   **A** Paul works in banking.
   **B** No, not Paul. He's _in Education_
**4** Matt draws pictures for books.
   **A** Matt works in administration.
   **B** Are you sure? I think he works _in publishing_

**Check your answers**
**1** in politics. **2** in banking. **3** in education. **4** in publishing.

**work for**

**Example from *The Story*:** 'I work for a big company.'

→ Write the words in the correct order.

**1** for/Sue/Kodak/works.

_____

**2** does/for/brother/which/your/company/work?

_____

**3** who/know/she/for/works/do/you?

_____

**Check your answers**
  **1** Sue works for Kodak.
  **2** Which company does your brother work for?
  **3** Do you know who she works for?

## Insight 45
  ★ In spoken English you can finish a question or sentence with a preposition.
  ★ In written English we sometimes avoid this.

_____

## Grammar and communication 3

**Asking** *Do you like it?*

Examples from *The Story*:

The woman says: 'I really enjoy teaching.'
Then she asks: 'Do you enjoy working in marketing?'

The man says: 'It's OK but I'm not very keen on all the travelling.'
→ Read the phrases and look at the symbols below.
→ Listen to Recording 4 and repeat the phrases.

## Insight 46

★ To answer only *yes* or *no* to the question *Do you like…?* can sound rude. Use one of these phrases instead.

### Recording 4

🔊 **CD1 TR 4, 06:44**

'I really enjoy it.' (++)       ☺
'I quite like it.' (+)
'I don't mind it.' (+/–)
'I'm not very keen on it, actually.' (–)
'Actually, I don't like it at all.'(– –)   ☹

★ With *actually*, the negative isn't so direct.
★ This is the other common use of the word *actually*.

*Do you like it?* – **responses**

→ Look at the questions and symbols (for example ++) below.
→ Listen to Recording 5 and respond.

**Example**: You are the woman in *The Story*.
Question: Do you like being a teacher?
You answer: (++) *Yes, I really enjoy it.*

These are from the vocabulary exercise earlier in this topic (pages 97–8).

1  Dan, do you enjoy being a waiter? (+) Yes, _really enjoy it_ quite like.
2  Pat, do you like working in reception? (–) No, _I'm not very keen on_
3  Carl, how do you like your job? (++) _I really enjoy it_
4  Kate, do you enjoy working in a shop? (+/–) _I don't mind it_
5  Jo, what's it like being a tour guide? (– –) _I don't like it at all_
6  Do you like working in travel, Jim? (+) Yes, _I quite like it_

> **1** 'Yes, I quite like it.'
> **2** 'No, I'm not very keen on it, actually.'
> **3** 'I really enjoy it.'
> **4** 'I don't mind it.'
> **5** 'Actually, I don't like it at all.'
> **6** 'Yes, I quite like it.'

## Grammar and communication 4

### Likes and dislikes – verb + *ing*/gerund

**Examples from *The Story*:**
   'I really enjoy teaching.'
   'I'm not very keen on all the travelling.'

After *enjoy, like, not mind* and *be keen on* the verb ends in *ing*.
This is the **gerund.**
   *enjoy* + verb/'*ing*'       *like* + verb/'*ing*',
   *mind* + verb/'*ing*'      *be keen on* + verb/'*ing*'

→ Read this interview with a schoolgirl, Sophie.
→ <u>Underline</u> all the verbs + gerunds.

| Interviewer | So, tell us about what you like doing and don't like doing, Sophie. |
|---|---|
| **Sophie** | Well, I really enjoy going out with my friends at the weekend. I like inviting them home, too. I don't mind doing my homework – I know that's important, but I'm not very keen on helping my Mum with the housework. |

## Check your answers

| Interviewer | Like doing... don't like doing... |
| --- | --- |
| Sophie | enjoy going out... like inviting... don't mind doing... not very keen on helping |

### Likes and dislikes

→ Complete these mini-dialogues using *enjoy, like, don't mind, not keen on*.

→ Use the verbs in the box below.

**1 A** What sort of thing do you like ~~doing~~ in the evening?

**B** Well, actually, I enjoy ~~watching~~ 📺 and I like ~~reading~~ 📖 too.

**2 A** Jack, can you help us with some housework on Saturday?

**B** OK I don't mind ~~hoovering~~ 🧹 but I'm not very keen on ~~ironing~~

**3 A** Do you like ~~cooking~~? 🥛

**B** Yes I really enjoy_____ 🍰

**4 A** That new film is on at the cinema.

**B** Actually, I'm ~~not going~~ ~~not very keen on going~~ out tonight. I'm very tired.

**5 A** I'm sorry but the dentist can't see you for another half an hour.

**B** That's OK I ~~don't mind waiting~~

---

Hoover   cook   go   do   watch TV   make
wait   iron   read

## Check your answers

**1 A** doing.

**B** watching TV, reading

**2 B** hoovering, ironing

**3 A** cooking

**B** making cakes

**4 B** not very keen on going

**5 B** don't mind waiting

# What's the right word or phrase?

### Work

→ Match 1–12 with a–l.
→ First try without a dictionary. Then use your dictionary if necessary.

1 Hannah works in the house for her family
2 Kate is 70.
3 Dawn hasn't got a job.
4 Sue works from 10–2.
5 Twenty people work for Julie.
6 May works 50 hours a week.
7 Denise works from 9–5.
8 Moyra is a student doctor at the hospital.
9 Chris's office is in her house.
10 Sheila works in the same office as her sister.
11 Lena works on short contracts for different companies.
12 Lucy goes to University.

a She works full-time.
b She's unemployed.
c She's a colleague.
d She does a lot of overtime.
e She's a housewife.
f She's a manager.
g She works part-time.
h She works freelance.
i She's retired.
j She works shifts.
k She works from home.
l She's a student.

### Check your answers
1 e 2 i 3 b 4 g 5 f 6 d 7 a 8 j 9 k 10 c 11 h 12 l

### How about you? – work

→ Write or prepare to tell a friend about your job/studies. What do you do/study?
→ Give some extra information about your job/studies.
→ Use some of the expressions in the vocabulary exercise above. How much do you enjoy your job/studies?

_____

_____

_____

_____

## British culture – work

▶ In Britain, usual office hours are 9.00 or 9.30 a.m.–5.00 or 5.30 p.m., Monday to Friday.
▶ The average working week is 36 hours.
▶ People usually take a break for lunch at some time between 12 and 2 o'clock.
▶ Four weeks per year is the average holiday.
▶ The company deducts some money from the salary before they pay it:
  – about 20% income tax on an average salary.
  – about 12% national insurance (N.I.). This is for medical services, state pension and other state benefits.
▶ The current average salary is about £22,000. It is not usual to ask people their salary.

→ Write or prepare to tell a friend about work in your country. Give information on the points above.

Use the phrases in the text to help you.

_____
_____
_____

### What would you say?

**1** You and John work for the same company. John leaves and goes to work for another company. Someone telephones and asks you, 'Can I speak to John, please?'

_____

**2** You work in a shop that is open seven days a week. You work on Saturdays and Wednesdays. It's the end of the day on Saturday. A colleague asks you, 'Are you in tomorrow?'

_____

**Possible answers**

**1** 'I'm sorry but John doesn't work here any more.'
**2** 'No, I'm not in again until Wednesday.'

★ Here 'to be in' means 'to be here, at work'.

## Revision

### How do you say it in your language?

→ Here are some examples of the important points in this topic.
→ Translate the sentences into your language in the spaces.
→ Remember – translate the idea, not the words.

**1** What do you do?                          I'm a... _____
**2** Do you like cooking?                     _____
    Yes, I really enjoy it.                  _____
    Yes, I quite like it.                    _____
    It's OK                                  _____
    I'm not very keen on it, actually.       _____
    Actually, I don't like it at all.        _____
**3** I don't mind waiting.                    _____
**4** I'm on my way home.                       _____

### Join the conversation

→ Look at the text of Recording 1 (page 86) – *The Story*, again.
→ Listen to Recording 6.

◀) **CD1 TR 4, 08:15**

→ Read the **man's** words.

## Test yourself 4

### Which one is right?

Choose **a** or **b**.

**1 a** What work does your brother?
 **b** What does your brother do?

**2 a** Like you your job?
 **b** Do you like your job?

**3 a** We're on our way there now.
 **b** We go to there now.

**4 a** Are you enjoy to travel?
 **b** Do you enjoy travelling?

**5 a** What sort of company does he work for?
 **b** For which sort of company he works?

**6 a** We can't use the car but I don't mind to walk.
 **b** We can't use the car but I don't mind walking.

Choose the correct stress

**7** My brother's a mechanic. **a** What does <u>your</u> brother do?
 **b** What does your <u>bro</u>ther do?

### Write your part of the dialogue

**Situation** You are at a party. You are in the middle of a conversation with a person you don't know.

**You**
**1** Say what you do.
 Ask his job

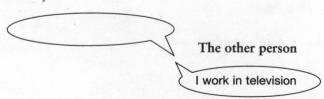

The other person

I work in television

**2** Ask for details

I read the news

**3** You think you know him.
You think his name is David West. Check

Yes, I am, actually

**4** Ask if he likes working in television

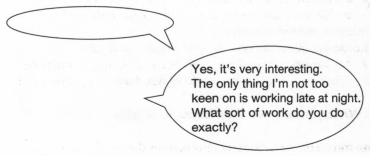

Yes, it's very interesting.
The only thing I'm not too
keen on is working late at night.
What sort of work do you do
exactly?

**5** Respond

Do you enjoy your job?

**6** Respond

His wine glass is empty. Offer more

**7**

Yes, please. That would be nice

**Check your answers**
**Which one is right?**
**1** b **2** b **3** a **4** b **5** a **6** b **7** a

**Dialogue: model answers**

**1** I'm a... What do you do? OR What's your job?

**2** What sort of work do you do in television?

**3** I think I know you. You're David West, aren't you?

**4** Do you like working in television?

**5** I... [details about you]

**6** I really enjoy it OR I quite like it OR I don't mind it OR I'm not very keen on it actually OR Actually I don't like it at all.

**7** Would you like some more wine? OR Would you like another glass of wine?

# 5

..............................................................................

# Giving explanations

Grammar and communication
- **Possessive pronouns** – *mine*, **etc.**
- **Present progressive**
  **– temporary actions in the present**
  **– present progressive and present simple**
- **Present progressive**
  **– future arrangements**
- **Saying why** – *to, so that, because*

Vocabulary
- **First names**
- **The family**

Pronunciation
- **Extra syllable, 3rd person singular, present simple**
- **Weak form** *to*

*The conversation on the plane continues... They exchange names, talk about their families and the reasons for their trips*

────────────────────

## Understanding the important information

→ Read the sentences below.
→ Listen to Recording 1, *The Story*.
→ Circle *Yes* for the things they talk about.
→ Circle *No* for the things they don't talk about.

They talk about
  **a** their names                        Yes/No
  **b** where he lives                      Yes/No
  **c** his family                          Yes/No
  **d** the reason for her trip             Yes/No
  **e** her mother                          Yes/No
  **f** her father                          Yes/No

**Recording 1 (and 5)** – *The Story*

🔊 **CD1 TR 5, 00:11**

| | |
|---|---|
| **Woman** | What's your name? |
| **Man** | Oliver. And yours? |
| **Woman** | My name's Tasha. It's short for Natasha, a Russian name. My mother's Russian. So, whereabouts in England do you live, Oliver? |
| **Man** | I live in Scotland, actually, in Edinburgh, but I'm staying in London for a couple of weeks, because of my job. And you? Are you on holiday? |
| **Woman** | Yes, I'm going to England to see some friends of mine. They live near London. |
| **Man** | Oh, right. And your family? |
| **Woman** | My father's working in the States at the moment – until next June. He works abroad quite a lot. It's nice because my mother organizes her work so that she can travel with him. Even if they aren't at home, I go to England every year because I need to see other relatives and friends. |

**Check your answers**
**a** yes  **b** yes  **c** no  **d** yes  **e** yes  **f** yes

## Understanding more

→ Read the questions below.
→ Listen to Recording 1 and circle ⬭ the right answer.

1 His name is <u>Oliver/Leo</u>.
2 Her name is <u>Sasha/Tasha</u>.
3 Her name is from <u>Greece/Russia</u>.
4 Her <u>mother/father</u> is from the same country.
5 The man lives in <u>Edinburgh/Glasgow</u>.
6 But for the next <u>2/3</u>weeks his work is in <u>Oxford/London</u>.
7 She's on her way to visit <u>her family/some friends</u>.
8 They live <u>in/near</u> London.
9 Her parents are in <u>South Africa/America</u>, for another <u>2 years/ 6 months</u>.
10 When her parents aren't in England <u>she goes/doesn't go home</u>.
11 When she goes to England she visits her friends and <u>museums/ her family</u>.

**Check your answers**
**1** Oliver **2** Tasha **3** Russia **4** mother **5** Edinburgh **6** 2 weeks …
London **7** some friends **8** near **9** America… 6 months **10** goes
**11** her family

---

## What do they say?

→ Read the sentences below.
→ Listen to the recording again and try to complete the words.
→ Then read the text of the recording to help you, if necessary.

**1** The woman asks the man his name.
He says, 'Oliver.' Then he asks the same question 'And /
y ouys?'

**2 a** Oliver has work in London for two weeks.
He says, 'I' / s taying / in London for a couple of weeks.'
**b** He says why.
'B ecause / o f / my job.'

**3** Oliver asks Tasha, 'Are you on holiday?'
She says, 'Yes,/ I' _ / g _ _ _ _ / t _ / England/ t _ / see some
friends / o _ / m _ _ _ .'

**4** Tasha's parents aren't in England now.
She says, 'My / f ather's / w orking / in the States at the
moment.'

**5** Tasha's mother likes travelling with her father but she works. Tasha says, 'My mother organizes her work s_o_/ t_h_a_t / s_h_e_/ c_a_n_ travel with him.'

**6** Why does Tasha go to England every year? She says, 'B_e_c_a_u_s_ e / I / n_e_e_d_ / t_o_ / see other relatives and friends.'

**Check your answers**

**1** And yours? **2 a** I'm staying in London for a couple of weeks. **b** Because of my job. **3** Yes, I'm going to England to see some friends (of mine). **4** My father's working in the States at the moment. **5** My mother organizes her work so that she can travel with him. **6** Because I need to see other relatives and friends.

---

## Find the words and phrases

→ Read the sentences below.
→ Read the text of Recording 1 on page 112 and complete the words.

**1** Tasha is the short name. Natasha is the long name.
Tasha is s_h_o_r_t / f_o_r_ Natasha.

**2** Tasha says, 'My mother's Russian.' Then she starts a new topic.
She says, ' _ _ / whereabouts in England do you live, Oliver?'

**3** Tasha asks, 'Whereabouts in England do you live, Oliver?' Oliver doesn't live in England, he lives in Scotland.
He says, 'I live in Scotland /, a_c_t_u_a_l_l_y_/.'

**4** Oliver's going to London. How long for? Two weeks.
He says, 'f_o_r_ / a / c_o_u_p_l_e_ / o_f_ / weeks.'

**5** Is Tasha working? No, she's _o_n_ holiday.

**6** Tasha says, 'I'm going to England to see some friends. They live near London.'
Oliver responds with another question.
He says, 'O_h_ / r_i_g_h_t. And your family?'

**7** Tasha's father works in other countries. He works a_b_r_o_a_d_.

**8** Does Tasha's father work in other countries all the time?
Not all the time but q_u_i_t_e_ / a_ / l_o_t_ of the time.

**9** Tasha goes to England when her parents are there and when her parents aren't there. She goes to England e_v_ _e_n / i_f_ her parents aren't there.

**10** How often does Tasha go to England? E_ve_ry / ye_a_r.

## Check your answers

**1** Tasha is short for Natasha. (preposition!)
**2** So, whereabouts in England do you live, Oliver?
**3** I live in Scotland, actually.
**4** I'm staying in London for a couple of weeks. (preposition!)
**5** She's on holiday. (Not: 'in holidays'). (preposition!)
**6** Oh, right.
**7** He works abroad.
**8** Not all the time but quite a lot of the time.
**9** She goes to England even if her parents aren't there.
**10** Every year. (Not: every ~~years~~).

······································································

# British culture – first names

▶ In Britain, it is common to have one first name, one middle name and one family name. It's also becoming popular to have two family names.

**Example:**

| Victoria | Ann | Smith |
|---|---|---|
| First | Middle | Family name or surname |

▶ Some people have more than one middle name. It is not common to use your middle name(s).
▶ First names and middle names often come from other members of the family.
▶ It is very common to shorten first names, e.g. Victoria → Vicky.
▶ If a first name has a short form, it can be more formal to use the long form. e.g. Michael can be more formal than Mike.

*(Contd)*

- When we write a name, we usually start with the first name, e.g. Collette Dickenson. 'Collette' is the first name, 'Dickenson' is the family name. On official papers and documents, the family name usually comes first.
- At work it is very common to use first names.
- You can give your child the name you like. There is no official list.

### Find the right first name

**Example from *The Story*:**

'Tasha is short for Natasha.'

→ Look at the names below and in the box.
→ Match the short and long names.

| **Girls** | | **Boys** | |
|---|---|---|---|
| **1** Jo | _____ | **1** Pat | _____ |
| **2** Alex | _____ | **2** Chris | _____ |
| **3** Liz | _____ | **3** Nick | _____ |
| **4** Sam | _____ | **4** Ricky | _____ |
| **5** Kate | _____ | **5** Sam | _____ |
| **6** Ros | _____ | **6** Joey | _____ |
| **7** Chris | _____ | **7** Mike | _____ |
| **8** Nicky | _____ | **8** Alex | _____ |
| **9** Pat | _____ | **9** Tom | _____ |
| **10** Di | _____ | **10** Dan | _____ |

| **Girls** | | **Boys** | |
|---|---|---|---|
| Patricia | Christine | Nicholas | Samuel |
| Joanna | Rosalyn | Michael | Daniel |
| Alexandra | Elizabeth | Richard | Thomas |
| Nicola | Catherine | Alexander | Christopher |
| Samantha | Diana | Patrick | Joseph |

## Check your answers

| | Girls | Boys |
|---|---|---|
| 1 | Jo/Joanna | Pat/Patrick |
| 2 | Alex/Alexandra | Chris/Christopher |
| 3 | Liz/Elizabeth | Nick/Nicholas |
| 4 | Sam/Samantha | Ricky/Richard |
| 5 | Kate/Catherine | Sam/Samuel |
| 6 | Ros/Rosalyn | Joey/Joseph |
| 7 | Chris/Christine | Mike/Michael |
| 8 | Nicky/Nicola | Alex/Alexander |
| 9 | Pat/Patricia | Tom/Thomas |
| 10 | Di/Diana | Dan/Daniel |

As you can see, some short names are the same for both men and women.

→ How many examples can you find in the lists? Write them here.

_____

## Asking someone about their name
→ Put these words in the right order:

for/name/what/your/'s/short? _what's your name short for?_

## Check your answers
Four. Alex, Sam, Chris and Pat are short names for both boys and girls. What's your name short for?

### About you: first names

→ Write answers to these questions or prepare to tell a friend.

Is your first name short for another name?_____
Does another member of the family have the same name?__
Where does your name come from?_____
Is it common or unusual in your country?_____
What does your first name mean?_____

## Using these words and phrases

**1** *So*

**Example from *The Story*:**

> **Tasha**   My mother's Russian. So, whereabouts in England do you
> live, Oliver?

## Insight 47

★ We can use *so* to change the topic.

★ In the conversation above, Tasha talks about her mother.

★ Then she asks Oliver where he lives. *So* starts the new topic

★ *So* is not essential.

*So,* **to start a new topic**

**Situation** John and Jean live in Miami. They have a party.
Two guests have a conversation.

→ Read the conversation below. The topic changes three times.

→ Write *so* where the topic changes.

| | |
|---|---|
| **Jo** | My name's Jo and yours? |
| **Sam** | Sam |
| **Jo** | Where do you come from Sam? |
| **Sam** | I'm from New York. I work in a bookshop there. |
| **Jo** | Do you like it? |
| **Sam** | Yes, I really enjoy it, actually. I love books. Do you know this town well? |
| **Jo** | Quite well. I come for a holiday from time to time. How about you? Where do you go on holiday? |
| **Sam** | I like going to Europe for my holidays – I love London and I know Paris and Rome and a few other places. How do you know John and Jean? |
| **Jo** | John's my brother. |
| **Sam** | Oh, right. |

## Check your answers

| | |
|---|---|
| **Jo** | My name's Jo and yours? |
| **Sam** | Sam. |
| **Jo** | <u>So,</u> where do you come from Sam? |
| **Sam** | I'm from New York. I work in a bookshop there. |
| **Jo** | Do you like it? |
| **Sam** | Yes, I really enjoy it, actually. I love books. <u>So,</u> do you know this town well? |
| **Jo** | Quite well. I come for a holiday from time to time. How about you? Where do you go on holiday? |
| **Sam** | I like going to Europe for my holidays – I love London and I know Paris and Rome and a few other places. <u>So,</u> how do you know John and Jean? |
| **Jo** | John's my brother. |
| **Sam** | Oh, right. |

### 2 Correcting people – *actually*

**Example from *The Story*:**

**Tasha:** 'So, whereabouts in England do you live, Oliver?'
Oliver doesn't live in England. He lives in Scotland.
He says: 'I live in Scotland, **actually**.'

He doesn't say the wrong information, 'I don't live in England.'
This can sound rude. He says 'I live in Scotland, actually.' He says
the correct information + *actually*.

With *actually* the correction is less direct.

## Insight 48

★ *Actually* goes at the beginning or the end of the correction,
**Example:** 'Actually, I live in Scotland' OR 'I live in Scotland,
actually.'

→ Read the short dialogues on the next page.
→ Correct the 'mistakes'.

## Recording 2

🔊 **CD1 TR 5, 01:13**

**Example:** A Good morning, Jo.      B ***My name's Sam, actually.***
(Your name's Sam)

**1 A** So, what's it like working     B ~~work for P actually~~
for Sony?                       (You work for Panasonic)

**2 A** Excuse me … here's your bag.  B _____
(The bag isn't yours)

**3 A** Would you like some wine?     B _____
(You don't drink alcohol)

**4 A** Please take me home.          B _____
(You can't drive)

**5 A** So, whereabouts in France     B _____
are you from?                   (You're from Italy)

**6 A** Peter's really nice, isn't he?  B _____
(You don't know Peter)

**7 A** (On the phone) Sue?           B _____
(You're Sue's mother)

**8 A** Lovely, isn't it?             B _____
(You're not very keen on it)

**9 A** What sort of work does        B _____
your husband do?                (You're not married)

## Check your answers

1 (Actually), I work for Panasonic, (actually).
2 (Actually), it's not mine, (actually).
3 (Actually), I don't drink alcohol, (actually).
4 (Actually), I can't drive, (actually).
5 (Actually), I'm from Italy, (actually).
6 (Actually), I don't know him, (actually).
7 (Actually) I'm her mother, (actually).
8 (Actually) I'm not very keen on it, (actually).
9 (Actually) I'm not married, (actually).

→ Listen to Recording 2 and say the responses.

### 3 Abroad

**Example from *The Story*:**

Tasha's father works abroad.

## Insight 49

★ *Abroad* has no preposition and no **article** ('the').

It isn't correct to say:
'He works ~~in the~~ abroad.'
'He goes ~~to~~ abroad for his holiday.'

→ Complete these answers with *abroad* and information about
   Oliver and Tasha from the recording.

**1** Is Tasha's mother in England?
   No, _____
**2** Does Tasha live in England?
   No, she_____
**3** Oliver _____ a lot for his job.
**4** Tasha's father _____ quite a lot.
**5** What sort of holidays do you like?
   I enjoy (travel) _____

**Check your answers**
**1** No, she's abroad. **2** No, she lives abroad. **3** Oliver travels
abroad a lot for his job. **4** Tasha's father works abroad quite a
lot. **5** I enjoy travelling abroad.

---

## How do you pronounce it?

*He, she, it and who?* **forms of present simple**

**Recording 3, part 1**

◄» **CD1 TR 5, 02:43**

**Example from *The Story*:**

> My mother organizes her work.

→ Read the question below.
→ Listen to the sentence on the recording and choose **a** or **b**.

The verb *organize* has three syllables – or-gan-ize.
'Organizes' has **a** three ⎫
⎬ syllables?
**b** four ⎭

**Check your answer**
'organizes' has four syllables - or-gan-iz-es. / ˈɔːgənaɪzɪz /
Remember, a syllable is part of a word with a vowel sound.

---

## Insight 50
★ Some verbs add an extra syllable / ɪz / with *he* and *she*, *it* and *who?*

---

→ Listen to Recording 3, part 2 and repeat these verbs.

**Recording 3, part 2**

◀ッ **CD1 TR 5, 03:02**

| close | fin-ish | re-lax | watch | dance |
|---|---|---|---|---|
| clos-es | fin-ish-es | re-lax-es | watch-es | danc-es |

**Pronunciation – 3rd person singular, present simple**

**Situation** Kate and Joey are married. Joey has a shop and his wife works in a supermarket. Who does what in their house?

→ Read Joey's sentences below and on page 123.
→ Complete the verbs and write the number of syllables in the brackets ( ). All the verbs here change.
→ Practise the extra syllable. Read the verbs aloud as you write.

## My wife and I

**Example:** I close (1) my shop at 6.00 but Kate's supermarket *closes* (2) at 9.00.

I finish ( ) work early but she _____ ( ) late.

At home I wash ( ) the dishes and she _____ ( ) the clothes.

I fix ( ) the car and she _____ ( ) things in the house.

I relax ( ) in the bath but she _____ ( ) with a book.

I watch ( ) sport on TV but Kate _____ ( ) news programmes.

I dance ( ) a bit but my wife _____ ( ) well.

I use ( ) soap but my wife _____ ( ) shower gel.

I change ( ) the baby in the morning and Kate _____ ( ) her at night.

I sneeze ( ) when I'm ill but she _____ ( ) every morning.

I organize ( ) the money and she _____ ( ) the holidays.

I kiss ( ) my wife and my wife _____ ( ) me.

> I close (1)...the supermarket closes (2)
> I finish (2)...she finishes (3)
> I wash (1)...she washes (2)
> I fix (1)...she fixes (2)
> I relax (2)...she relaxes (3)
> I watch (1)...Kate watches (2)
> I dance (1)...my wife dances (2)
> I use (1)...my wife uses (2)
> I change (1)...Kate changes (2)
> I sneeze (1)...she sneezes (2)
> I organize (3)...she organizes (4)
> I kiss (1) my wife and my wife kisses (2) me.

→ Listen to the answers above on Recording 3, part 3 and repeat.
→ Pay special attention to the extra syllable for *she*.

### Asking *who?* – pronunciation 3rd person singular '*-es*'

Who does these things? Kate or Joey?

→ Complete the questions with one word only.

| | |
|---|---|
| Who _____ ( ) the dishes? | Joey. |
| Who _____ ( ) work at 9.00? | Kate does. |
| Who _____ ( ) sport on TV? | Joey does. |
| Who _____ ( ) things? | They both do. |

## Insight 51
**Check your answers**

**1** Who washes the dishes? Not: ~~Who does wash the dishes?~~
**2** Who finishes work at 9.00 When *who* is the subject of the verb, there is no 'does'. Use who + verb with 's' of 'es'.

**3** Who watches sport on TV?
**4** Who fixes things?

## Insight 52

*Q When do we add an extra syllable for 'he, she, it' and question 'who'?*

*A* When it's difficult to say the 's' without adding an extra vowel sound. An extra vowel sound = extra syllable (It's the same reason as the plural nouns in Topic 3.)

→ Look at the summary below.

_____

## Pronunciation and spelling summary

### 3rd person singular

★ For *he, she, it and who* add an extra syllable to verbs ending in:

| - se | -ce | -ge | -ze | -ss | -sh | -tch | -x |
|------|-----|-----|-----|-----|-----|------|-----|
| close | dance | change | sneeze | kiss | wash | watch | relax |
| use | | | | | finish | | fix |
| organize | | | | | | | |

Here, the spelling changes too. Add 'es'

→ Look at the verbs below.
→ Which ones change with *he, she, it* and question *who*?

| touch | cross | read | think | want | drink |
|-------|-------|------|-------|------|-------|
| fax | pass | manage | pronounce | wish | |

Touch, cross, fax, pass, manage, pronounce, wish. All these words have an extra syllable in 3rd person singular.

---

## What's the right word?

### The family: close relatives

**Who's who in this family?**

→ Look at the family diagram below and the vocabulary in the boxes.
→ Complete the sentences on page 127.
→ Use your dictionary if necessary.

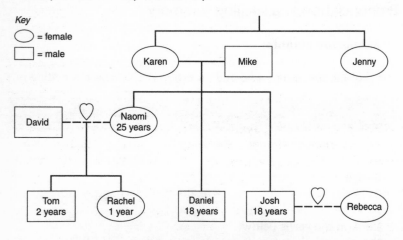

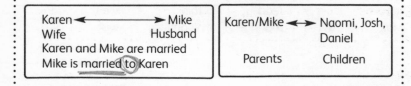

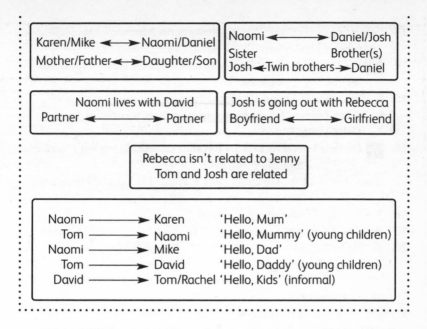

→ Now complete these sentences with the vocabulary from the diagram and boxes above.

1 🔳 Mike: Could I speak to Karen, please? It's her _husband_ here.'
2 🔳 This is Karen, Josh's mother. Is my _son_ there, please?'
3 I'm Naomi, Daniel's sister. Is my _brother_ here, please?
4 **A** Who's David? **B** Naomi's _partner_.
5 **A** Josh, are you _related to_ Mike? **B** Yes, he's my dad.
6 Mike: Naomi's a lovely _daughter_.
7 Mike: I'm married to Karen now. Sue's my first _wife_.
8 Naomi: Daniel's my _brother_.
9 Josh is Daniel's _twin / bro_. They look exactly alike.
10 Josh is in love with his _girlfriend_. He wants to marry her. He asks her, 'Will you marry me?'
11 When David goes to work, little Tom says, 'Bye, bye _Daddy_,'
12 **A** Naomi, is Daniel a _relative_ of yours? **B** Yes, he's my brother.'

**13** 'We always give our ~~mother~~ _____ flowers on Mother's Day.'
  *Mother's Day is usually in April in Britain.

**14** ❱ It's Daniel here, Naomi's brother. Can I leave a message
  for my ~~sister~~, please?'

**15 a** Naomi and David have got two ~~children~~
  **b** When Naomi takes them out, she says 'Come on ~~kids~~.
  We're going out.'

**16** ❱ Daniel: I need to talk to Mum. Naomi:?Mum isn't here but
  ~~dad~~ is. Shall I get him?'

**17** Tom is in a shop. He can't find Naomi. He says, 'Where's my
  ~~mummy~~?'

**18** Naomi and Josh are ~~sister~~ and ~~brother~~.

**19 A** Who's Karen ~~married to~~? **B** Mike

**20 A** Who's Rebecca ~~going out with~~? **B** Her ~~boyfriend~~'s
name's Josh.

## Check your answers

**1** husband **2** son **3** brother **4** partner **5** related to (preposition!
Not: '~~related with~~') **6** daughter **7** wife **8** brother **9** twin brother
**10** girlfriend **11** Daddy **12** relative/relation **13** Mum **14** sister
**15 a** children **b** kids (It is rude to use the singular in this way.
Instead we use the name e.g. 'Come on David', not '~~Come on
kid~~'.) **16** Dad **17** Mummy **18** brother and sister **19** married to
(preposition! Not: ~~married with~~') **20** going out with/boyfriend

## Family relationships

**Possessive's contraction of** _is_ **and** _has_
A sentence can have more than one possessive 's.

→ Look at the examples below.

**1** Who's Karen? Mike's wife (Not: ~~The wife of Mike~~)
      is          possessive 's

**2** Karen's daughter's name's Naomi. (Not: ~~The name of the~~
  possessive 's          is      ~~daughter of Karen is Naomi~~)

**3** What's David's son's name? (Not: ~~What's the name of the~~
    is     possessive 's    ~~son of David~~)
OR    What's the name of David's son?
    is     possessive 's
**4** Daniel has a friend, Jack.
    Who's Jack? A friend of Daniel's. (Not: ~~A friend of Daniel.~~)
    is              possessive 's

**1** **A** Who's Josh? **B** M___'_/ s___
**2** **A** Who'_ Mike? **B** K___'_/ h_____
**3** Daniel'_/ m___'_/ n___'_/ Karen.
**4** Josh'_/ f_____'s/ n___'_/ Mike.
**5** Mike'_/ d_____'_/ n___'_ Naomi.
**6** **A**: What'__/ K___n'_ / d_____'_ / n____? **B**: Naomi.
**7** **A**: Who'_ Daniel? A f _____ / o__/ J ____'_.

## Check your answers
**1** Mike's son. **2** Karen's husband. **3** Daniel's mother's name's
Karen. **4** Josh's father's name's Mike. **5** Mike's daughter's name's
Naomi. **6** What's Karen's daugher's name? **7** Who's Daniel? A
friend of Jack's. (It is normal usage to add 's to a name when it
follows a person + *of*).

## *Write about you and your family*

→ Choose the right information below to make a paragraph about
   you and your family.
→ Delete, circle, complete or tick the right answers about you.
→ Use your dictionary if necessary.

For example: I'm { married
               ~~not married~~

My   husband's
      wife's       name's Mary/John
      partner's
      girlfriend's
      boyfriend's

I've got **1**
      **2** children ✓
      **3**

## About you

My name's _____
My family and friends
 call me _____
I'm { married
    { not married
I've got a { partner
        { girlfriend
        { boyfriend

## About your partner

My { husband's
   { wife's name's _____
   { partner's
   { girlfriend's
   { boyfriend's

OR

I haven't got a partner/girlfriend/boyfriend

OR

I'm too young to have a girlfriend/boyfriend

## About your brothers and sisters

I've got  **1** brother    His name's _____
       **2** brothers  Their names are _____ and _____
       **3** brothers  Their names are _____,____ and ____
       **4** etc. brothers Their names are _____
                        _____ and _____

I've got   **1** sister      Her name's _____

               **2** sisters     Their names are _____ and _____

               **3** sisters     Their names are \_\_\_\_\_, \_\_\_\_\_ and\_\_\_\_

               **4** etc. sisters    Their names are _____

                                      _____ and _____

OR

I haven't got any brothers or sisters. I'm an only child

### About your parents

Both my parents are alive. They live in _____

{ Both my parents are alive but they aren't together.

{ My mother lives in _____ and my father lives in _____

My mother's alive but my father's dead. She lives in _____

My father's alive but my mother's dead. He lives in _____

Both my parents are dead

### About your children

I haven't got any children

I've got one child, a son. His name's _____

I've got one child, a daughter. Her name's _____

I've got two, three, four etc. children. Their names are \_\_\_\_\_

_____ and _____

---

# Grammar and communication 1

### Possessive pronouns – *mine*, etc.

**Examples from** *The Story*:

**1**   The woman asks the man his name.
He says, 'Oliver.' Then he asks the same question.
He says, 'And *yours?*'

**2** Why is Tasha going to England?
She says, 'To see some friends of mine.'

## Insight 53

★ 'They're friends of mine' is more common than 'they're my friends.'

→ Use the possessive pronouns in the box to complete the table below.

| Subject | | Possessive adjective | | Possessive pronoun |
|---|---|---|---|---|
| I | ⟶ | my | ⟶ | *mine* |
| he | ⟶ | his | ⟶ | *his* |
| she | ⟶ | her | ⟶ | *hers* |
| you | ⟶ | your | ⟶ | *yours* |
| we | ⟶ | our | ⟶ | *ours* |
| they | ⟶ | their | ⟶ | *theirs* |

> ours   mine   theirs   his   yours   hers

### Check your answers

| Subject | Possessive adjective | Possessive pronoun |
|---|---|---|
| I | my | mine |
| he | his | his |
| she | her | hers |
| you | your | yours |
| we | our | ours |
| they | their | theirs |

### Possessive pronouns

→ Complete the sentences below with the correct possessive pronoun.

**1 A** My birthday's in April. When's ___*yours*___ ? **B** In November.
**2** We're seeing friends of ___*ours*___ for dinner tomorrow.
**3 A** Does David know Jack? **B** Yes, Jack's a friend of ___*his*___
**4** That isn't their car. ___*Theirs*___ is blue.

**5 A** Is Jo a classmate of _yours_? **B** Yes, we're in the same English class.

**6** The family is going on holiday.

    **a** Which bag is yours?      That big one's _mine_

    **b** And John's?      The red one's _his_

    **c** Where's Mary's?      _hers_ is this black one.

    **d** How about Kay's and Mike's?      _Theirs_ are in the car.

    **e** And we can take _ours_.      Come on, let's go.

**Check your answers**

**1** yours **2** ours **3** his **4** theirs **5** yours **6 a** mine **b** his **c** hers
**d** theirs **e** ours

---

## Grammar and communication 2

### Present progressive – temporary actions

**Example from _The Story_:**

**1** Tasha's parents aren't in England now.
    She says, '**My father's working** in the States until June.'
                  **is**

The name of the tense is the **Present Progressive**.
What's the meaning and form?

→ Choose the right answers.

**Meaning**

**1** Here the present progressive is for   **a** the past.
                                  **b** the present.
                                  **c** the future.

**2** The action is                **a** permanent.
                                  **b** temporary.

**Form**

**1** The verb has    **a** one word.
                         **b** two words.

**2** The present of 'be'   **a** is
                        **b** isn't   } part of this tense

**Check your answers**

**Meaning 1 b** the present **2 b** temporary.
**Form**      **1 b** two words **2 a** The present of 'be' is part of this tense.

## Insight 54

   ★ Here the **present progressive** is for **a temporary action** in the present.

### Present progressive – form

→ Complete the table below with the correct part of the verb *be*.
→ Write the contractions in the brackets, for example I am (I'm).

| Affirmative ('yes') | | Negative ('no') | |
|---|---|---|---|
| I _am_<br>('m) | | I _ _ not<br>('m) | |
| He<br>She _i s_<br>It  ('_) | working. | He<br>She _ _ not<br>It  ('_)<br>OR _ _ n't | working. |
| You<br>We _are_<br>They ('_ _) | | You _ _ _ not<br>We ('_ _)<br>They<br>OR _ _ _ n't | |

134

| Questions | | Question tags – to make conversation | |
|---|---|---|---|
| | | Echo questions – to express interest | |
| | | **Positive** | **Negative** |
| _ _ I | | _ _ I? | aren't I? |
| _ _ he she it | working? | _ _ he she? it? | _ _ n't he she? it |
| _ _ _ you we they | | _ _ _ you? we? they? | _ _ _ n't you? we they |

**Check your answers**

| Affirmative ('yes') | | Negative ('no') | |
|---|---|---|---|
| I am ('m) | | I am not ('m) | |
| he she is it ('s) | working | he she is not it ('s) OR isn't | working |
| you we are they ('re) | | you are not we ('re) they OR aren't | |
| **Questions** | | Question tags – to make conversation Echo questions – to express interest | |
| | | **Positive** | **Negative** |
| Am I | | am I? | aren't I? |
| Is he she it | working? | is he? she? it? | isn't he? she? it? |
| Are you we they | | are you? we? they? | aren't you? we? they? |

## More questions! Present progressive – form

→ Answer *Yes/No* to these questions

**1** The main verb is always with 'ing'.   ~~Yes~~/No

**2** To make questions, you use auxiliary *do*.   Yes/~~No~~

**3** To ask a question, you change the word order.   ~~Yes~~/No

**4** In questions the verb *be* is before the person.   Yes/No

**5** The negative can have two forms.   Yes/No

**6** The 'I' form of the negative question tag is irregular.   Yes/No

### Check your answers
**1** Yes **2** No **3** Yes **4** Yes **5** Yes **6** Yes (aren't I?)

## Temporary actions in the present – present progressive

**What's happening at home?**

**Situation** Mark arrives home. He's talking to his brother, Dave. They've got one sister, Sharon and a brother, Jamie.

→ Complete the conversation. Use the correct parts of the present progressive and appropriate verbs.

| | |
|---|---|
| **Mark** | Where's Dad? |
| **Dave** | He'_/_____ the car. This water's for him. |
| **Mark** | And Mum? |
| **Dave** | She's in the kitchen – _____ a cake for your birthday. |
| **Mark** | What' __ Jamie _____? |
| **Dave** | _____ TV in his room. |
| **Mark** | __/__? |
| **Mark** | _____ Sharon _____ her homework? |
| **Dave** | Of course she __'__. She's upstairs with some friends. They'_/_I_____/ to music. |
| **Mark** | They a____'t /I_____/__ my new CD, a___/ they? |

**[Mark goes to Sharon's room]**

**Mark**    Sharon, what / __/you/ I_____/ t__?

**Sharon**  Your new CD. It's great! I'__ really _____ it!

**Mark**    A____/y____? Now come on. Give it back to me.

**Sharon**  Sorry! Here you are.

## Check your answers

**Mark**    Where's Dad?

**Dave**    He's washing the car. This water's for him.

**Mark**    And Mum?

**Dave**    She's in the kitchen – making a cake for your birthday.

**Mark**    What's Jamie doing?

**Dave**    Watching TV in his room.

**Mark**    Is he?

**Mark**    Is Sharon doing her homework?

**Dave**    Of course she isn't. She's upstairs with some friends.
           They're listening to music.

**Mark**    They aren't listening to my new CD, are they?

**[Mark runs up to Sharon's room]**

**Mark**    Sharon, what are you listening to?

**Sharon** Your new CD. It's great! I'm really enjoying it!

**Mark**    Are you? Now come on. Give it back to me.

**Sharon** Sorry! Here you are.

# Insight 55

*Q In the conversation above, what's the difference between the
two answers below?*

**Mark**    What's Jamie doing?

**a Dave    He's watching TV.**

**b Dave    Watching TV.**

*A* Both are correct and common.
  **a** is always appropriate.  **b** is more informal.

## Insight 56

*Q In the story, why is it:*

**'My father's living in the States until June'?**
*(present progressive)*

**Can I also say, 'My father lives in the States'?**
*(present simple)*

*A* This is a very important question. The grammar in both sentences is correct.

They mean different things.

With the **present progressive**, ('My father's living') the situation is **temporary**.

With the **present simple**, ('My father lives'), the speaker thinks the situation is **permanent**. So, 'My father lives in the States until June' is wrong. *✗*

## Insight 57

*Q* Situation **It's 3.00. Where's Sharon?**
*A* Is it correct to say, 'She's sleeping'?

This answer is not wrong but it's not common. 'She's asleep' is more common. It's the same with questions and the negative.

'Is she asleep?' is more common than 'Is she sleeping?'.
'She isn't asleep' is more common than 'She isn't sleeping'.

## Present simple or present progressive?

→ Circle the correct verb form. Choose present simple for permanent situations. Choose present progressive for temporary situations.

1  Your teacher's ill, so today <u>I teach/I'm teaching</u> your class.
2  Are you in a hotel? No, <u>I stay/I'm staying</u> with friends.
3  My son <u>lives/is living</u> with me until his new flat is ready.
4  Now, come on Joseph, <u>you are/you're being</u> very naughty today. Stop that and sit down. Usually <u>you are/you are being</u> a very good boy.
5  Normally, <u>I work/I'm working</u> hard but this month <u>I don't/I'm not</u>. It's very quiet.
6  <u>Does your daughter live/Is your daughter living</u> at home? Yes, she's only 14.

### Check your answers
**1** I'm teaching. **2** I'm staying. **3** Is living. **4** You're being... You are. **5** I work... I'm not. **6** Does your daughter live?

## Present progressive – future arrangements

**Example from *The Story*:**

Oliver is on a plane on his way to London.
He says, 'I'm **staying** in London for a couple of weeks.'

### Meaning
→ Answer these questions. For 1, 2 and 4 find the right answer. For 3 answer 'Yes' or 'No'.

**1** Here, this tense is for an action in the
    (a) **Past**           (b) **Present**         (c) **Future**

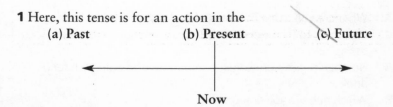

Now

**2** The decision to stay in London is
(a) In the past      (b) In the present      (c) In the future

Now

**3 a** The plan is for Oliver to spend two weeks in London. Yes/No
  **b** Action to arrange the time in London is in the past. Yes/No
**4** The arrangement is **a** personal **b** part of a timetable?

**Check your answers**
**1 c** future  **2 a** in the past  **3 a** yes – planned **b** yes – arranged
**4 a** personal

---

**Insight 58**
  * Here the **present progressive** is for **personal future arrangements**.

---

→ Complete this conversation between two friends.

**A** What _/you _ this evening?
**B** I'_/_ to the cinema with Don. Would you like to come with us?
**A** No, thanks, Jim'_/_ in a minute. We'_/_ out for a drink.
**B** Which pub _/you/ _ _?
**A** The one by the river.

**Check your answers**

**A** What are you doing this evening?
**B** I'm going to the cinema with Don. Would you like to come with us?
**A** No, thanks. Jim's arriving in a minute. We're going out for a drink.
**B** Which pub are you going to?
**A** The one by the river.

140

**Example:**

'I'm going to the cinema this evening.'

---

## Insight 59

*Q Can I also say, 'I go to the cinema this evening'?*
*A* No. This is a personal arrangement in the future.
The present progressive is the only correct tense.

(The present simple is only used for the future to talk
about a one-off action that is part of a timetable, schedule or
itinerary – see Topic 8.)

---

### Present and future actions

→ Read the sentences below. They are all in the present
  progressive.
→ Which sentences refer to an action in the present?
→ Which sentences refer to a personal future arrangement?
→ Write 'present' or 'future'.

**1** I'm doing it right now!
**2** I'm leaving soon.
**3** Is he arriving on Friday?
**4** I'm busy talking on the phone at the moment.
**5** I'm seeing him in the morning.
**6** The telephone's ringing – Can someone please
  answer it?
**7** I'm having dinner with him tomorrow evening.
**8** They're having a holiday at the end of the contract.
**9** You're not meeting John after work, are you?
**10 A** Mummy, I can't sleep.
  **B** I'm coming in a minute, darling.

### Check your answers
**1** Present  **2** Future  **3** Future  **4** Present  **5** Future  **6** Present
**7** Future  **8** Future  **9** Future  **10** Future

## Future arrangements – present progressive

→ Read the mini-dialogue below about arrangements for next weekend.
→ Underline the personal future arrangements.

> **A** So, what are you doing next weekend?
> **B** Well, on Saturday morning I'm visiting a friend. Then, in the evening we're having dinner in the new pizza restaurant. On Sunday my parents are coming for the day.

### Check your answers

> **A** So, what <u>are you doing</u> next weekend?
> **B** Well, on Saturday morning <u>I'm visiting</u> a friend. Then, in the evening <u>we're</u> having dinner in the new pizza restaurant. On Sunday my parents <u>are coming</u> for the day.

## Find the mistakes with the verbs

→ There are five mistakes in this mini-dialogue. Write the correct dialogue below.

> **A** Do you come to class tomorrow? **B** No, I won't.
> **A** Why you can't come? **B** Because tomorrow comes my mother from Germany. I go to the airport to meet her.

**A** <u>Are you coming ...</u>   **B** <u>No, I'm not</u>
**A** <u>Why can't you come</u>   **B** <u>Because tomorrow is coming my mother I'm going to ...</u>

### Check your answers

> **A** Are you coming to class tomorrow? **B** No, I'm not.
> **A** Why can't you come? **B** Because tomorrow my mother is coming from Germany. I'm going to the airport to meet her.

142

→ What are you doing next weekend? Write or prepare to tell a friend.

→ Write a minimum of three things about your arrangements for next weekend.

---

## Grammar and communication 3

**Saying why** – *to, so that, because*

**Examples from *The Story*:**

**1** Tasha: 'I'm going to England to see some friends.'
**2** Tasha: 'My mother organizes her work so that she can travel with my father.'
**3** Why does Tasha go to England every year?
She says, 'because I need to see other relatives and friends.'
**4** Why is Oliver staying in London for 2 weeks?
**Because of** his job.

| |
|---|
| **Summary** – *Saying why* |

**A** Why is Tasha travelling to England?
To
**B** Because she wants to/likes to/needs to } visit friends and family.
So (that) she can

**A** Why is Oliver staying in London?
**B** Because of his job        (because of noun +)

**Answers to** *'Why?'*

→ Why is Tasha travelling to England?
→ Write *because*, *because of* or *so (that) she can*.

**a** .....*So that she can*..... buy new books for her job.
**b** .....*For what Because of*..... her friends and relatives.
**c** .....*Because*..... it's her country.
**d** .....*So that she can*..... have a holiday.

## Check your answers

**a** So that she can buy new books for her job.
**b** Because of her friends and relatives.
**c** Because it's her country.
**d** So that she can have a holiday.

## Insight 60

### Common mistake – saying why

**Example from** *The Story*:

Tasha says 'I'm going to England to see some friends.'

This is **the infinitive of purpose**. In other words, it answers the question *Why?* or *What for?*

Not: 'I'm going to England ~~for to see~~ some friends.'

Not: 'I'm going to England ~~for seeing~~ some friends.'

## How do you pronounce it?

### Infinitive of purpose – *to* + verb

→ Look at the words with stress in the phrase below.
   ... to <u>see</u> some <u>friends</u>.'

The pronunciation of *to* is weak / tə /. The important word in the phrase 'to see' is *see*.

→ Complete sentences 1–8 with an expression from the box below.

**Example:** We go to France *to buy nice wine*.

1 I'm phoning
2 I go to the coffee bar
3 I need some change
4 I'm going to the kitchen
5 You call 999
6 I swim
7 She's in Italy
8 I'd like to go to London

*[handwritten:]*
to tell you ...
to get an ambulance
to have some tea
to make a phone call
to talk abd
to get an ambulance
to relax and keep fit
to learn italian
to write the answers

---

to relax and keep fit

to learn Italian

to make a phone call

to have some tea

to tell you about the party

to get an ambulance    to buy nice wine

to visit the museums

to talk to my friends and have a snack

---

**Check your answers** (*Recording 4*)

🔊 **CD1 TR 5, 05:20**

1 I'm phoning to tell you about the party.
2 I go to the coffee bar to talk to my friends and have a snack.
3 I need some change to make a phone call.
4 I'm going to the kitchen to have some tea.
5 You call 999 to get an ambulance.
6 I swim to relax and keep fit.
7 She's in Italy to learn Italian.
8 I'd like to go to London to visit the museums.

→ Listen to the sentences above on Recording 4 and repeat them.
→ Pay special attention to weak form *to* / tə /. The stress is on the verb after *to*.

### *Saying why*

→ Read the questionnaire below and tick ✓ the right answers for you.

## Why are you learning English?

☐ Because I like it. It's a hobby.
☐ Because I need it for my job.
☐ Because I need it for my studies.
☐ Because I want to visit England.
☐ So I can travel independently.
☐ So I can understand and talk to my colleagues and/or visitors.
☐ So I can get a better job.
☐ To pass exams.
☐ Because I want to understand the words of songs in English.
☐ Because I like to watch films in English.
☐ To help my children with their English studies.
☐ Because there is an English-speaking person in my family.
What are your main reasons? _____

## Why are you using this Complete English as a Foreign Language book?

☐ To improve and practise my English in general.
☐ To learn how to communicate better in English.
☐ To understand speakers of English when they talk.
☐ To improve my pronunciation.
☐ To improve my vocabulary.
☐ To improve my grammar.
☐ To find out more about British life and customs.
☐ Because I can't go to classes.
☐ Because I study on my own.
What are your main reasons? _____

### *What would you say?*

**1** You are next in a queue in a shop. The shop assistant asks 'Who's next? The person behind you says 'Me'.

_____

**2** The phone rings. Your friend answers it. You're in your room. Your friend calls you and says 'It's for you'.

_____

**Possible answers**

**1** 'I think it's my turn, actually' OR 'Excuse me, I think I'm next.'

**2** (I'm) coming.'

_____

## Revision

### How do you say it in your language?

→ Here are some examples of the important points in this topic.
→ Translate the sentences below into your language in the spaces.
→ Remember – translate the idea, not the words.

**1** Here's my car. Where's yours?

_____

**2** Maria's a friend of mine.

_____

**3** I'm studying English because of my job.

_____

**4** I listen to the CD to improve my pronunciation.

_____

**5** I'm working tomorrow.

_____

**6 A** Where's Pat? **B** She's having a bath.

_____

**7** I don't work so that I can be with my children.

_____

### Join the conversation

→ Look at the text of Recording 1 (page 112), *The Story*, again.
→ Listen to Recording 5.

◄» **CD1 TR 5, 06:23**

→ Read the woman's words in the spaces.

_____

## Test yourself 5

### Which one is right?

Choose **a** or **b**.

**1** Where's Sue? **a** She's in holidays.
  **b** She's on holiday.

**2 a** Do you go out this evening?
  **b** Are you going out this evening?

**3** I go to the cinema a lot **a** because of I like new films.
  **b** because I like new films.

**4** I'm working hard **a** so as to can travel **a** abroad.
  **b** so that I can travel **b** in the abroad.

**5** Why are you calling David? **a** To invite him to the party.
  **b** For to invite him to the party.

**6** We go there **a** all the weekends.
  **b** every weekend.

**7** I like playing tennis **a** even if it's raining.
  **b** if even it's raining.

**8** **a** I don't wait any more. I leave right now.
  **b** I'm not waiting any more. I'm leaving right now.

**9** **a** Susan is the girlfriend of Paul and Paul's a friend of me.
  **b** Susan is Paul's girlfriend and Paul's a friend of mine.

**10** **a** She's a friend of Peter.
  **b** She's a friend of Peter's.

For 11 and 12 choose the appropriate answer.

**11** You live at number 2, don't you? **a** No.
  **b** Actually, my house is
  number 3.

**12** I'm a friend of your brother's. **a** Oh, right.
  **b** Yes.

**Situation** You are in a new English class in England. You meet another student. She is not the same nationality as you.

**You**

**1** You say your name
You ask her name

**Gloria**

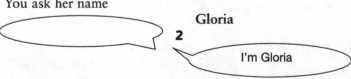

**2**

I'm Gloria

**3** You ask why she's studying English

**4** Because of my job.

She asks you the same question

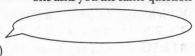

**5** You answer (work/tourism)

You ask about her arrangements
for after the class

**6** She answers (library/
homework)
She asks you the same
question

**7** You answer (lunch/cafeteria/friends)

**Write a dialogue**

**Check your answers**
**Which one is right?**
**1** b **2** b **3** b **4** b a **5** a **6** b **7** a **8** b **9** b **10** b
**11** b **12** a

**Dialogue: model answers**

| | | |
|---|---|---|
| **1** You | Hello, My name's... What's yours? |
| **2** Gloria | I'm Gloria. |
| **3** You | Why are you studying English? |
| **4** Gloria | Because of my job. How about you? |
| **5** You | I'm studying English because I want to work in tourism in my country. What are you doing after the class? |
| **6** Gloria | I'm going to the library to do my homework. And you? |
| **7** You | I'm having lunch in the cafeteria with some friends. |

# Staying in contact

Grammar and communication
- ***Future plans* – going to**
- ***Making arrangements: possibilities, suggestions and offers***
- ***Telephone language***
- ***Asking for things (2)***

Vocabulary
- ***Numbers (1)***
- ***The alphabet***

Pronunciation
- ***Using stress to correct mistakes***

*Tasha and Oliver continue their conversation… They exchange personal details and plan future contact.*

# Understanding the important information

→ Read the sentences below.
→ Listen to Recording 1 and answer *Yes* or *No*.

| | |
|---|---|
| **1** Oliver would like to see Tasha again. | Yes/No |
| **2** Tasha would like to see Oliver again. | Yes/No |
| **3** He gives her his contact details. | Yes/No |
| **4** She gives him her contact details. | Yes/No |
| **5** They arrange a meeting. | Yes/No |
| **6** They arrange a telephone call. | Yes/No |
| **7** They're arriving in London soon. | Yes/No |

**Recording 1 (and 16) –** *The Story*

◀» **CD2 TR 1, 00:19**

| | |
|---|---|
| **Oliver** | As I'm working in London for two weeks, we could … we could meet for a drink one evening, if you like. |
| **Tasha** | Yes, that would be nice. |
| **Oliver** | I don't know where I'm staying but you can phone me at the office, and we can arrange something. Shall I give you my number? |
| **Tasha** | OK Where's my diary? |
| *Tasha opens her bag and gets her diary.* | |
| **Tasha** | What's your surname? |
| **Oliver** | Rees. |
| **Tasha** | Is that R double E, C, E? |
| **Oliver** | No, its R, double E, S actually, and the telephone number of the London office is 020 7402 3277. |
| **Tasha** | 020 7402…? |
| **Oliver** | 3277. You can get me on extension 159, I think it is. Yes, 159. If you have access to e-mail, my e-mail address is orees@fastpost.com. |
| **Tasha** | I can give you the telephone number of my friend's house, too. |
| **Oliver** | Why not? Then I can call you. Just a minute. |
| | *(Contd)* |

> *Oliver opens his diary.*
>
> **Tasha**  My other name's Harrison by the way. Tasha Harrison.
>
> **Oliver**  Harrison, 'H', Tasha Harrison. And your friend's number is…?
>
> **Tasha**  020 8549 6682.
>
> **Oliver**  020 8949…
>
> **Tasha**  No, it's 020 8549 6682… Yes, that's it.
>
> **Oliver**  When would you like me to call, during the day or in the evening?
>
> **Tasha**  I don't mind. I'm going to visit relatives and do other things but I'm going to spend time at home with my friends, too. So, any time's alright with me, really. I'm on holiday!
>
> **Oliver**  Right then, I'll telephone you some time next week, Tasha, if that's OK
>
> **Tasha**  Yes, I'll look forward to it.
>
> **Oliver**  Oh, look, the 'Fasten your seat belts' sign is on. We're landing in a minute.

**Check your answers**
1 Yes  2 Yes  3 Yes  4 Yes  5 No  6 Yes  7 Yes

---

## Understanding more

→ Cover the text of Recording 1, *The Story*.
→ Read the questions below.
→ For 1 and 5 listen and tick ALL the correct answers.
→ For 2, 3 and 4 complete the information where possible.

**1** Oliver talks about  **a** dinner  
                            **b** a drink   } next week.  
                            **c** the cinema

**2** Oliver's details    **a** his family name _____
    **b** the name of his hotel _____
    **c** his home telephone number _____
    **d** his office telephone number _____
    **e** his e-mail address _____

**3** Tasha's details    **a** her family name _____
    **b** her friend's name _____
    **c** her friend's address _____
    **d** her friend's telephone number _____
    **e** her e-mail address _____

**4** Tasha's plans for her holiday    **a** _____
    **b** _____
    **c** _____

**5** Who's phoning who and when?    **a** Oliver's phoning Tasha
    **b** Tasha's phoning Oliver
    **c** next weekend
    **d** next week
    **e** in the day
    **f** in the evening

**Check your answers**
**1 b. 2 a** Rees **b** X. **c** X. **d** 020 7402 3277. **e** orees@fastpost.com.
**3 a** Harrison. **b** X. **c** X. **d** 020 8549 6682. **e** X. **4 a** visit relatives.
**b** do other things. **c** spend time with her friends. **5 a d e f.**

---

## What do they say?

→ Read the sentences below.
→ Listen to Recording 1 again and try to complete the words.
→ Then read the text of the recording on pages 153–4 to help you if necessary.

**1 a** Oliver would like to see Tasha again.
He suggests a drink. He says, 'We c _ _ _ d meet for a drink…'

**b** Tasha responds. 'Yes, t_ _ t / w _ _ _ d / be / n _ _ e.'

**2 a** Oliver talks about possible contact.
He says, 'I don't know where I'm staying but you / c _ _ /
phone me at the office and we / _ _ _ / arrange
something.'

**b** Tasha also talks about possible contact.
She says, 'I / _ _ _ / give you the telephone number of my
friend's house.'

**3** Oliver offers to give Tasha his telephone number.
He says, 'S _ _ _ _ / _ / give you my number?'

**4 a** Oliver offers to phone Tasha next week.
He says, 'I'_ _ / telephone you some time next week.'

**b** Tasha feels positive about it.
She says, 'I'_ _ / l _ _ k / f _ _ w _ _ d / t _ / i _ .'

**5 a** Oliver asks Tasha for a time.
He says, 'When w _ _ _ _ / you / l _ _ _ / m _ / t _ / call?'

**6** Tasha talks about her plans for her holiday.
She says, 'I' _ / g _ _ _ _ / t _ / v _ _ _ t / relatives and do
other things but I'm / g _ _ _ _ / t _ / s _ _ _ _ / time at home
with my friends, too.'

## Check your answers

**1 a** 'We could meet for a drink…'

**b** 'Yes, that would be nice.'

**2 a** 'You can phone me… and we can arrange something.'

**b** 'I can give you…'

**3 a** 'Shall I give you…?'

**4 a** 'I'll telephone you…'

**b** 'I'll look forward to it.'

**5 a** 'When would you like me to call?'

**6** 'I'm going to visit relatives and do other things but I'm going to
spend time at home with my friends, too.'

## What's the right word?

### Numbers 1–10

→ Write the numbers next to the words. Use your dictionary if necessary.

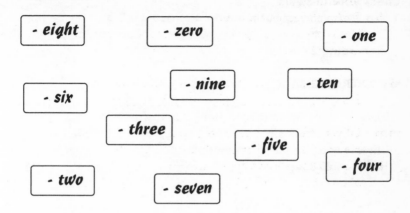

### Check your answers

0 – zero; 1 – one; 2 – two; 3 – three; 4 – four; 5 – five; 6 – six;
7 – seven; 8 – eight; 9 – nine; 10 – ten

→ Practise saying the numbers backwards as fast as possible: ten, nine, etc.
→ Practise counting in twos.
→ What are the *even* numbers? 2, 4, etc.
→ What are the *odd* numbers? 1, 3, etc.

### How do they say it?

### Telephone numbers

→ Read the sentences below.
→ Listen to the telephone numbers on Recording 2 and choose a or b

**1** For 'o' they say   **a** zero

                           **b** O (the name of the letter).

**2** For 8549 they say   **a** eight – five – four – nine

                            **b** 85 – (eighty-five), 49 (forty-nine).

**3** When two numbers are the same, for example '77', they say
**a** 'two sevens' or **b** 'double seven'.

**Check your answers**

**1 b** (**a** is also correct but it is more formal.) **2 a 3 b**

### Recording 2

🔊 **CD2 TR 1, 02:33**

| | |
|---|---|
| **Oliver** | ...and the telephone number of the office is 020 7402 3277. |
| **Oliver** | And your friend's number is...? |
| **Tasha** | 020 8549 6682. |

---

## Find the words and phrases

→ Read the sentences below.

→ Read the text of Recording 1 again (pages 153–4) and complete the words.

**1**     Oliver would like to meet Tasha for a drink. Does he say exactly when?
No. He says, 'We could meet o _ _ / e _ _ _ _ _ g.'

**2 a**   Oliver checks it is alright with Tasha. He says,
'We could meet for a drink..., i _ / y _ _ / l _ _ _ .'

   **b**   Later he checks that a phone call is alright.
He says, ' i _ / t _ _ _ ' s / _ _ .'

**3**     He doesn't know the telephone number of his hotel. He says,
'You can phone me / _ _ / t _ _ / o _ _ _ _ _ .'

**4** Is the meeting fixed? No.
Oliver says, 'You can phone me... and we can a _ _ _ _ _ _ /
s _ _ _ _ _ _ _ g.'

**5** People often write names and telephone numbers in the
special pages in their d _ _ _ _ .

**6** S _ _ _ _ _ _ means the same as family name.

**7** 7402 3277 isn't Oliver's direct number. His telephone is
e _ _ _ _ _ _ _ n 159.

**8** Tasha hasn't got a computer in London but perhaps her
friends have got e-mail. Oliver says, 'If you h _ _ _ /
a _ _ _ _ s / t _ / e-mail.'

**9** Oliver gives Tasha his phone number and she gives him
her number t _ _ .

**10** Oliver needs time to find his diary. He says 'J_ _ _ /
a minute.'

**11** Does he need Tasha's surname? Yes. Has he got it? No.
Tasha gives him this information. She says 'My other
name's Harrison, b_ / t _ _ / w _ _.'

**12 a** Does Tasha choose 'day' or 'evening' for the phone call?
No. She says, 'I / d _ _ ' _ / m _ _ d.'
   **b** Oliver can phone in the day and he can phone in the
   evening. He can phone / a _ _ / t _ _ _.

**13** Tasha accepts Oliver's suggestion. Oliver starts his promise
to call her next week with the phrase, 'R _ _ _ _ / t _ _ n.'

**14** Which day is Oliver calling Tasha? We don't know
exactly. He says 'S _ _ _ / t _ _ _ / next week.'

**15** This is a 'fasten your seatbelts' /
s _ _ _ . Is it _ _? Yes. Why?
Because they're arriving soon.

FASTEN
SEATBELTS

**16**   Planes take off and l _ _ _.

**17**   Verb *get*.
   **a** Why does Tasha open her bag? – to *get* her diary.
   **b** Oliver says, 'You can *get* me on extension 159.'

   Which one means *contact*, which one means *take*?

**Check your answers**
**1** We could meet one evening. **2 a** We could meet for a drink, if you like. **b** If that's OK **3** at the office (preposition!) **4** You can phone me and we can arrange something. **5** diary **6** surname **7** extension **8** If you have access to e-mail. (electronic mail) **9** too **10** Just a minute. **11** My other name's Harrison, by the way. **12 a** I don't mind. **b** any time **13** Right then. **14** Some time next week. **15 a** sign **b** on (preposition!) **16** land **17 a** take **b** contact

---

## Using these words and phrases

   **1** *Some time* **and** *any time*

For example, 'I'm going home **some time** next week.'

### Insight 61
   **Some time* means:*
   **a** I'm going next week.
   **b** The time of the trip is fixed.
   **c** I don't know the time OR I don't remember the time.

   **Any time* means:*    **a** the time isn't fixed.
                          **b** The person can choose the time.

For example, 'You can call me *any time* tomorrow.'
The person can call at 9, or 10, or 11, etc. – when they like.

Another example: 'We can meet *at any time* between 11 and 1.'
The person can choose a time between 11 and 1.

→ Complete these sentences with *some time* or *any time*:

**1** When's John coming back from Australia?
_____ tomorrow, I think.
**2** When can I use the computer?
_____ you like.
**3** When can we visit him in hospital?
_____ between 10 a.m. and 9 p.m.
**4** When's your appointment at the dentist's?
_____ next Wednesday.

**Check your answers**
**1** Some time tomorrow. **2** Any time you like. **3** Any time between
10 a.m. and 9 p.m. **4** Some time next Wednesday.

**2** *By the way*

We know that indirect language is very common in English. *By the
way* is another example.

In the story, Oliver opens his diary to write Tasha's telephone
number. He needs her surname. Before he asks, she gives him the
extra information. She says, 'My other name's Harrison, *by the way*.'

.........................................................................................

# Insight 62
   * Without *by the way* the sentence or question is:
      – correct
      – communicative
      – direct.
   * With *by the way* the sentence or question is:
      – correct
      – communicative
      – indirect.

*(Contd)*

When do I use this expression?

✱ Use *by the way* to

    **a** give extra information

    **b** introduce a new topic in an indirect way
    (*so* on page 119 is more direct)

    **c** introduce a difficult topic.

✱ *By the way* can go at the beginning or the end of the sentence.

→ What would you say in these situations?

**1**    Your colleague's talking to you about her husband. You want to know her husband's job. Ask her.

_____

**2**    You're talking to a friend. You can't remember her boyfriend's name.

_____

**3**    Your colleague's baby is very ill. He is in hospital. You're talking to your colleague. Ask about the baby.

_____

**4**    You buy a new computer. You're at work, talking to your colleagues. Tell them.

_____

**5**    You're at a friend's house. Your friend is having a party tomorrow. You would like your new girlfriend to come to the party. Ask your friend.

_____

**6**    Your friend Mary is thinking about a trip to England. You want to know her decision.

_____

**7**    Your friend promises to give you the telephone number of a new friend. It's a week later. Ask for the number.

_____

**8**   You invite a new friend to dinner. You want to cook fish. You're talking to the friend on the phone. Check that he likes fish.

_____

**9**   A colleague is having a meeting with a new client. You join the meeting and introduce yourself.

_____

### Check your answers
**1** By the way, what does your husband do*? **2** By the way, what's your boyfriend's name*? **3** By the way, how's your baby*? **4** By the way, I've got a new computer* **5** By the way, is it OK if my new girlfriend comes to the party*? **6** By the way, are you going to England*? **7** By the way, have you got X's phone number*? **8** By the way, do you like fish*? **9** Hello, *my name's X, by the way.

\* _By the way_ can go here, too.

_____

## How do you pronounce it?

### Using stress to correct mistakes

## Insight 63
*   In English we often use stress to correct mistakes. How do you correct, for example, a wrong telephone number in your language? Some languages use extra words. For example, 'No, it's not 3 it's 2'.

→ Listen to this example from _The Story_ on Recording 3, part 1.

### Recording 3, part 1

◄» **CD2 TR 1, 03:00**

> **Oliver**   And your friend's number is…?
> **Tasha**   020 8549 6682.
>
> _(Contd)_

> **Oliver**  020 8949…
> **Tasha**  No, 020 8<u>5</u>49.

★  To correct a person, we stress the right number(s).

→ Read the four mini-dialogues below.
→ Underline the different number in **B** – the number(s) where
there is a mistake.

**Recording 3, part 2**

◄) **CD2 TR 1, 03:22**

**1 A**  Is that 8954 6210?
　**B**  Sorry, this is 8954 3210.

**2 A**  I'm calling 01223 55 31 13.
　**B**  Sorry, you've got the wrong number. This is 01223 55 31 31.

**3 A**  Good morning. Kodak.
　**B**  I'm trying to get 8749 4168.
　**A**  Sorry, this is 4178.

**4 A**  Hello! Vicky?
　**B**  Sorry, there's no-one called Vicky here.
　**A**  Isn't that 01932 214218?
　**B**  No, I'm afraid it's not. This is 01532 214218.

**Check your answers**
**1** <u>3</u>210. **2** 55 31 <u>31</u>. **3** 4<u>178</u>. **4** 01<u>5</u>32.

→ Now listen to the four mini-dialogues above on Recording 3,
part 2 and correct the mistakes.

**Correcting other 'mistakes'**

Where are the 'mistakes' in the mini-dialogues below? Some of the
'mistakes' are only a different opinion.

→ Underline the 'corrections', the syllable with stress in **B**.

### Recording 3, part 3

🔊 **CD2 TR 1, 04:26**

**1 A** I'd like to meet your girlfriend.
   **B** Julie? She's my sister.

**2 A** The meeting's on Thursday.
   **B** I think it's on Wednesday.

**3 A** He's a good singer.
   **B** He's a fantastic singer.

**4 A** We need some sandwiches.
   **B** We need lots of sandwiches.

**5 A** The dictionary's not on the desk.
   **B** No, it's under the desk, on the floor.

**6 A** I can telephone you tomorrow.
   **B** No, it's my turn, I'll call you.

**Check your answers**
**1** <u>sis</u>ter **2** <u>Wed</u>nesday **3** fan<u>tas</u>tic **4** <u>lots</u> **5** <u>under</u>, <u>floor</u>, **6** <u>my</u>, <u>I'll</u>, <u>you</u>

→ Now, listen to the dialogues on Recording 3, part 3 and correct the mistakes, using stress.

---

## Grammar and communication 1

**Future plans –** *going to*

**Example from *The Story*:**

Tasha talks about her holiday plans.

She says, '**I'm going to** visit relatives and do other things but **I'm going to** spend time at home with my friends, too.'

## Insight 64

*The name of this tense is the *'going to'* future.

**Meaning**

Here, *going to* is for future plans.

**Form**

The form is the verb *go* in present progressive + *to* + verb.

→ Make mini-dialogues. Match sentences **1–9** with the correct sentence or question (**a–i**) from the second box below.

| | | |
|---|---|---|
| **1** | **A** | _____ |
| | **B** | Because he's not at home. |
| **2** | **A** | _____ |
| | **B** | After the news. |
| **3** | **A** | _____ |
| | **B** | Oh, is he? Who to? |
| **4** | **A** | _____ |
| | **B** | Is he? I hope he passes. |
| **5** | **A** | _____ |
| | **B** | Are you? That's nice. |
| **6** | **A** | _____ |
| | **B** | Oh, just a sandwich, I think. |
| **7** | **A** | _____ |
| | **B** | Yes, I think they are. |
| **8** | **A** | _____ |
| | **B** | I can, if you like. |
| **9** | **A** | _____ |
| | **B** | Aren't you? Why not? |

**a** I'm going to visit my parents next week.
**b** Are your friends going to buy that house?
**c** He's going to take his driving test soon.

**d** We aren't going to invite them.
**e** What are you going to have for lunch?
**f** Why aren't you going to call him?
**g** Who's going to make some tea?
**h** When are you going to put the TV off?
**i** He's going to get married.

**Check your answers**
**1** f **2** h **3** i **4** c **5** a **6** e **7** b **8** g **9** d

---

## Grammar and communication 2

### Making arrangements: possibilities, suggestions and offers

**Examples from *The Story*:**

'**We could** meet for a drink one evening.'
'**You can** phone me at the office.'
'**I'll call** you some time next week.'
'**Shall I** give you my number?'
'**When would you like me to** call you?'

## Insight 65

* Here, *can, could, I'll, shall I? would you like me to?* are all similar in meaning.

**Situation** Your friend is ill, in hospital. You want to visit him/her. You are talking to his/her partner.

| Summary – *Possibilities, suggestions, offers* | | |
|---|---|---|
| I can<br>I could<br>I'll | } | go to the hospital tomorrow. |
| Shall I<br>Would you like me to | } | go to the hospital tomorrow? |

## Insight 66

* All these expressions are correct and appropriate.
* *Could* is a little less direct than the others.
* *Shall I?* and *Would you like me to?* are questions. Here, *I can, I could* and *I'll* aren't questions but they need a response.
* To say *yes* you can use an echo question. (Echo questions are in Topic 2.)
* *Can you? Could you?* and *Would you?* are echo questions for the expressions above.
* The offer and the echo question can have different verbs.

Examples:  1  A  I'll do that for you.
                 B  Can you?
            2  A  I could ask him.
                 B  Would you?

## Insight 67

*Q Can I say 'It's possible for me to (go to the hospital tomorrow)' for offers?*

*A The grammar is correct.*

Students of English often say *It's possible, Is it possible? It isn't possible*. It is more common to say *I can, I could, I'll, shall I?* or *Would you like me to?* for offers.

### Possibilities, suggestions and offers

**Situation**  Debbie is my neighbour. She's got four young children. I arrive at her house.

→ Read the conversation on page 169 and answer these two questions.

**1** Debbie is   **a** fine
                  **b** not very well

**2** I offer to do four things for her. Write them below with her answers:

– a tick for *yes* ✓
– a cross for *no* ✗

**a** Take _____ Answer ☐   **c** _____ Answer ☐
**b** _____ Answer ☐   **d** _____ Answer ☐

### Recording 4

◄» **CD2 TR 1, 05:25**

| | |
|---|---|
| **Me** | Hi! Debbie. Isn't it cold today? How are you? |
| **Debbie** | Not very well at all actually, and it's nearly time for school. |
| **Me** | I can take the children to school for you if you like. |
| **Debbie** | Really? Are you sure? |
| **Me** | Yes, of course. |
| **Debbie** | That's very kind of you. I feel really terrible! |
| **Me** | Right, now you just go and sit down and I'll make you a cup of tea. Shall I call the doctor? |
| **Debbie** | Could you? Thanks. |
| **Me** | Where can I find the number? |
| **Debbie** | In the little book by the phone. Could you ask for an appointment as soon as possible, please? |
| **Me** | No problem. How about dinner this evening? Would you like me to cook for you all? The children could eat at my house. |
| **Debbie** | Thanks for the offer, but it's alright. My husband doesn't mind cooking, actually. |

### Check your answers
**1b. 2a** Take the children to school – yes. **b** Make a cup of tea – yes.
**c** Phone a doctor – yes. **d** Cook dinner – no.

## Insight 68
* 'Really? Are you sure?' It is common to check an offer of help before you say yes.
* 'Not very well at all, actually' is more common than 'I'm ill'.

→ Read the sentences below. Find the exact words in the dialogue above.

**1** I offer to take the children to school.  Debbie says Yes.
  I say _____  She says _____
**2** I offer to make a cup of tea.
  I say _____
**3** I offer to call the doctor.  Debbie says Yes.
  I say _____  She says _____
**4** I need help to find the number.
  I ask _____
**5** I offer to cook dinner.
  I say _____
**6** I suggest the children eat at my house.  Debbie says No.
  I say _____  She says _____

**Check your answers**
**1** I can take the children to school for you if you like. Debbie says
yes. She says, ' That's very kind of you.' **2** I'll make you a cup of
tea. **3** Shall I call the doctor? Debbie says yes. She says, 'Could
you?' **4** Where can I find the number? **5** Would you like me to
cook? **6** The children could eat at my house. Debbie says no. She
says 'Thanks for the offer, but it's alright.'

→ Now listen to the dialogue on Recording 4 and repeat it.

## Insight 69
### Common mistake – offers and suggestions
'Would you like me to make some tea?'
(Not: ~~Would you like that I make some tea?~~)

| would like | 🧍 | to+ verb |
|---|---|---|
| Would you like | us | to help you? |
| When would you like | Richard | to do the job? |
| I'd like | the children | to come with us. |

## Possibilities, suggestions and offers

**Situation** You are on the phone to your friend. Your friend is bored.

→ Read the conversation below and complete with the correct phrase.

| | |
|---|---|
| **Your friend** | I'm bored. |
| **You** | _____(1) go to the cinema (?) |
| **Your friend** | That's a good idea. _____(2) go to the ABC(?) They've got nine screens there. |
| **You** | Why not? I've got the car tonight. _____(3) pick you up on the way (?) |
| **Your friend** | _____?(4) Great! Thanks! |
| **Your friend** | Do you know what time the films start there(?) |
| **You** | I've got no idea. _____(5) call and ask(?) |
| **Your friend** | Don't worry, I think it's usually about 8 o'clock. |
| **You** | Fine. _____(6) get to your house around seven(?) Is that OK? |
| **Your friend** | Yes, an hour is plenty of time to get there, decide which film to see and buy the tickets. |
| **You** | See you later, then. Bye. |
| **Your friend** | Bye! |

## Check your answers

**1** We can ⎫
We could ⎬ go to the cinema.
Shall we ⎭ go to the cinema?

**2** We can ⎫
We could ⎬ go to the ABC.
Shall we ⎭ go to the ABC?

**3**
I can
I could          } pick you up on the way.
I'll

Shall I
Would you like me to  } pick you up on the way?

**4**
Can
Could          } you?
Would

**5**
I can
I could          } call and ask.
I'll

Shall I
Would you like me to  } call and ask?

**6**
I can
I could          } get to your house around seven.
I'll

Shall I
Would you like me to  } get to your house around seven?

→ Now look at these responses from the dialogue above. Do they mean *yes* or *no*?

→ Write a tick ✓ or cross ✗ in the boxes.

**Suggestions/offers**
**1** We could go to the cinema.
**2** Shall we go to the ABC?
**3** Shall I pick you up on the way?

**4** I'll call and ask (the times).

**Responses**
That's a good idea. ☐
Why not? ☐
Can you? or Could you?
or Would you? ☐
Don't worry. ☐

**Check your answers**
**1** ✓ **2** ✓ **3** ✓ **4** ✗

Here's a summary of all the responses from the three conversations about offers and suggestions in this topic. (Recording 1 and 5 and the dialogue above.)

| **Summary** – *Saying Yes and No to offers and suggestions* | |
|---|---|
| Yes | No |
| That's very kind of you | Thanks (for the offer), but it's |
| (Yes), That's a good idea | alright |
| (Yes), Why not? | Don't worry |
| (Yes), that would be nice | |
| OK | |
| Could you? | |
| Can you? | |
| Would you? | |

## Insight 70

You can see from these expressions that

* It is very common to say *yes* without the word 'yes'.
* It is very common to say *no* without the word 'no'.
* These are more examples of indirect language.

## What's the right word?

## British culture – surnames/family names

*Q How do I answer the question, 'What's your name?'*
*A* In an informal situation give your first name.

In a more formal situation give your first name and then your family name(s). In official situations give your family name.

▶ Nowadays, at work most people are informal – they use first names.

▶ When women get married they usually change their name to their husband's surname, for example, Brenda Dickens marries Jack Green. Her new name is Brenda Green or Mrs Green.

▶ Nowadays, some women don't change their surname. Some of them keep their maiden surname and add their husband's surname, e.g. Sylvia Jessop-Bourne.

▶ What are the most common family names in Britain? Here are some from the telephone book: Baker, Mills, Walker,

*(Contd)*

Moore, Brown, Ward, Campbell, Newman, Reid, Wilson, O'Brien, Harris, Evans, Dixon, Fisher, Hall, Dickinson, King, Mann, Woods, Lee, Green, Young, Taylor, Thomas, Matthews, Palmer, West, White.

▶ The most common name for a man is David Jones and for a woman Margaret Smith.

▶ Some surnames are male first names + 's'.

For example,

First name: Edward; family name: Edwards.

→ Look at the two lists below. They are the same except for the 's' at the end of the surname.

| First names | Surnames |
|---|---|
| William | Williams |
| Daniel | Daniels |
| Peter | Peters |
| Richard | Richards |
| Steven | Stevens |
| Hugh | Hughes |
| Matthew | Matthews |
| Edward | Edwards |

**First names and surnames**

Which name is it, the first name or surname?

→ Recording 5 below has eight mini-dialogues – one for each pair of names in the box above.

→ Listen and tick the 'first name' or the 'surname' in the boxes above.

**Check your answers** (*Recording 5*)
🔊 **CD2 TR 1, 08:02**

1 Hello, my name's **Williams**.
2 **A** What's your name? **B Daniel.**
3 Hi! I'm **Peter.**
4 **A** And your name is…? **B Richards.**

### *Names in your country*
→ Read the questions below.
→ Either write your answers or prepare to tell a friend.

How many names do people usually have in your country?

_____

Which names do people use more at work, first names or family names?

_____

What happens to a woman's name when she gets married?

_____

What are the most common family names in your country?

_____

In your language have you got special words or names for people who are special to you? Give some examples.

_____

Do you have special titles for older people?

_____

## British culture – special telephone services
→ Cover the text of Recording 6.
→ Read the information below.
→ Listen to the recording and complete the numbers for Britain.

**International phone calls**                           And in your country?
The international code for Britain is ____    _____

**Special services**
▶ Emergency –  fire                                    _____
                police       } This number   _____
                ambulance        is free      _____

*(Contd)*

- ▶ Operator     National _____     _____
                   International _____     _____
- ▶ Directory enquiries
                   National _____     _____
                   International _____     _____

**Check your answers** (*Recording 6*)
🔊 **CD2 TR 1, 08:53**

> To phone a number in Britain from abroad, the international
> code is 44.
> For emergency services – fire, police or ambulance – dial 999.
> This is a free number.
> Operator services are on 100 – one, zero, zero.
> For the international operator, dial 155.
> To ask for a telephone number call 192 for numbers in
> Britain or 153 for international directory enquiries.

→ What are these numbers in your country? Complete the list on
the right above.

## Grammar and communication 3

### Using the telephone

What do these **telephone sounds** mean?

→ Read the sentences on page 177.
→ Listen to Recording 7 and match **1–6** with **a–e**.

### Recording 7

🔊 **CD2 TR 1, 09:35**

| 1 — | 4 — |
|-----|-----|
| 2 — | 5 — |
| 3 — | 6 — |

**a** It's engaged. Try again later.
**b** Oh dear! It's out of order.
**c** That means you've got a line. You can dial now.
**d** **A** What's happening? **B** The computer is dialling the number.
**e** Wrong number? Dial it again.
**f** It's ringing. Someone'll answer it in a minute.

**Check your answers**
**1** d **2** c **3** f **4** a **5** e **6** b

*Hello!* – **Telephone language**

.....................................................................................
## Insight 71

 ＊   We say 'This is', (Not: 'I am…')
        'Is that?' (Not: 'Are you…?')
   { 'Speaking' (Not: 'Yes, I am X')
   { 'John speaking'
   { 'It's John speaking'
   { 'It's John here' (Not: 'I am John')
   { 'John here'
.....................................................................................

→ Listen to the two mini-dialogues on Recording 8.

**Recording 8**

◀ **CD2 TR 1, 10:53**

[Ring ring]
**Rachel**   6537. Hello?
**Richard**  Can I speak to Rachel, please?
**Rachel**   Speaking.
[Ring ring]
**Rachel**   Hello?
**Matt**     This is Matt. Is that Rachel?
**Rachel**   Yes, it's me.

→ Complete these dialogues with the phrases above.

**1**

Tom
> Hi, _____ Tom. _____ Andrea?

Vicky
> Hello, Tom. No, _____ Vicky. Hang on a minute and I'll call her. Andrea, _____ Tom on the phone for you.

**2**

> Hello. Is David there, please?

Peter

> _____

David

### Check your answers
1  **Tom**  Hi, This is Tom. Is that Andrea?
   **Vicky**  Hello, Tom. No, this is Vicky … Andrea, it's Tom on the phone for you.
2  Speaking *or* This is David *or* This is David speaking.

### Asking for numbers on the telephone
**Situation** You need the codes for some of the big towns in the British Isles. You phone Directory Enquiries on 192 and ask for the codes.

→ Cover the text of Recording 9.
→ Look at the map below.
→ Read the names of the towns.
→ Listen to the recording and write the code number under the name of the town.

## British culture
Most codes begin with 01. The list is in alphabetical order.

Edinburgh

Dublin •

Birmingham

• Norwich

Oxford

Cardiff • Bath London

Canterbury
01227

• Dover

Brighton

Plymouth •

## Recording 9

🔊 **CD2 TR 1, 11:27**

| **Example: Operator** | Directory Enquiries. Which name, please? |
|---|---|
| **Caller** | Hello, yes. Could I have the code for Canterbury, please? |
| **Operator** | Yes, the code for Canterbury is 01227. |
| **Caller** | Thank you. Goodbye. |

**1** **Operator** Directory enquiries, Lynn speaking. Which name, please?

**Caller** Yes, Could you tell me the code for Bath, please?

**Operator** Yes, the code for Bath is 01225.

**Caller** Thanks. Bye.

**2** **Operator** Directory enquiries. Which name, please?

**Caller** Hello. I'd like the code for Birmingham, please.

**Operator** Birmingham – that's 0121.

**Caller** Many thanks. Goodbye.

**3** **Operator** Directory enquiries, Nick speaking. Can I help you?

**Caller** Yes, can you give me the code for Brighton, please?

**Operator** Brighton – yes that's 01273.

**Caller** Thanks very much. Bye.

**4** **Operator** Directory enquiries. Which name, please?

**Caller** Hello. Could I have the code for Dover, please?

**Operator** Yes, Dover's 01304.

**5** **Operator** Directory enquiries, Diane speaking. Which name, please?

**Caller** Hello, yes. What's the code for Edinburgh, please?

**Operator** One second please. Yes, that's 0131.

**6** **Operator** Directory Enquiries. Which name, please?

**Caller** Hello. Could you tell me the code for London, please?

**Operator** Yes the new code for inner London is 020 7. And 020 8 for outer London.

**7** **Operator** Directory Enquiries. Which name please?

**Caller** Hello. Can you give me the code for Plymouth, please?

**Operator** Sorry, which town, caller?

**Caller** Plymouth, please.

**Operator** The code for Plymouth is 01752.

**Check your answers**

**1** Bath – 01225 **2** Birmingham – 0121 **3** Brighton – 01273
**4** Dover – 01304 **5** Edinburgh – 0131 **6** Inner London – 020 7,
Outer London – 020 8 **7** Plymouth 01752

---

## Grammar and communication 4

### Asking for things

→ Read the text of Recording 9 on page 180.
→ Find five expressions to ask for things.
→ Write them below.

**a** C _ _ _ _ / I / h _ _ _ ...?
**b** C _ _ _ _ / y _ _ / t _ _ _ / me...?
**c** I ' _ / l _ _ _ ...
**d** C _ _ / y _ _ / g _ _ _ / m _...?
**e** W _ _ _ ' _ / t _ _ / code for...?

**Check your answers**
**a** Could I have...? **b** Could you tell me...? **c** I'd like... **d** Can you
give me...? **e** What's the code for...?

### Asking for telephone numbers

→ Look again at the map on page 179.
→ Cover the text of Recording 10 below.
→ You need the codes for the other four places on the map,
  (1) Cardiff, (2) Oxford and (3) Norwich and (4) Dublin.
→ Listen and use the questions above to ask for the codes.
→ Write the codes on the map.

**Check your answers** (*Recording 10*)

🔊 **CD2 TR 1, 13:25**

| **1** | **Operator** | Directory enquiries. Which name, please? |
|---|---|---|
| | **You** | _____ . |
| | **Operator** | Yes, the code for Cardiff is 029 20. |
| **2** | **Operator** | Directory enquiries. Mandy speaking. Which name, please? |
| | **You** | _____ . |
| | **Operator** | The code for Oxford is 01865. |
| **3** | **Operator** | Directory enquiries. Which name would you like? |
| | **You** | _____ . |
| | **Operator** | The code for Norwich is 01603. |
| **4** | **Operator** | Directory enquiries. Which name would you like? |
| | **You** | _____ . |
| | **Operator** | The code for Dublin is 003531. |

---

## How do you pronounce it?

### Do you know your a, b, c (alphabet) in English?

A a Apple     B b Bus     C c Cup

.....................................................................

## Insight 72

*Q How many letters are there in the alphabet?*
*A* 26.

*Q How many sounds are there in English?*
*A* 44

*Q How many vowels are there in the alphabet?*
A Five, 'a', 'e', 'i', 'o', 'u'. But there are 20 vowel sounds in English.

*Q How many consonants are there in the alphabet?*
A 21. But there are 24 consonant sounds in English.

* English spelling doesn't always help with the pronunciation. (This is why I always suggest you listen to the recordings several times before you read the words. Listening to English before you read it always helps with good pronunciation.)
* In English one pronunciation can have different spellings and different meanings.

For example      *no* and *know*
                     *see* and *sea*
                     *right* and *write*
                     *meet* and *meat*

* Because English sounds can have different spellings, it is very common to ask for spellings of words, especially names and addresses.

→ Look at the columns of letters below.
   The letters in each column have the same sound.
→ Listen to Recording 11, part 1 and repeat the names of the letters. You will hear each letter twice.

**Recording 11, part 1**

◀) **CD2 TR 1, 14:34**

| a | b | f | i | o | q | r |
|---|---|---|---|---|---|---|
| h | c | l | y |   | u |   |
| j | d | m |   |   | w |   |
| k | e | n |   |   |   |   |
|   | g | s |   |   |   |   |
|   | p | x |   |   |   |   |
|   | t | z |   |   |   |   |
|   | v |   |   |   |   |   |

## Can you say the names of the letters?

→ Listen to the first letter from each column on Recording 11, part 2.
→ Say the others with the same vowel sound.

### Spelling

**Situation** I teach a class of people who want to be English teachers. Here is my register (list of students). Some names are missing. The spelling of some names is wrong.

→ Listen to Recording 12 and write or correct the surnames.

CLASS REGISTER

**1** Lesley_____
**2** Denise Varnish
**3** Matt Hanant
**4** Anne _____
**5** Simon _____
**6** John Pierson
**7** Joan _____
**8** Liz Thomson-Smith

### Recording 12

◀) **CD2 TR 1, 08:08**

| | |
|---|---|
| **Me** | So, could you tell me your surnames, please? Lesley, What's your surname? |
| **Lesley** | Crowley. |
| **Me** | How do you spell that, Lesley? |
| **Lesley** | C – R – O – W – L – E – Y. |
| **Me** | And yours, Denise? |
| **Denise** | My family name's Farnish. |
| **Me** | Is that with an 'F' or a 'V'? |
| **Denise** | With an 'F'. F – A – R – N – I – S – H. |
| **Me** | And how about you, Matt? What's your other name? |
| **Matt** | Hannant. That's H – A double N – A – N – T. |
| **Me** | Anne, your surname is…? |

| | |
|---|---|
| **Anne** | Johnson, spelt J – O – H – N – S – O – N. |
| **Me** | Simon, yours next, please. |
| **Simon** | Lawrence. |
| **Me** | How do you spell it? |
| **Simon** | L – A – W – R – E – N – C – E. |
| **Me** | And John? I've got Pierson here. Is that right? |
| **John** | Yes. P – E – A – R – S – O – N. |
| **Me** | Oh, I've got P – I – E. |
| **John** | No, it's P – E – A at the beginning. |
| **Me** | And Joan – How about you? What's your other name? |
| **Joan** | Rawlings. R – A – W – L – I – N – G – S. |
| **Me** | And the last one is Liz, please. |
| **Liz** | My surname's Thompson-Smith. |
| **Me** | Is that Thompson with a 'P' or without? |
| **Liz** | With a 'P' and 'Smith' at the end. |
| **Me** | Thanks very much everybody. Now let's start the lesson. |

**Check your answers**
**1** Lesley Crowley **2** Denise Farnish **3** Matt Hannant **4** Anne Johnson **5** Simon Lawrence **6** John Pearson **7** Joan Rawlings **8** Liz Thompson-Smith

→ What's the question?

The answer is S – M – I – T – H.
The question is _____?

(Answer: 'How do you spell it?' (Not: 'How do you write it?')

_____

## How do you spell it?

It is easy to confuse some letters, for example 's' and 'f' or 'p' and 'b', especially on the telephone. To make the difference, we say, for example, 'F for 'Foxtrot' or 'S for Sierra'. Some people use other common words or names for this, for example, A for 'apple'.

Below is the International Phonetic Alphabet (NATO Alphabet).

→ Look at this example:

| | |
|---|---|
| **Telephonist** | What name is it, please? |
| **Caller** | Eva Rach. |
| **Telephonist** | Is that R – A – T for Tango? |
| **Caller** | No, it's R – A– C for Charlie – H. |

→ Listen to Recording 13 and repeat the letters and words.

**Recording 13**

◄)) **CD2 TR 1, 19:58**

| | |
|---|---|
| A – Alpha | N – November |
| B – Bravo | O – Oscar |
| C – Charlie | P – Papa |
| D – Delta | Q – Quebec |
| E – Echo | R – Romeo |
| F – Foxtrot | S – Sierra |
| G – Golf | T – Tango |
| H – Hotel | U – Uniform |
| I – India | V – Victor |
| J – Juliet | W – Whisky |
| K – Kilo | X – X-Ray |
| L – Lima | Y – Yankee |
| M – Mike | Z – Zulu |

→ Help to spell aloud this Japanese surname correctly
S A K O T A
It's 'S' for _____
'A' _____
_____
_____
_____
_____

**Check your answers**

'S' for Sierra
'A' for Alpha
'K' for Kilo
'O' for Oscar
'T' for Tango
'A' for Alpha

## Which letter is it?

Example from the class register exercise on page 184:

**A** My name's 'Farnish'
**B** Is that with an 'F' or a 'V'?
**A** With an 'F'.

→ Look at the pairs of names below.
→ Listen to Recording 14 and choose the correct spelling **a** or **b**.

| | | | | |
|---|---|---|---|---|
| **1** | a | Hallis | b | Harris |
| **2** | a | Fraser | b | Frazer |
| **3** | a | Stephens | b | Stevens |
| **4** | a | Simms | b | Sims |
| **5** | a | Stupps | b | Stubbs |
| **6** | a | Initial 'F' | b | Initial 'S' |

## Recording 14

◀) **CD2 TR 1, 21:24**

**1**
**A** My name's Hallis.
**B** Double 'R' is that?
**A** No, double 'L', H – A – double L – I – S.
**2**
**A** The name's Frazer.
**B** Do you spell that with an 'S' or a 'Z'?
**A** With a 'Z'.

*(Contd)*

**3**

**A** My name's Stevens.

**B** Is that with 'PH' or a 'V'?

**A** With a 'V'.

**4**

**A** My name's Simms.

**B** Is that one 'M' or two?

**A** S - I - double M - S.

**5**

**A** Her name's Helen Stubbs.

**B** Is that 'P' for Papa or 'B' for Bravo?

**A** Double 'B' for Bravo.

**6**

**A** What's your initial?

**B** 'S'.

**A** Is that 'F' for Foxtrot or 'S' for Sierra?

**B** 'S' for Sierra.

**Check your answers**

**1** a **2** b **3** b **4** a **5** b **6** b

### Spelling vowels

Many learners of English have problems with the names of English vowels (a,e,i,o,u). Here's some practice.

→ Listen to Recording 15 and complete the spelling of these surnames.

```
1 P _ P _ R
2 S N _ _ T H _
3 S M _ _ T _ N
4 T _ Y L _ R
5 S H _ R _ D _ N
6 R _ _ D _ R
7 S _ M _ _ L S
```

**Check your answers** (*Recording 15*)
**◄ CD2 TR 1, 22:36**

| |
|---|
| **1** Piper, that's P–I–P–E–R. |
| **2** My name's Snaithe, spelt S–N–A–I–T–H–E. |
| **3** Yes, it's Smeaton, S–M–E–A–T–O–N. |
| **4** And my surname is Taylor, T–A–Y–L–O–R. |
| **5** The family name's Sheridon, S–H–E–R–I–D–O–N. |
| **6** And the second name is Reeder, that's spelt R–E–E–D–E–R. |
| **7** Samuels, S–A–M–U–E–L–S. |

*Spelling your name aloud and giving your contact details*

→ Practise spelling your names and address aloud – clarify difficult letters.
→ Practise saying the numbers aloud.

First name _____

Middle name(s) _____

Surname(s) _____

Telephone number (home) _____(work)_____(mobile) _____

E-mail address_____

Address _____

Passport number _____

*What would you say?*

**1** You telephone a friend in England from your country. You get a wrong number.

_____

**2** You are on the telephone. The line is very bad. You can't hear the other person.

_____

**Possible answers**
**1** I'm very sorry. It's the wrong number.
Advanced alternative: Sorry to disturb you. I think I've got the wrong number.

**2** I'm sorry, this line's terrible. I can't hear you.
Advanced alternative: I'm sorry, this line's terrible. Could you speak up a bit, please?

---

## Revision

### How do you say it in your language?

Here are some examples of the important points in this topic.

→ Translate the sentences below into your language.
→ Remember – translate the idea, not the words.

**1** **a** We could go out for a pizza tonight. **b** That's a good idea!

---

**2** **a** I'll book the restaurant for tomorrow. **b** I'll look forward to it.

---

**3** **a** Shall I make some coffee? **b** Yes, please.

---

**4** **a** Can I help you? **b** It's very kind of you, thank you, but it's alright.

---

**5** By the way, how's your mother today – is she better?

---

**6** I'm going to buy a car tomorrow.

---

### Join the conversation

→ Look at the text of Recording 1 (pages 153–4), *The Story*, again.
→ Listen to Recording 16.

◀)) **CD2 TR 1, 23:55**
→ Read **Oliver's** words in the spaces.

## Test yourself 6

**Which one is right?**

→ Choose **a** or **b**.

**1** Three and five is
   **a** nine.
   **b** eight.

**2** 'surname', 'family name' and 'other name' mean
   **a** the same.
   **b** something different.

**3** You ask someone to wait. You say,
   **a** 'A moment.'
   **b** 'Just a minute, please.'

**4** Beer or wine?
   **a** I don't mind.
   **b** It is not matter.

**5** I can't speak to Peter. His number is
   **a** occupied.
   **b** engaged.

**6** I can't use the machine. It's
   **a** out of operation.
   **b** out of order.

**7** On the telephone
   **i** **a** Here speaks Rodica.   **ii** **a** Is that Peter?
      **b** This is Rodica.          **b** Are you Peter?

**8** **a** Please, it is possible I speak with Jenny?
   **b** Could I speak to Jenny, please?

**9** Your telephone number is in my
   **a** diary.
   **b** agenda.

**10** The shop is open 24 hours a day. You can go shopping
   **a** all the times.
   **b** at any time.

**11** **a** Would you like that I go with you?
   **b** Would you like me to go with you?

**12** Shall I ask him?

    **a** Yes, you shall. **b** Yes, please.

**13** Shall we go out for a drink after work?

    **a** Sorry, I go out with my wife to a family dinner.

    **b** Sorry, I'm going out with my wife to a family dinner.

**14**  **a** Why he is going to sell the house?

    **b** Why is he going to sell the house?

### Which one is better?

**15** Would you like me to translate that for you? I speak Japanese.

    **a** Yes, I would.

    **b** Thanks.

**16** Shall I do that?

    **a** No.

    **b** I'm alright, thanks.

### Which ones are right?

**17** I'll do that for you, shall I?

    **a** Can you? Thanks.

    **b** Could you? Thanks.

    **c** Would you? Thanks.

### Write a dialogue

**Situation** You are on the phone to your friend.

**1 You**            **Your friend**

                       What can we do this evening?

Suggest a Chinese meal and
a DVD at his house.

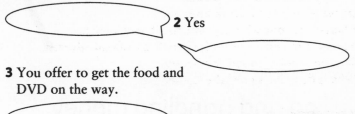

**2** Yes

**3** You offer to get the food and
DVD on the way.

**4** Yes. He asks you to get Chinese
chicken with rice.

**5** You say yes.
You offer to get some beer.

**6** No. He's got some.

**7** You ask what type of film
he'd like to see.

**8** He has no preference.

## Check your answers
**1** b **2** a **3** b **4** a **5** b **6** b **7** i b ii a **8** b **9** a **10** b **11** b **12** b **13** b **14** b
**15** b **16** b **17** a, b, c

## Dialogue: model answers

| **1 You** | We could have a Chinese meal and watch a DVD at your house. |
| **2 Your friend** | Yeah, why not? |
| **3 You** | Shall I get the food and the DVD on the way? |
| **4 Your friend** | That would be good. Could you get me a Chinese chicken with rice, please? |
| **5 You** | No problem. I could get some beer, too. |
| **6 Your friend** | No, don't worry about that. I've got some. |
| **7 You** | What sort of film would you like to see? |
| **8 Your friend** | I don't mind. |

# Travelling and handling money

Grammar and communication
- ***Inviting people to do things***
- ***Suggesting doing something together –*** *let's*
- ***Asking people to do things***
- ***Asking for help – indirect questions***

Vocabulary
- ***Numbers (2)***
- ***Money***
- ***Travel***

Pronunciation
- ***Pronouncing groups of words – linking***

*The plane is arriving in London at Heathrow Airport*

## Understanding the important information

**Situation** The pilot of the plane talks to all the passengers.
He makes an announcement.

→ Cover the text of Recording 1, *The Story* below.
→ Read the sentence above it.
→ Listen to the recording and choose ALL the correct answers.

The captain talks about

    **a** seat belts
    **b** passports
    **c** the time
    **d** the arrival time
    **e** the temperature
    **f** the weather

### Recording 1 – The Story

◀) **CD2 TR 2, 00:20**

**Pilot** Good morning, ladies and gentlemen. This is your captain speaking again. In a few moments, we will begin our descent into London's Heathrow Airport. Please return to your seats and fasten your seatbelts. If you would like to adjust your watches, the time in London is now 6.50 in the morning and the temperature on the ground is −2 degrees centigrade, that's 29 degrees Fahrenheit. Our estimated time of arrival is 7.15. That's a quarter past seven on the ground in London. The forecast for today is cold ... but bright.

**Check your answers**
a c d e f

## Understanding more

→ Cover the text of Recording 1, *The Story*.
→ Read the questions below.
→ Listen and choose a or b.

**1** The time in London is now **a** six fifteen (6.15) **b** six fifty (6.50).
**2** The temperature is **a** 2 degrees *centigrade **b** -2 degrees centigrade.
**3** They're landing at **a** seven fifteen (7.15) **b** seven fifty (7.50).

**Check your answers**
**1** b **2** b **3** a

*In Britain we measure temperature in both centigrade (Celsius) and Fahrenheit. °C = 32°F.

## How do they say it?

### Pronouncing groups of words – linking words

## Insight 73

★ When we speak, we often join a word to the next word.
★ This happens when one sound is a consonant and the other a vowel.
★ Two examples from the story above are, 'ladies and', 'this is'.
★ Sometimes the last letter isn't a consonant. It's the last sound that's important, for example, 'time in London' – the last sound in 'time' is /m/.

→ Read the phrases below. They are from *The Story* on page 195.
→ Listen to these phrases on Recording 2 and repeat them.
→ Pay special attention to linking the words marked.

**Recording 2**

◀) **CD2 TR 2, 10:04**

> Ladies‿and gentlemen
> This‿is your Captain speaking again
> In‿a few moments
> The time‿in London‿is now 6.50
> That's‿a quarter past seven‿on the ground‿in London

## What's the right word?

### Numbers to 100

→ Complete this table with the numbers below.

| | | | |
|---|---|---|---|
| 1 one | 11 _____ | | |
| 2 two | 12 _____ | 20 _____ | |
| 3 three | 13 *thirteen* | 30 _____ | |
| 4 four | 14 _____ | 40 _____ | |
| 5 five | 15 _____ | 50 _____ | |
| 6 six | 16 _____ | 60 _____ | |
| 7 seven | 17 _____ | 70 *seventy* | |
| 8 eight | 18 _____ | 80 _____ | |
| 9 nine | 19 _____ | 90 _____ | 100 *a hundred* |

## Check your answers

| | | | |
|---|---|---|---|
| 1 one | 11 eleven | | |
| 2 two | 12 twelve | 20 twenty | |
| 3 three | 13 thirteen | 30 thirty | |
| 4 four | 14 fourteen | 40 forty | |
| 5 five | 15 fifteen | 50 fifty | |
| 6 six | 16 sixteen | 60 sixty | |
| 7 seven | 17 seventeen | 70 seventy | |
| 8 eight | 18 eighteen | 80 eighty | |
| 9 nine | 19 nineteen | 90 ninety | 100 a hundred |

→ Write these numbers in figures.

ninety-nine ___    twelve ___    forty-three ___    thirty-one ___

eleven ___    seventy-six ___    eighty-five ___    twenty-two ___

sixty-four ___    fifty-seven ___    seventeen ___    a hundred ___

## Check your answers

Ninety-nine – 99; Twelve – 12; Forty-three – 43; Thirty-one – 31;
Eleven – 11; Seventy-six – 76; Eighty-five – 85; Twenty-two – 22;
Sixty-four – 64; Fifty-seven – 57; Seventeen – 17; A hundred – 100

→ Write these numbers in words.

Example: 72 – *Seventy-two*

| | | |
|---|---|---|
| 18 _____ | 59 _____ | 13 _____ |
| 93 _____ | 15 _____ | 21 _____ |
| 86 _____ | 16 _____ | 45 _____ |
| 19 _____ | 37 _____ | 12 _____ |
| 14 _____ | 68 _____ | 100 _____ |

## Check your answers

→ Now try some mental maths. Say these sums aloud when you do them.

**1** Eleven and five and seventeen and forty-two is _____
You say, 'Eleven and five is sixteen, and seventeen is… and forty-two is…

**2** Nine and six and twenty-three and eighteen is _____

**3** Four and twelve and two and fourteen is _____

## Check your answers

**1** Eleven and five is sixteen, and seventeen is thirty three and forty-two is seventy-five. **2** Nine and six is fifteen, and twenty-three is thirty-eight and eighteen is fifty-six. **3** Four and twelve is sixteen, and two is eighteen and fourteen is thirty-two.

→ Say these numbers aloud as quickly as possible.

**a** Say the **even** numbers up to twenty – two, four, six, etc…
**b** Say the **odd** numbers up to twenty – one, three, five, etc…
**c** Count in 5s up to 50. Five, ten, etc…
**d** Count in 3s up to 36. Three, six, etc…
**e** Can you say the 'eight times table' in English?
One eight is eight
Two eights are sixteen
Three eights are …

## Check your answers

**a** Two, four, six, eight, ten, twelve, fourteen, sixteen, eighteen, twenty

**b** One, three, five, seven, nine, eleven, thirteen, fifteen, seventeen, nineteen

**c** Five, ten, fifteen, twenty, twenty-five, thirty, thirty-five, forty, forty-five, fifty

**d** Three, six, nine, twelve, fifteen, eighteen, twenty-one, twenty-four, twenty-seven, thirty, thirty-three, thirty-six

**e** One eight is eight      Two eights are sixteen
Three eights are twenty-four      Four eights are thirty-two
Five eights are forty      Six eights are forty-eight
Seven eights are fifty-six      Eight eights are sixty-four
Nine eights are seventy-two      Ten eights are eighty

## Maths talk

→ Write the sums below in figures.

Use the numbers and signs in the box to help you.

**a** Twenty plus ten equals thirty 20_____10_____30
**b** Twelve minus one is eleven _____
**c** Four multiplied by six equals twenty-four_____
**d** Twenty-seven divided by three is nine_____

| 4 | 12 | 30 | 11 | 3 | 10 | 27 | 6 | 1 | 24 | 9 | 20 |
|---|----|----|----|---|----|----|---|---|----|---|----|
|   |    | +  | −  | × | ÷  | =  |   |   |    |   |    |

## Check your answers

**a** 20 + 10 = 30. **b** 12 − 1 = 11. **c** 4 × 6 = 24. **d** 27 ÷ 3 = 9.

## Insight 74

*Q How do you say this? 3 × 6 = 18.*
*A* There are 3 ways

**a** three sixes are
**b** three times six is      } eighteen
**c** three multiplied by six equals
(more formal/technical)

## Find the words and phrases

→ Read the sentences below.
→ Read the text of Recording 1 (page 195), *The Story*, and find the correct words and phrases.

1 The pilot wants to talk to all the people on the plane.
He says 'Good morning, l _ _ _ _ s / and g _ _ _ l e _ _ n.'
2 Does he say 'I am your captain?' No, he uses telephone language. He says, 'T _ _ _ / _ _ / your captain.'
3 We don't call the pilot 'Pilot Smith', we say 'C _ _ _ _ _ _ Smith'.
4 The pilot invites the passengers to change the time on their watches. He says 'I_ / y _ _ / w _ _ _ _ / l _ k _ / t _ / adjust your watches, the time in London is...'
5 Does the pilot know the exact time they are arriving in London? No, he says, 'Our e _ _ _ _ _ _ _ d / time / o _ / a _ r _ _ _ l / is 7.15.'
6 What television programme is immediately after the news? Usually it's the weather f _ _ _ _ _ _ _ where they talk about the weather for the rest of today, tomorrow, etc.

### Check your answers
1 ladies and gentlemen. (These words are often on public toilet signs.) 2 This is. 3 captain. 4 If you would like to adjust your watches. 5 estimated time of arrival. 6 forecast.

## Grammar and communication 1

### Inviting people to do things

**Example from *The Story*:**

The pilot invites the passengers to change the times on their watches.

He says, 'If you **would like to** adjust your watches...'

## Insight 75

★ We use *if you would like to* for two situations:

**1** to invite people.
**2** to ask and tell people to do things in a polite, indirect way.

**For example:**

**1** 'We're having a small dinner party on Saturday. If you would like to join us...' Meaning: I'm inviting you to the dinner party.
**2** 'If you would like to take a seat for a moment...' Meaning: Please sit down and wait.

★ When you are asking someone to do something, it is common not to finish the sentence.

**For example:**

**Situation** At the reception of a small hotel.

Receptionist: 'If you would just like to follow me, please...'
(and s/he doesn't say 'I can show you to your room' – the meaning is clear from the situation. She doesn't need to finish the sentence.)

★ This expression is particularly common in formal and new situations.

### Asking someone to do something

Where can you hear these 'invitations'?

→ Read the 'invitations' on page 203 and match each one with a place below. You can use each place more than once.

office     dentist's     shop

BANK

CLASSES ↓

school     dinner party

**1** If you would like to come back for your watch some time later this afternoon... around 4...

**2** If you would like to sit there, Kevin, next to my husband...

**3** I've got your son here. I'm afraid he's not very well so if you would like to come and pick him up...

**4** I'm sorry but Mr Smith isn't here this afternoon. If you would like to give me your name and number...

**5** If you would like to come with me to the cash desk...

**6** If you would like to go through to the waiting room...

**7** If you would like to go in, the manager can see you now...

**8** If you would like to just open your mouth and say 'aah'... oh yes...

**9** If you would all like to come to the table...

**10** If everybody would like to be quiet now, please...

**Check your answers**
**1** shop **2** dinner party **3** school **4** office **5** shop **6** dentist's
**7** office **8** dentist's **9** dinner party **10** school

## Insight 76
   *Q What are the possible responses to these 'invitations'? Is it OK to say 'Yes'?*
   *A* 'Yes' alone isn't appropriate. ☹

→ Look at these responses.

**1** You can say,    'Thank you'

                       'Yes, that's fine'

                       'Yes, of course'

                       'Yes, I'll' + verb

**2** You say nothing and 'do' the action.

**3** If you are following someone, you can say, 'After <u>you</u>.'

→ Match these sentences from the exercise above with an appropriate response from the box on page 204.

**1** In a shop:

**A** If you would like to come back for your watch some time later this afternoon... around 4...

**B** _____

**2** In a school:

**A** I've got your son here. I'm afraid he's not very well so if you would like to come and pick him up...

**B** _____

**3** In an office:

**A** I'm sorry but Mr Smith isn't here this afternoon. If you would like to give me your name and telephone number...

**B** _____

**4** In a shop:

**A** If you would like to come with me to the cash desk...

**B** _____

**5** In an office:

> **a** If you would like to go in, the manager can see you now.
>
> **b** _____
>
> **a** Thank you
> **b** Yes, I'll be there as soon as I can
> **c** Yes, of course, have you got pen and paper, it's 7859…
> **d** Yes, that's fine
> **e** After you

**Check your answers**
**1** d **2** b **3** c **4** e **5** a

*Our story continues. Oliver and Tasha get off the plane*

→ Look at pictures 1–6 on page 206.

In Recording 3 on pages 207–8, the conversation between Oliver and Tasha is in six parts, **a–f**. The parts are in the wrong order.

→ Listen and write the correct letter **a–f** in the first box under the pictures.

**a**

| | |
|---|---|
| **Oliver** | Well, it's been really nice talking to you, Tasha. |
| **Tasha** | Yes, and thanks for the help with the luggage. |
| **Oliver** | I'll be in touch next week, then. |
| **Tasha** | Yes, bye. |
| **Oliver** | Bye. |

**b**

| | |
|---|---|
| **Oliver** | Wow, this suitcase is a bit heavy – is that it now? |
| **Tasha** | The suitcase, the small bag and my handbag – yes, that's everything. |

**c**

| | |
|---|---|
| **Oliver** | Now, it's this way. You haven't got anything to declare, have you? |
| **Tasha** | No, nothing. |
| **Oliver** | We can go through the green channel, then. Over there. |

**d**

| | |
|---|---|
| **Immigration officer** | Thank you madam. Sir, your passport please. Thank you. |

**e**

| | |
|---|---|
| **Oliver** | Do you need a trolley? |
| **Tasha** | That would be a good idea – I've got quite a lot of luggage. |
| **Oliver** | They're just over here. Now, let's find the rest of the luggage. |

**f**

| | |
|---|---|
| **Tasha** | Would you mind waiting for just a minute, Oliver? |
| **Oliver** | Of course not. The suitcases aren't here yet, anyway. |
| **Tasha** | Could you look after my trolley, oh, and can you take my coat, please? |
| **Oliver** | Sure, go ahead. |

*(Contd)*

> *Tasha asks for help at the information desk.*
> **Airport employee**    Can I help you?
> **Tasha**    Yes, could you tell me where the ladies' is, please?
> **Airport employee**    Of course, madam. Just over there. Can you see the sign?

### Recording 3 – The Story

🔊 **CD2 TR2, 02:02**

**Check your answers**
1 d 2 e 3 f 4 b 5 c 6 a

→ Write the correct words on the signs in the pictures on page 206.

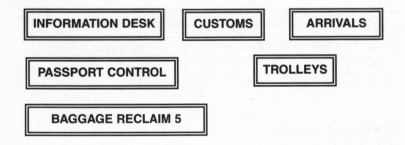

| INFORMATION DESK | CUSTOMS | ARRIVALS |
| PASSPORT CONTROL | | TROLLEYS |
| BAGGAGE RECLAIM 5 | | |

**Check your answers**
1 Passport Control 2 Trolleys 3 Information desk 4 Baggage Reclaim 5 5 Customs 6 Arrivals.

→ Read the sentences and mini-dialogues below. Where are the people?
→ Write the letters A to F in the second box, under the correct picture (1–6) on page 206.

**A** 'Could you open your bag for me, please?'
   'Yes, of course.'
**B** 'Hello, Rachel, it's lovely to see you again. How are you?'

**C** 'Excuse me, I'm from this flight but my suitcase isn't here.'

**D** 'Have you got a visa?'
'Yes, it's on the next page.'

**E** 'I think we need two, don't you? One isn't enough for all this luggage.'

**F** 'How can I help you, sir?'
'Where can I change some money, please?'

**Check your answers**
**1** D **2** E **3** F **4** C **5** A **6** B

---

## Understanding more .

→ Read the sentences 1–3 below.
→ Read the text of Recording 3 on pages 207–8 and choose **a** or **b**.

**1** **a** Tasha has got    1 piece   ⎫
    **b**              2 pieces ⎬ of luggage.

**2** **a** They go to the    red     ⎫
    **b**             green ⎬ channel at customs.

**3**     Tasha needs to   **a** change some money.
                     **b** go to the toilet.

**Check your answers**
**1** b **2** b **3** b

---

## What do they say?

→ Read the sentences below.
→ Read the text of Recording 3 on pages 207–8 and complete the sentences.

**1**    They get the trolley. Oliver suggests they find their suitcases. He says, 'Now, l _ _ ' _ / find the rest of the luggage.'

**2 a** Tasha asks Oliver to wait for her. She says,
'W _ _ _ _ / you / m _ _ _ / w _ _ _ _ _ g/ for just a minute?'

**b** Oliver responds, 'Of / c _ _ _ _ e / n _ t.'

**c** Tasha asks Oliver to look after her trolley and take her coat.
She says, 'C _ _ _ _ / y _ _ / look after my trolley?
Oh, and / c _ _ / y _ _ / take my coat, p _ _ _ _ _ ?'

**d** Oliver responds, /'S _ _ _ -/ g _ / a _ _ _ d.'

**3 a** The person at the information desk offers Tasha help.
She says, 'C_ _ / I / h _ _ _ / y _ _ ?'

**b** Tasha asks for help to find the ladies' toilets.
She asks, 'C _ _ _ _ / y _ _ / t _ _ _ / m _ / where the ladies'/
_ _ /, please?'

**Check your answers**

**1** Now let's find the rest of the luggage. **2 a** Would you mind
waiting for just a minute? **b** Of course not. **c** Could you look after
my trolley and can you take my coat, please? **d** Sure. Go ahead.
**3 a** Can I help you? **b** Could you tell me where the ladies' is
please?

---

**Insight 77**

★ The ladies' is the short expression for *'the ladies' toilets'*.

★ The men's or gents' are short expressions for *'the (gentle)
men's toilets'*.

★ We say 'the ladies'/men's is over there'. (Not: ~~are~~)

★ The words *ladies* and *gents* are for public toilets only.

---

## Find the words and phrases

→ Read the questions below.

→ Read the text of Recording 3 again and complete the words and
phrases.

**1** Oliver has only got one suitcase but Tasha's got q _ _ _ _ / a / l
_ _ / of / l _ _ g _ _ e.

**2** Are the suitcases on the way? Yes.
Are the suitcases there? No, not y _ _.

**3** Tasha asks Oliver to wait. To wait isn't a problem because the suitcases aren't there. Oliver says, 'The suitcases aren't here yet, a _ _ w _ _.

**4** How can you ask, 'Is that all (your luggage?)' in two other ways?
'Is that / _ _ /? ' or 'Is that e _ _ _ _ t _ _ _ g?'

**5** When you take someone somewhere, you can say, 'It's t _ _ _ / w _ _.'

**6 a** Oliver checks Tasha hasn't got anything to declare.
He says, 'You / h _ _ _ _' _ / got / a _ _ th _ _ _ / to declare, / h _ _ _ / y _ _ ?'

**b** Has Tasha got anything to declare? No, n _ _ _ _ _ g.

**7** Oliver is happy about meeting Tasha on the plane. He says, 'I _ ' _ / b _ _ n / r _ _ _ _ y / n _ _ e / t _ _ k _ _ g / t _ / you / Tasha.'

**8** Tasha thanks Oliver f _ _ the help with her suitcase.

**9** He says he'll contact her next week. He says, 'I' _ _ / b _ / i _ / t _ _ _ _ /next week.

**10** Verb *get*: In part e 'I'll go and *get* one' (trolley).
Here, *get* means  **a** buy  **b** bring one here?

## Check your answers

**1** Tasha's got quite a lot of luggage. **2** No, not yet. **3** The suitcases aren't there, anyway. **4** 'Is that it?' 'Is that everything?'('Is that it?' is informal, 'Is that everything?' is always appropriate.) **5** It's this way. **6 a** You haven't got anything to declare, have you? **b** No nothing. **7** It's been really nice talking *to* you Tasha (Preposition!) **8** Tasha thanks Oliver *for* his help (Preposition!) **9** I'll be *in* touch next week (Preposition!) **10** b.

## Insight 78

*Q What are the differences between suitcase, luggage and baggage?*

*A* Answer:

### Meaning

**1** This is a suitcase.

**2** This is luggage.

**3** This is baggage.

### Form

*Suitcase* is countable – one *suitcase* (two syllables), two *suitcases* (three syllables).

*Luggage* and *baggage* are uncountable/mass words.

**Example:**   Our suitcases and bags are in the car OR
Our luggage is in the car.

★ The unit word for *luggage* is *piece*. For example, an airport employee: 'How many pieces of luggage have you got?'
★ We sometimes say *case* for *suitcase*.

→ Complete the sentences below with *(suit)case(s)*, *luggage*, *pieces* of *luggage* or *baggage*.

1 People take guitars, boxes, and all sorts of _____ on planes.
2 Passengers can take one small piece of hand _____ into the plane with them.
3 On flights from Europe to America you can take two _____ of _____ .
4 Let's go kids! Are your _____ in the car?

**Check your answers**
1 baggage  2 hand luggage  3 pieces of luggage  4 (suit)cases
(Luggage is wrong here because the verb is plural – *are*)

---

## Grammar and communication 2

### Suggesting doing something together – *let's*

**Example from *The Story*:**

They get the trolley. Oliver suggests they find their suitcases. He says, 'Now let's find the rest of the luggage.'

**Meaning**
Who is making a suggestion? Oliver.
Does the suggestion include Oliver? Yes.

**Insight 79**
★ Use *let's* when the suggestion includes *you*.

## Form

*Let's* + verb

★ The negative is *let's not* + verb.
★ The short answer is, *Yes, let's.*
★ The question tag is *Let's (go), shall we?*

| Let's – summary of responses | |
| --- | --- |
| Positive responses are | OK/Alright<br>Yes, why not?<br>That's a good idea  ☺<br>Yes, why don't we? |
| Possible negative responses are | Do you really want to?<br>I'm not too sure  ☹<br>Perhaps not<br>Actually, I'm not too keen |

**Situation** You live with Chris, a friend of yours.

→ Write suggestions and responses for these situations.

**1** It's very hot. You and Chris are sitting in the garden, talking. You're thirsty.

**You** _____

**Chris** _____  ☺

**2** **Situation** You both have a friend, Hilary. Hilary is ill. Suggest you both go and visit her this afternoon.

**You** _____, _____?

**Chris** _____  ☹

**3** Chris puts the TV on. There's a football match on. You don't like football and there's a good film on Channel 5.

**You** _____the football. Why don't we watch the film on Channel 5 instead?

**Chris** _____  ☺

**4** You are talking about a holiday. Suggest Mexico.
**You** _____Mexico.
**Chris**_____ ☺
Chris suggests inviting Sam (another friend) too.
**Chris** _____
**You** _____ ☹

**5** You are going to a party tonight. You're very tired. You don't want to go.
**You** _____to the party. _____ stay here instead.
**Chris** Shall we have a Chinese meal?
**You** Yes ____'__!

## Check your answers

**1** Let's have a drink. **2** Let's go and visit Hilary this afternoon, shall we? **3** Let's not watch the football. Why don't we watch the film on Channel 5 instead? **4** Let's go to Mexico. Let's invite Sam, too. **5** Let's not go to the party. Let's stay here instead. Yes, let's!

## Responses

☺ Any response from the ☺ list in the box on page 214.
☹ Any response from the ☹ list in the box on page 214.

## Insight 80

*Q What's the difference between*   *'We could'*     *(Topic 6)*
                                     *'We can...'*
*and 'Let's'...?*
*A* **Here are two examples:**

**Situation** You're with a friend, talking about this evening.

**a** 'We could go to the cinema.'
**b** 'Let's go to the cinema.'

With a *We could...* the cinema is a possibility.

With b *Let's...* you would like to go to the cinema and you would like the other person to go, too.

In summary, *we could* is less direct.

# Grammar and communication 3

### Asking people to do things

**Examples from** *The Story*:

**1** Tasha asks Oliver to wait for her. She says, 'Would you mind waiting for just a minute?'
Oliver responds, 'Of course not.'

**2** Tasha asks Oliver to look after her trolley and take her coat. She says, 'Could you look after my trolley, oh, and can you take my coat, please?'
Oliver responds, 'Sure. Go ahead.'

## Insight 81

★ A response isn't always necessary. The person can 'do' the action without a response.

| Grammar summary – Asking someone to do something | | |
|---|---|---|
| **Request** | **Responses – it's OK** | **Responses – it isn't OK** |
| Can you + verb...? <br> Could you + verb...? | Sure <br> Of course <br> Of course I can/could <br> Yes, that's no problem | I'm afraid I can't <br> I'm sorry but I can't <br> I'm sorry but + reason |
| Would you mind <br> + verb/ing? | Of course not <br> Not at all | |

★ It is very common to say *please* when you ask someone to do something.
★ Answers *Yes, I can, Yes, I could, No, I can't, No, I wouldn't*, etc. alone are not usually appropriate. ☹

★ *Would you mind?* means 'Is it a problem for you to...?'
If it is not a problem, the response is negative, *No, of course not.*

★ When you say *no*, it is common to give a reason.
Example 'Could you cook the dinner tomorrow, please?'
'I'm sorry, I can't. I'm going out to dinner with Julie.'

★ *Could* is less direct than *can*.

★ *Would you mind...?* can be more formal than *can you?/could you?*

## Asking someone NOT TO do something

Would you mind not +verb/'ing'?

Positive response
Oh! I'm sorry
Negative response
Is it really a problem?

### Asking people to do things – *Can you...? Could you...? Would you mind...?*

→ Read the situations below.
→ Complete the requests.
→ Choose an appropriate response from the box on page 218, where necessary.

**1** Someone speaks to you in English but you don't understand. Ask them to say it again.
You  *Ca*_____, please?

**2** You are eating with friends. You would like some water. The bottle is at the other end of the table.
You  *Co*_____
Your friend _____

**3** Your child asks for help with his/her English homework.
*Mum/Dad, ca* _____?
You _____

**4** You are a tourist and you've got a camera. You want a photo with your friends. You ask another tourist.

W _____?

The tourist _____

**5** The telephone rings. You are just going in the shower. Ask the person to call you back in 10 minutes.

Ca _____ ?

The caller _____

**6** A friend is staying in your house. She smokes in the kitchen. You really don't like it. Ask her not to.

You W_____

Your friend _____

**7** Someone tells you a new word in English. You want to write it but you don't know the spelling.

You Co _____?

The other person _____

## Responses

Of course. What is it?
I'm sorry but I'm going out right now and it's urgent
Oh, sorry!
Not at all – what do I do?
Yes, it's T – H – A…
Yes, here you are

**Check your answers**
**1** Can you say that again, please? *This is more common than 'Can you repeat that, please?' **2** Could you pass the water, please? Yes. Here you are. **3** Mum/Dad, can you help me with my homework? Of course. What is it? **4** Would you mind taking a photo of us, please? Not at all. What do I do? **5** Can you call me back in 10 minutes, please? I'm sorry but I'm going out right now and it's urgent. **6** Would you mind not smoking in the kitchen? Oh, sorry! **7** Could you spell that for me, please? Yes, it's T – H – A…

## Asking people to do things – official announcements

**Situation**  On a plane or at an airport.

→ Cover the text of Recording 4.
→ Read the flight attendants' requests and invitations below (a–h)
→ Listen to the announcements on Recording 4, (1–8). Just try to understand the message – it is not necessary to understand all the words.
→ Match the requests and the announcements, for example 1–f.
→ Write the number in the box.

**a**  'Could you please go back to your seat, sir? We're landing soon.' ☐

**b**  'Would you mind not smoking, please, sir? This is a non-smoking flight.' ☐

**c**  'I'm sorry, could you please sit down again, madam? The plane is still moving.' ☐

**d**  'Could you put those bags in the overhead compartments, please?' ☐

**e**  'Could you please hurry, sir? The aircraft is ready to leave.' ☐

**f**  'Could you please stay in your seat, sir, and fasten your seatbelt? It's a little bumpy ahead.' ☐

**g**  'If you wouldn't mind filling this in, madam…You'll need it at passport control.' ☐

**h**  'If you would like to report to the special desk sir, when you get off the plane…' ☐

### Recording 4

🔊 **CD2 TR 2, 03:35**

> **1**  Passengers are requested to remain in their seats with their seat belts fastened – we are entering an area of turbulence.
>
> **2**  Passenger Smith going to Rome is requested to go immediately to Gate 12 where the flight is now closing.
>
> **3**  All transfer passengers are requested to report to the transfer desk.
>
> *(Contd)*

**4** All passengers are requested to return to their seats. We are beginning our descent.

**5** Passengers are requested to put all hand luggage in the storage space above your heads.

**6** All passengers are required to complete a landing card for the immigration authorities.

**7** Passengers are requested to remain in their seats until the plane comes to a complete halt.

**8** Passengers are respectfully reminded that smoking is not allowed on this flight.

**Check your answers**
**a** 4 **b** 8 **c** 7 **d** 5 **e** 2 **f** 1 **g** 6 **h** 3

## Insight 82

★ In hotels, restaurants, airports, shops, etc., the staff say *sir* to a man and *madam* to a woman. Clients and customers don't use *sir* or *madam* with staff.

★ If we use the family name, we say *Mr* or *Mrs* + family name.

## Grammar and communication 4

### Asking for help – indirect questions

The person at the information desk offers Tasha help.
She says, 'Can I help you?'

Tasha asks for help to find the toilets.
She says, 'Could you tell me where the ladies' is please?'

Direct question     'Where's the ladies', please?'
Indirect question   'Could you tell me where the ladies' is, please?'

## Insight 83

★ Both are grammatically correct.
★ *Could you...* is very common because it is indirect.*
★ Use *Could you tell me...*
   *Can you show me...*  } to ask for help.
   *Would you mind explaining...*
★ In other words, expressions for 'asking for help' and
   'asking someone to do something' are the same.

**Common mistake – word order in indirect questions**

## Insight 84

'Can you tell me how much this is, please?' ✓
                    (subject + verb ✓)
(Not: 'Can you tell me how much is this, please?) ✗
                    (Verb + subject ✗)
★ Word order is important with indirect questions.

*Q Where is the question form in indirect questions?*
*A* At the beginning.
*Can you...*
*Could you...*  } is the question. (verb + subject)
*Would you mind...*

The question is at the beginning.
The second part of the sentence is not a question. For this
reason there is no question form here.

| Grammar summary – Indirect questions – verb *be* | | | |
|---|---|---|---|
| **Indirect question phrase** | **question words** | **subject** | **verb** |
| Can you tell me | where | | |
| Could you tell me | how much | it | is? |
| Would you mind telling me | when | | |
| | who | | |

→ Below are six direct questions asking for help.
→ Ask the questions in a polite (indirect) way.
→ Start with *Excuse me,...*

**1** 'Where's the coffee bar?'
*Excuse me, ca*_____

**2** 'Where are the toilets?'
*Excuse me, co*_____

**3** 'How much is this?'
*Excuse me, co*_____

**4** 'How much are these?'
*Excuse me, w*_____

**5** 'How much is this magazine?'
*Excuse me, ca*_____

**6** 'How much are these crisps?'
*Excuse me, co*_____

## Check your answers
**1** Excuse me, can you tell me where the coffee bar **is**, please?
**2** Excuse me, could you tell me where the toilets **are**, please?
**3** Excuse me, could you tell me how much this **is**, please?
**4** Excuse me, would you mind telling me how much these **are**, please?
**5** Excuse me, can you tell me how much this magazine is, please?
**6** Excuse me, could you tell me how much these crisps **are**, please?

## British culture – money – sterling
▶ The currency (unit of money) in Britain is the pound (£). (Today £1 is about US $1.60.)
▶ The sign '£' goes in front of the number, for example £15. (Not: 15£)
▶ There are 100 pence (we often say 'p') in £1.
▶ The coins are:
  1p 2p 5p 10p 20p 50p £1 £2

▶ The notes are: £5 £10 £20 £50

## Insight 85

*Q How do we say, for example, £3.20?*
*A* We can say, 'Three pounds, twenty pence' (more formal).

or 'Three pounds, twenty'   } less formal
or 'Three pounds, twenty p'

*About your country: money*

→ Read the questions below.
→ Either write your answers or prepare to tell a friend.

**1** What is the currency in your country?
_____

**2** What are the coins?
_____

**3** What are the notes?
_____

**4** How do you write it?

_____

**5** How do you say it?

_____


*Our story continues. Oliver is in a shop in the airport*

## Understanding the important information

→ Cover the text of Recording 5.
→ Read the questions below.
→ Listen to Recording 5 and answer the questions.

**1** Oliver buys 1, 2, 3, 4, things?
**2** Oliver's got the right money. Yes/No

**Recording 5**

◀ **CD2 TR 2, 05:58**

| | |
|---|---|
| **Oliver** | Excuse me, do you sell Computing Weekly? |
| **Seller** | Yes, sir, they're here. |
| **Oliver** | And a packet of mints – have you got Polos? |
| *The seller gets a packet of Polos.* | |

| Oliver | £2.86 please, sir. |
|---|---|
| Oliver | Sorry, I haven't got any change. Is £20.00 alright? |
| Seller | Yes, no problem. Seventeen pounds, 14p change. |
| Oliver | Thanks. |

## Check your answers

**1** Oliver buys two things. **2** No, Oliver hasn't got the right money.

---

## Understanding more

→ Cover the text of Recording 5 again.
→ Read the sentences below.
→ Listen and choose the correct answer.

**1** Oliver buys     **a** a newspaper.
                      **b** a magazine.

**2** He buys   **a** a Mars bar
               **b** a packet of Polos   } too.
               **c** a packet of crisps
               **d** a bar of chocolate

**3** The total price is
   **a** £1.86.
   **b** £2.68.
   **c** £2.86.

**4** Oliver gives the man
   **a** £5.
   **b** £10.
   **c** £20.

**5** The change is
   **a** £17.40.
   **b** £7.14.
   **c** £7.40.
   **d** £17.14.

**6** The change is
   **a** right.
   **b** wrong.

## Check your answers
**1** b **2** b **3** c **4** c **5** d **6** a

## What's the right word?

### Snacks

→ Label the pictures. Choose one expression from **Box 1** and one
  word from **Box 2** below.
→ Use your dictionary if necessary.

Example
*a packed of polos*

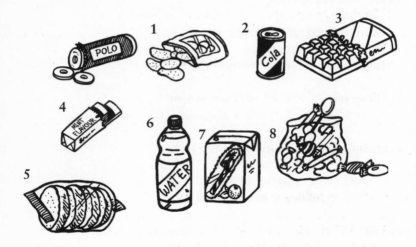

| Box 1 | |
|---|---|
| a bar of | a carton of |
| a can of | a packet of |
| a bottle of | |

| Box 2 | |
|---|---|
| water | sweets |
| fruit juice | crisps |
| chocolate | biscuits |
| chewing gum | Coke |

226

| | | |
|---|---|---|
| **1** a packet‿of crisps | **4** a packet‿of chewing gum | **7** a carton‿of fruit juice |
| **2** a can‿of Coke | | |
| **3** a bar‿of chocolate | **5** a packet‿of biscuits | **8** a packet‿of sweets |
| | **6** a bottle‿of water | |

## How do you pronounce it?

### Saying groups of words together – linking

## Insight 86

→ Look at the link lines and stress on the expressions above.

The word *of* is weak in all the sentences, so the vowel is *schwa* / ə /.

→ Listen to Recording 6 and repeat the list.

Pay special attention to
**a** stress **b** linking words **c** weak *of*.

## British culture – snacks

▶ Snacks are very common in Britain.
▶ Sweet things are very popular, especially sweets and chocolate, for example, Polos (mint sweets) and Mars bars.
▶ It is common to have biscuits and cakes, especially with tea and coffee.
▶ Nowadays, savoury snacks, for example, crisps and nuts, are also popular.
▶ All the snacks in the exercise above are very common.
▶ People eat snacks at any time of the day.
▶ At work, a snack with tea and coffee is very usual.
▶ In the summer, ice cream is a popular snack.
▶ In recent years, interest in healthy eating has increased.

### *About you: snacks*

→ Write answers to the questions below or prepare to tell a friend.

**1** What do people eat and drink between meals in your country?

_____

**2** Write two lists:
   **a** snacks you like.
   **b** snacks you don't like.

### Understanding numbers
### Is it 13 or 30?

Look at the stress pattern.

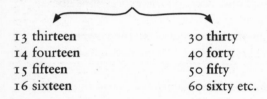

13 thirteen          30 **thirty**
14 fourteen          40 **forty**
15 fifteen           50 **fifty**
16 sixteen           60 **sixty** etc.

### Can you hear the difference?

→ Listen to Recording 7 and tick ✓ the correct picture.

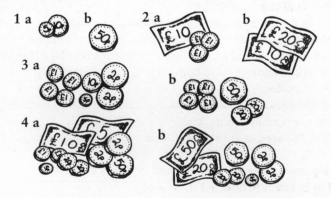

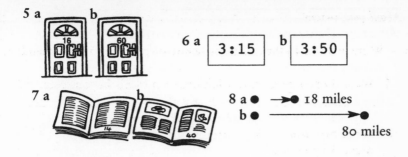

5 a    b

6 a 3:15    b 3:50

7 a    b

8 a ●——●18 miles
b ●————————●
80 miles

**Recording 7**

◄)) CD2 TR 2, 07:42

| | | |
|---|---|---|
| **1** | **A** | Excuse me, how much is this, please? |
| | **B** | 50p. |
| **2** | **A** | How much does this cost, please? |
| | **B** | £13. |
| | **A** | Sorry, is that £13 or £30? |
| | **B** | £13, sir. |
| **3** | **A** | Do you know how much this is, please? |
| | **B** | £4.90. |
| **4** | **A** | Excuse me, could you tell me how much this costs, please? |
| | **B** | Of course. That's £17.99. |
| | **A** | Is that one, seven or seven '0'? |
| | **B** | One seven, seventeen. |
| **5** | **A** | Where do you live? |
| | **B** | At number 60. |
| **6** | **A** | At what time? |
| | **B** | At 3.15. |
| **7** | **A** | Where is it? |
| | **B** | On page 14 or 40. |
| **8** | **A** | How far is it to the town? |
| | **B** | 18 miles. |

**Check your answers**
1 b 2 a 3 b 4 a 5 b 6 a 7 b 8 a

# What do they say?

### Asking the price

→ Read questions 1–4 of Recording 7 above.
→ Copy below the four questions to ask the price.
→ Choose *direct* or *indirect* for each one.

**1** _____? Direct/Indirect
**2** _____? Direct/Indirect
**3** _____? Direct/Indirect
**4** _____? Direct/Indirect

## Check your answers

**1** Excuse me, how much is this, please? (Direct) **2** How much does this cost, please? (Direct) **3** Do you know how much this is, please? (Indirect) **4** Excuse me, could you tell me how much this costs, please? (Indirect)

→ Listen to Recording 7 again and repeat the questions and answers.

## Insight 87
### Common mistake – indirect questions

★ The word order in indirect questions is always the same. The question is at the beginning and the rest is normal word order – subject first, then verb.

'Excuse me, could you tell me how much **this costs**, please?'

(Not: 'Excuse me, could you tell me how much ~~does this cost~~, please?')

★ Use *if* with yes/no indirect questions.
For example: Direct question. 'Does this shop open on Sundays?'
Indirect question. 'Do you know if this shop opens on Sundays?'

## Asking for help – indirect questions

→ Which one is correct? Complete the questions with a, b or c.

**1** Excuse me, do you know how much _____, please?
**a** are these **b** these are

**2** Could you tell me _____, please?
**a** where the coffee bar is **b** where is the coffee bar

**3** Do you know when _____ ?
**a** starts the film **b** the film starts

**4** Excuse me, can you tell me _____?
**a** where this train goes **b** where does this train go

**5** Do you know what _____?
**a** does he do **b** he does

**6** Excuse me, can you tell me _____ to the town centre, please?
**a** how far is it **b** how far it is

**7** Could you tell me _____ there?
**a** how do I get **b** how to get

**8** Do you know when _____?
**a** he is arriving **b** is he arriving

**9** Can you tell me what _____ in English?
**a** is this **b** this is

**10** Can you tell me _____ to London?
**a** does this train go **b** if this train goes

**11** Could you tell me _____ the right bus for the airport, please?
**a** if this is **b** is this

**12** Do you know _____ ?
  **a** what means this word
  **b** what this word means
  **c** what does mean this word

This one's difficult for very many learners of English – have you got it right?

**Check your answers**
1 b 2 a 3 b 4 a 5 b 6 b 7 b 8 a 9 b 10 b 11 a 12 b

*What would you say?*

**1** You buy something in a shop.
  The person gives you the wrong change.

  _____

**2** You are at baggage reclaim at the airport. Your suitcase
  doesn't come.

  _____

**Possible answers**
**1** How much is it again? OR I'm sorry but I don't think this
  change is right.

  *I don't think X is right* is more common than 'x is wrong'.
  *I don't think X is right* is less direct.
Advanced alternative: I'm sorry but I think there's a mistake here.

**2** Excuse me, I don't know where my suitcase is. Could you help
  me please?

_____

## Revision

**How do you say it in your language?**

→ Here are some examples of the important points in this topic.

→ Translate the sentences into your language in the spaces.
→ Remember – translate the idea, not the words.

**1** You arrive at a restaurant. The person working there says 'If you would like to follow me... (I'll show you to your table)

_____

**2** A 'What shall we do today?' B 'Let's go to my brother's.' A 'Fine, why not?'

_____

**3** A 'Shall we walk there?' B 'I'm not too keen on that idea. Let's go by car.'

_____

**4** A 'Can I help you?' B 'Yes, Could you tell me where the coffee bar is, please?'

_____

**5** A 'I'm sorry I can't go tomorrow. Would you mind changing the meeting to Wednesday?' B 'Of course not – that's no problem.'

_____

**6** At the end of a conversation you say, 'It's been nice talking to you.'

_____

**7** 'Do you need a trolley? I'll go and get one.'

_____

### Join the conversation

→ Look at the text of Recording 8 on page 234. It's the complete conversation from Recording 3, when Oliver and Tasha get off the plane. Notice the linking.
→ Listen to Recording 8 and read Tasha's words in the spaces.
→ Pay special attention to the linking between the words.

## Recording 8

🔊 CD2 TR 2, 09:32

| | |
|---|---|
| **Immigration officer** | Thank you madam. Sir, your passport please. Thank you. |
| **Oliver** | Do you need ‿a trolley? |
| **Tasha** | That would be a good ‿idea – I've got quite ‿a lot ‿of luggage. |
| **Oliver** | They're just over here. Now, let's find the rest ‿of the luggage. |
| **Tasha** | Would you mind waiting for just ‿a minute,‿ Oliver? |
| **Oliver** | Of course not. The suitcases ‿aren't here yet anyway. |
| **Tasha** | Could you look ‿after my trolley, oh, and can you take my coat, please? |
| **Oliver** | Sure, go ahead. |

*Tasha asks for help ‿at the information desk.*

| | |
|---|---|
| **Airport employee** | Can ‿I help you? |
| **Tasha** | Yes, could ‿you tell me where the (ladies'/gents') is, please? |
| **Airport employee** | Of course, (madam/sir). Just ‿over there. Can you see the sign? |
| **Oliver** | Wow, this suitcase ‿is ‿a bit heavy – is that ‿it now? |
| **Tasha** | The suitcase, the small bag ‿and my handbag – yes that's ‿everything. |
| **Oliver** | Now, it's this way. You haven't got ‿anything to declare, have you? |
| **Tasha** | No, nothing. |
| **Oliver** | We can go through the green channel, then. Over there. |
| **Oliver** | Well, it's been really nice talking to you, Tasha. |
| **Tasha** | Yes ‿and thanks for the help with the luggage. |
| **Oliver** | I'll be in touch next week, then. |
| **Tasha** | Yes, bye. |
| **Oliver** | Bye. |

## Test yourself 7

### Which one is right?

→ Choose **a** or **b**.

**1** Thirty-five and twenty-nine are
  **a** forty-six.
  **b** sixty-four.

**2** If you would like to go in now, madam...
  **a** Yes, I would.
  **b** Thank you.

**3** **a** Would you mind to wait, please?
  **b** Would you mind waiting, please?

**4** **a** I'm hungry. Let's have something to eat!
  **b** I'm hungry. Let's to have something to eat!

**5** Could you help me, please?
  **a** Yes. What do you want?
  **b** Of course. What would you like me to do?

**6** Excuse me, can you tell me where the station is, please?
  **a** Yes, I can.
  **b** Yes, it's just over there.

**7** **a** I'll get a trolley for the luggages.
  **b** I'll get a trolley for the luggage.

**8** The information desk?
  It's  **a** in this way.
        **b** this way.

**9** **a** 'Bye, I'll see you tomorrow.'
  **b** 'Bye, I see you tomorrow.'

**10** Would you mind coming back later? (You can go back later.)
   **a** Yes.
   **b** Sure, it's no problem.

**11** **a** Can you tell me where are the taxis, please?
    **b** Can you tell me where the taxis are, please?

**12** £24.75. This is
   **a** pounds twenty four, seventy-five.
   **b** twenty-four pounds, seventy-five.

### Write a dialogue

**Situation**  Eva is an au-pair with the Lewis family. (She works in the family, helping with the children and the house.) It's the morning and Barbara, Lewis and Eva are talking about the day.

**Barbara**                                     **Eva**
  **1** Barbara asks Eva to take the
     children to school. She's
     working this morning.                   **2** Eva says 'yes'

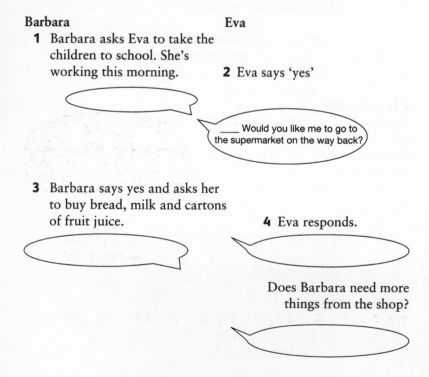

_____ Would you like me to go to the supermarket on the way back?

  **3** Barbara says yes and asks her
     to buy bread, milk and cartons
     of fruit juice.                          **4** Eva responds.

Does Barbara need more
things from the shop?

**5** Barbara says no and asks Eva to
take the children to the park
after school.

She also asks her to work
on Saturday evening.

**6** Eva can take the children
to the park but she can't
work on Saturday evening.
She's going to a party.

**7** It's the afternoon
Eva is in the park with the children.
One of the children sees an
ice cream van and suggests they
all have an ice cream.

*OK. Which one
would you like?*

**Check your answers**
**1** b **2** b **3** b **4** a **5** b **6** b **7** b **8** b **9** a **10** b **11** b **12** b

## Dialogue: model answers

**1 Barbara**    Could you take the children to school, please? I'm working this morning.

**2 Eva**    Of course. Would you like me to go to the supermarket on the way back?

**3 Barbara**    Could you? Can you get some bread, some milk and some cartons of fruit juice?

**4 Eva**    Fine. Do you need anything else?

**5 Barbara**    No, thanks. Could you take the children to the park after school and would you mind working on Saturday evening?

**6 Eva**    I can take the children to the park but I'm sorry, I can't work on Saturday evening – I'm going to a party.
[In the afternoon]

**7 Child**    Let's all have an ice cream!

# 8

# Using public transport

Grammar and communication
- **Prepositions at the end of questions**
- **Asking for instructions, giving instructions**
- **Asking for and understanding travel information**
- **– the time, timetables, itineraries**

Vocabulary
- **Public transport**
- **The time**

Pronunciation
- **Stress – place names**

*Oliver is at the information desk at the airport. He needs to get to the centre of London.*

## Understanding the important information

→ Cover the text of Recording 1, *The Story*.
→ Read the question below.
→ Listen to the recording and answer the question.

How is Oliver going to the centre? – By train, by bus or by taxi?

### Recording 1 – The Story

🔊 **CD2 TR 3, 00:13**

| | |
|---|---|
| **Airport employee** | Can I help you? |
| **Oliver** | Yes, could you tell me how to get to the centre of town, please? |
| **Airport employee** | You can go by bus, by train or by underground, sir. Which part of London are you going to? |
| **Oliver** | I need to get to Victoria Station. |
| **Airport employee** | Then you can take the A1 Airbus. It goes all the way to Victoria. |
| **Oliver** | The A1, right. And where do I get the bus from? |
| **Airport employee** | Just over there, sir. You see the sign that says, 'Airbus?' You follow that sign. |
| **Oliver** | Oh, I see! Do you know when the next bus leaves? |
| **Airport employee** | In ten minutes, sir – at 8.05. |
| **Oliver** | And how long does it take to get there? |
| **Airport employee** | I'm not sure – the best thing to do is ask the driver. |
| **Oliver** | Many thanks for your help. |

**Check your answer**
By bus

## Understanding more

→ Cover the text of Recording 1 again.
→ Read the questions below.
→ Listen and choose the right answers.

**1** Choose ALL the right answers.
The man says Oliver can go by bus, or by
**a** coach
**b** taxi
**c** underground
**d** train

(2–6 Choose the right answer.)
**2** Where exactly in London is Oliver going?
**a** Waterloo Station
**b** Paddington Station
**c** Victoria Station
**d** Euston Station

**3** What's the name of the bus?
**a** London bus
**b** Airbus
**c** Central bus
**d** Express bus

**4** **a** It's a long walk to the bus.
**b** The bus is very near.
**c** The bus goes from the train station.
**d** The bus is downstairs.

**5** The next bus leaves
**a** in an hour
**b** in half an hour

**c** in two minutes' time
**d** in ten minutes' time

**6** When does the bus arrive in London?
  **a** we don't know
  **b** in one hour
  **c** in half an hour
  **d** in ten minutes

**Check your answers**
**1** c and d **2** c **3** b **4** b **5** d **6** a

---

## What do they say?

→ Read the sentences below.
→ Listen to Recording 1 again and try to complete the words.
→ Then read the text on page 240 to help you if necessary.

**1 a** Oliver doesn't know how to get to the centre of town. He asks for help. He says, 'C _ _ _ _ / you / t _ _ _ / me / h _ _ / t _ / g _ _ / t _ / the centre of town, please?'
  **b** There are three possibilities.
The man says, 'You / c _ _ / g _ / b _ bus, / b _ / train or b _ / underground.'

**2 a** The man asks where exactly in London Oliver is going. He says, 'Which part of London / a _ _ / y _ _ / g _ _ _ g / t _ ?'
  **b** Oliver answers, 'I / n _ _ _ / t _ / g _ _ / t _ Victoria Station.'

**3 a** The man suggests the Airbus.
He says, 'Y _ _ / c _ _ / t _ _ _ / the A1 Airbus.'

**4 a** Oliver doesn't know where the buses are. He asks, 'Where / d _ / I / g _ _ / t _ _ / b _ _ / f _ _ _?'

**b** The man gives Oliver instructions.
'Y _ _ / f _ ll _ _ / the sign that says 'Airbus'.'

**5** Is it necessary to change?
No, the A1 bus goes a _ _ / t _ _ / w _ _ / to Victoria Station.

**6** Oliver wants to know the time the journey takes. He asks,
'H _ _ / l _ _ _ / d _ _ _ / it / t _ _ _ / t _ / g _ _ / there?'

**Check your answers**
**1 a** Could you tell me how *to* get to the centre of town, please?
(preposition!) **b** You can go *by* bus, *by* train or *by* underground
(preposition!). **2 a** Which part of London are you going *to*?
(preposition!). **b** I need to get to Victoria Station. **3** You can take
the A1 Airbus. **4 a** Where do I get the bus *from*? (preposition!)
**b** You follow the sign that says 'Airbus'. **5** No, the A1 bus goes all
the way to Victoria Station. **6** How long does it take to get there?

---

## How do you pronounce it?

### London's main stations – stress

*The logo is a registered trademark in the name of the Secretary of State for the Environment, Transport and the Regions.*

**Example from *The story*:**

The man asks Oliver: 'Which part of London are you going to?'
Oliver answers: 'I need to get to Vic<u>to</u>ria.'

→ Cover the text of Recording 2 below.
→ Look at the Underground map on page 245 with the names of the main train stations.
→ Listen to Recording 2.
→ Repeat the names and <u>underline</u> the stress for each one.

**Check your answers** (*Recording 2*)
◆) **CD2 TR 3, 01:14**

1 Vic<u>to</u>ria
2 <u>Pad</u>dington
3 <u>Mar</u>ylebone
4 King's <u>Cross</u>
5 St <u>Pan</u>cras
6 <u>Eus</u>ton
7 <u>Liver</u>pool Street
8 Water<u>loo</u>

## Understanding the important information

→ Read the sentences below.
→ Read the text about the London Underground and answer True or False.

| | | |
|---|---|---|
| 1 | London has twelve Underground lines. | True/False |
| 2 | There are ninety-five Underground stations. | True/False |
| 3 | Each line has a number. | True/False |
| 4 | There is only one fare. | True/False |
| 5 | It costs the same all day. | True/False |
| 6 | You can use a travelcard on the buses and trains. | True/False |
| 7 | It doesn't cost much to use public transport in Britain. | True/False |

# British culture – the London Underground or 'the Tube'

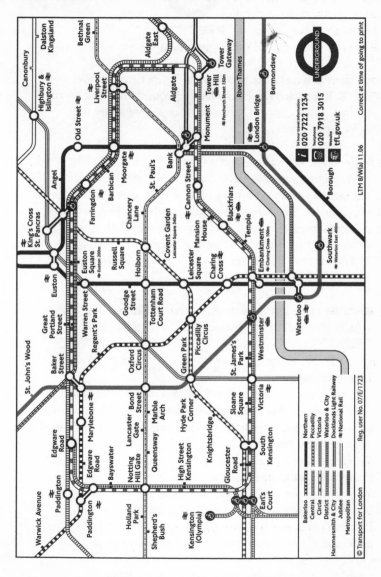

London Travel Information
**020 7222 1234**
24 hours

Textphone
**020 7918 3015**

- There are just over 450 kms of Tube tunnel under London's streets, with 12 Underground lines and more than 250 stations. Over 100,000 people a day use Victoria station.

- Each line has a name and a colour. For example, the District Line is green and the Circle Line is yellow. London is divided into six fare zones. Central London is Zone 1. The fare you pay depends on the number of zones you travel in. It is cheaper to travel after 9.30 in the morning when you can buy a one-day travelcard. You can use this ticket on the buses and trains too. Family tickets are also available.

- Public transport is quite expensive in Britain. The cheapest way to travel in London is with an Oyster card.

### Check your answers
The correct answers are in brackets. **1** True. **2** False (more than 250). **3** False (each line has a name). **4** False (the fare depends on the number of zones). **5** False (it's cheaper after 9.30). **6** True. **7** False (it's quite expensive).

### Famous places in London – stress

You are on a tourist bus in central London.

→ Look at the bus route below with the famous places.
→ Listen to the announcement on Recording 3.
→ Underline the syllable with stress for each place.

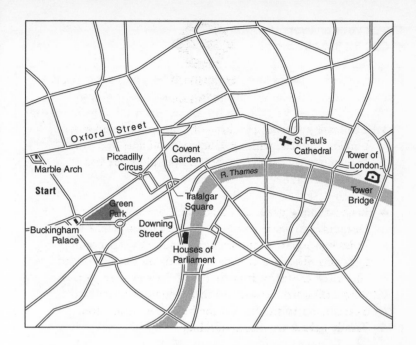

1 Marble Arch    2 Oxford Street    3 Green Park

4 Buckingham Palace    5 Piccadilly Circus    6 Trafalgar Square

7 Downing Street    8 Houses of Parliament    9 Covent Garden

10 St Paul's Cathedral    11 London Bridge    12 The Tower of London

*He's getting off the bus and she's getting on the bus.*

Good morning, ladies and gentlemen. Welcome to the Tour of London bus. If you would like to look at your maps for a moment, I can tell you a little bit about our route. This bus stops at the following famous places:

1  Marble <u>Arch</u>
2  <u>Ox</u>ford Street
3  Green <u>Park</u>
4  Buckingham <u>Pal</u>ace
5  Piccadilly <u>Cir</u>cus
6  Trafalgar <u>Square</u>
7  <u>Down</u>ing Street
8  The Houses of <u>Par</u>liament
9  Covent <u>Gar</u>den
10  St Paul's Ca<u>the</u>dral
11  Tower <u>Bridge</u>
12  The Tower of <u>Lon</u>don

Passengers are reminded that you can get on or off the bus at any one of these stops. We hope you enjoy your tour with us this morning.

## Insight 88
★ The stress is at the beginning on two names, <u>Ox</u>ford Street and <u>Down</u>ing Street.
★ For most place names the stress is on the second word, like *Park*, *Palace*, *Square*, *Road*, *Bridge*, for example, London <u>Bridge</u>, Kensington <u>Pal</u>ace.
★ *Street* is different – the stress is on the first word.

→ Listen to Recording 3 again and repeat the names of these famous places.

## How do you pronounce it?

### Stress on place names – addresses

**Insight 89**
★ English has lots of words for *Road* or *Street*.

→ Listen to Recording 4 and repeat these street names.
→ Underline the syllable with stress.

| | | |
|---|---|---|
| *Park Road* | *High Street* | *Eton Avenue* |
| *Buckingham Gardens* | *Tudor Drive* | *Moor Close* |
| *West Hill* | *Elm Crescent* | *Rose Walk* |
| *River Lane* | *Church Grove* | *Esher Place* |
| *Orchard Way* | *Maple Court* | *Nova Mews* |

**Check your answers** (*Recording 4*)
◀)) **CD2 TR 3, 02:56**

Abbreviations are in brackets ( ).

| | | |
|---|---|---|
| Park <u>Road</u> (Rd) | <u>High</u> Street (St) | Eton <u>Av</u>enue (Ave) |
| Buckingham <u>Gar</u>dens (Gdns) | Tudor <u>Drive</u> (Dr) | Moor <u>Close</u> (Cl) |
| West <u>Hill</u> | Elm <u>Cres</u>cent (Cres) | Rose <u>Walk</u> (Wlk) |
| River <u>Lane</u> (La) | Church <u>Grove</u> (Gr) | Esher <u>Place</u> (Pl) |
| Orchard <u>Way</u> | Maple <u>Court</u> (Ct) | Nova <u>Mews</u> |

★ When we say or write an address, the number is first, before
the name of the street, for example, 2 Park Road, 57 Eton
Avenue.

# Grammar and communication 1

### Prepositions at the end of questions

**Examples from *The Story*:**

**1** The man asks Oliver exactly where in London he's going
He says, 'Which part of London are you going to?'
(preposition!)

**Affirmative** 'I'm going to Victoria.'

**Question** 'Which part of London are you going to?'

**2** Oliver doesn't know where the buses are.
He asks 'Where do I get the bus from?' (preposition!)

**Possible answer** 'You get the bus from the bus stop outside the terminal.'

## Insight 90

★ The grammar is correct with the preposition at the end.
★ Nowadays it is common to put the preposition at the end of the question.

→ Complete these mini-dialogues with the correct question from the box below.

**1** A _____? B My brother – I call him every week.

**2** A _____? B This picture. Isn't it attractive?

**3** A _____? B My girlfriend. It's her birthday today.

**4** A _____? B My boyfriend. I miss him.

**5**  **A** _____? **B** My keys. Do you know where
they are?

**6**  **A**  There's an urgent e-mail for you. **B** _____?

**7**  **A**  I like reading. **B** _____?

**8**  **A**  She's married. **B** _____?

**9**  **A**  I'm going to that new restaurant this evening.
**B** _____?

**10**  Taxi-driver **A** _____?
**B** The station please.

**11**  **A**  We could go and see that new film this weekend.
**B** _____?

**12**  **A**  I'd like to book a Eurostar ticket to Paris, please.
**B** _____?

> **a** Do you know who it's from? **b** Oh, is she? Who to?
> **c** They're nice flowers. Who are they for? **d** Who are you talking to?
> **e** Of course, sir. When for? **f** Are you really? Who are you going with?
> **g** What are you looking at? **h** What's it about?
> **i** Do you? What sort of books are you interested in?
> **j** What are you looking for? **k** Who are you writing to?
> **l** Where to, madam?

**Check your answers**
**1** d **2** g **3** c **4** k **5** j **6** a **7** i **8** b **9** f **10** l **11** h **12** e

## What's the right word?

### Public transport

→ Write the names of these vehicles. Choose words from **Box 1** on
page 252.

→ Where do they go from? Choose the place from **Box 2** and write
it next to the picture.

→ Use your dictionary if necessary.

| Box 1 | |
|---|---|
| taxi | train |
| underground (train) | |
| coach | bus |

| Box 2 | |
|---|---|
| station | coach station |
| bus-stop | taxi-rank |
| | platform |

## Check your answers
**1** Train/station/platform **2** underground (train)/station/platform
**3** bus/bus stop **4** coach/coach station **5** taxi/taxi-rank

### Getting around on public transport

→ Read the mini-dialogues in Recording 5 on page 253 and look at the words in the box. Ignore the pictures below for the moment.

→ Listen to Recording 5 and complete the dialogues with the correct word(s) from the box.

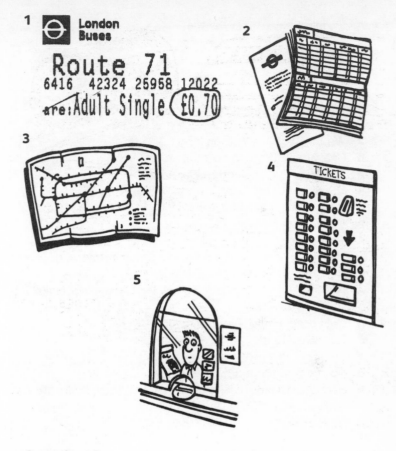

**1** London Buses

**Route 71**
6416  42324  25958  12022
are: Adult Single £0.70

**2**

**3**

**4** TICKETS

**5**

**Recording 5**

🔊 **CD2 TR 3, 04:25**

**1 A** I don't know the Underground.
Could you give me a _____ please?

  **B** Of course. Here you are.

**2 A** Excuse me, do you know the time of the next train, please?

  **B** I'm not sure. There's a _____ over there, on the wall.

**3 A** Excuse me, how much is a _____ to London?

  **B** Is that a _____ ?

  **A** No, a _____ please. I'm coming back this evening.

*(Contd)*

**4 A** I want to buy a ticket but the _____/_____ is closed.

**B** You can get one at the _____ / _____ over there.

**5 A** Which _____ does the train go from, please?

**B** Number five, right at the end, over there.

**6 A** What's the _____ to the town centre please?

**B** 70p.

**7 A** Which _____ is Victoria in?

**B** One, I think. It's in the centre, isn't it?

**8 A** Which _____ is Heathrow on?

**B** The blue one, but I don't know the name of it.

**9 A** Are you going to Edinburgh?

**B** I'd like to but it takes I hours.

**A** That's a long _____

**10 A** Is this a _____ train? **B** No, I'm afraid it stops at all stations.

**11 A** Is this a _____ train? **B** No, sorry, change at the next stop.

**12 A** I'm not sure which platform to go to.

**B** Let's listen to the _____.

**13 A** We're going on an _____ to Cambridge tomorrow.

**B** Oh, are you? What time does your coach leave?

**14 A** In a taxi. 'The fare is £4.50. How much _____ shall I give him?'

**B** 'If you give him £5.00 that's fine.'

---

direct  platform  journey  ticket machine  timetable  fare  line
ticket  excursion  fast  announcements  tip  zone  single  return
map  ticket office

**Check your answers**
**1** map **2** timetable **3** ticket, single, return **4** ticket office, ticket machine **5** platform **6** fare **7** zone **8** line **9** journey **10** fast **11** direct **12** announcements **13** excursion **14** tip

## Label the pictures

→ Now label the pictures on page 253.

**Check your answers**
**1** fare **2** timetable **3** map **4** ticket machine **5** ticket office

---

# Insight 91
### Common mistake
'This is a long travel.'✘
'This is a long journey.' ✓

*Q What's the difference between 'travel' and 'journey'?*
*A Journey* is usually a countable noun.
  *Journey* is the time and/or distance from A to B.

**For example:** 'It's a long journey from England to North America.'

*Travel* can be **a** a verb **b** an uncountable noun

Travel is general movement.
**For example: a** 'I travel a lot for my job.'
              **b** 'Foreign travel is good for a person's education.'

---

*Travel* **or** *journey?*

→ Complete with *journey* or *travel*.

**1** It's a long _____ to get here.
**2** He's a _____ agent.
**3** Foreign _____ helps people understand other cultures.
**4** How long does the _____ take?

**Check your answers**
**1** journey **2** travel **3** travel **4** journey

## What's the right word?

### Trips

→ Choose the correct phrase from the box to complete the sentences below.
→ Use your dictionary if necessary.

> change your ticket    get on    book a ticket    go on the excursion
> find out about times and prices    get off    cancel the trip

You would like to go on an excursion.

1 First you _____
2 Then you _____
3 If something happens and you can't go, you can either
   **a** _____ or **b** _____
4 On the day of the trip you **a** _____ the coach. When you get there you **b** _____ the coach and have a good time!

**Check your answers**
**1** First you find out about times and prices. **2** Then you book a ticket. **3** You can either change your ticket or cancel the trip.
**4 a** You get on the coach **b** You get off the coach.

## Grammar and communication 2

### Asking for instructions, giving instructions

Examples from *The Story*:

**Asking for instructions**

1 The man at the information desk says, 'Can I help you?' Oliver says, 'Yes, could you tell me how to get to the centre of town, please?'

**2** The man says 'You can take the A1 Airbus.'
Oliver asks, 'Where do I get the bus from?'

### Giving instructions

The man answers, 'You **follow** the sign that says 'Airbus'.'

→ Answer these questions about instructions.
  Examples: 'Where do I get the bus from?' 'You **follow** the sign...'

### Meaning
In the two examples above, *get* and *follow* are **a** in the past.

  **b** in the present.

  **c** in the future.

### Form
The tense is **a** present simple.

  **b** present progressive.

  **c** future simple.

### Check your answers
Meaning c
Form a

# Insight 92
  ★ We can use the present simple to ask for and give instructions.

### Asking for instructions

→ Read the seven questions below.
→ How many are correct?

### Direct questions

How do I get to the town centre?
How can I get to the town centre?
How could I get to the town centre?

Can you tell me how to get to the town centre?
Could you tell me how I get to the town centre?
Do you know how I can get to the town centre?
Do you know how I could get to the town centre?

**Check your answers**
All the questions are correct.

## Insight 93

*Q What are the differences?*
*A* All the questions are appropriate in most situations.

The indirect questions are very common.

*Could* is the most indirect.

### Summary – Instructions

#### 1 Asking for instructions

**Direct questions**

|  | do |  |
|---|---|---|
| How | can | I get to the town centre? |
|  | could |  |

**Indirect questions**

| Can |  | tell | me |  | I | get to the |
|---|---|---|---|---|---|---|
|  | you | show |  | how | I can | town centre? |
| Could |  |  |  |  | I could |  |
|  |  | explain | to me |  | to |  |

| Do you know how I |  | can | get to the town centre? |
|---|---|---|---|
|  |  | could |  |

#### 2 Giving instructions – present simple

You go… You follow… You take…

#### 3 For more than one possibility

You can + verb (without 'to') +'or'+ verb (without 'to')

For example: 'You can walk or go by bus.'

## Asking for instructions

→ Put the words in the right order to complete the question.

**1** Excuse me, _____ the station from here, please?
       to/how/I/do/get

**2** Excuse me, _____ a ticket for tomorrow?
       can/where/I/book

**3** Excuse me, _____ excursions to Oxford?
       out/I/how/find/about/could

**4** Can you show me _____ a ticket from this machine, please?
       to/how/buy

**5** Could you tell me _____ the coach station, please?
       to/get/I/how

**6** Do you know _____ this door, please?
       how/open/can/I

**7** Do you know _____ my return ticket, please?
       change/I/could/how

## Check your answers
**1** how do I get to **2** where can I book **3** how could I find out about
**4** how to buy **5** how I get to **6** how I can open **7** how I could change

## Giving instructions

**Example from *The Story*:**

Oliver asks: 'Where do I go to get the bus?'
The man says: 'You follow the sign that says Airbus".'

## Insight 94
★ To give instructions, use the present simple.

**Situation** You want to make a trip from London to Paris on the Eurostar train. You ask a friend for instructions.

→ Complete your friend's instructions with the correct verb phrases from the box overleaf.

→ It's not necessary to understand all the words. Just try to get the general idea.

*She's going down the escalator.*

*He's going up the escalator.*

*He's going through the door.*

When you get to St Pancras Station, _____(1) the signs to 'Eurostar'. _____(2) the escalator and _____(3) your ticket from the ticket office. Then _____(4) ticket check and security control. After that _____(5) in the departure lounge. When you hear the announcement to board the train _____(6) the right escalator or travelator for your part of the Eurostar platform and _____(7) the train, _____(8) your luggage in the special luggage racks and _____(9) your seat. If you need refreshments during the journey – tea, coffee, something to eat, _____(10) the buffet car.

> you go to   you put   you go up   you wait   you go down
> you look for   you get on   you go through   you follow
> you collect

## Check your answers
**1** you follow **2** you go down **3** you collect **4** you go through **5** you wait **6** you go up **7** you get on **8** you put **9** you look for **10** you go to

### Asking for help

→ Correct these questions if necessary. Some of the verbs are wrong.

**1** Where I sign? _____
**2** Can you tell me what do I write in this card?_____
**3** Where pay I, please? _____
**4** Can you tell me where I go now, please? _____
**5** How do I get a taxi? _____
**6** How I open this door? _____
**7** Do I write this in English or my language?_____
**8** I give a tip or not? _____

## Check your answers
**1** Where do I sign? **2** Can you tell me what to write/what I write in this card? **3** Where do I pay, please? **4** correct – Can you tell me

where I go now, please? **5** correct – How do I get a taxi? **6** How do I open this door? **7** correct – Do I write this in English or my language? **8** Do I give a tip or not?

→ Now match the questions (1–8) above with the possible answers (a–h) below.

**a** If you could just wait over there, please sir.
**b** At the bottom, just here.
**c** At the cash desk over there please.
**d** Yes, people usually give about 10%.
**e** 'Happy Birthday' is fine.
**f** I can call one for you, madam.
**g** They open automatically when the train stops.
**h** Either, it doesn't matter.

**Check your answers**
**1** b **2** e **3** c **4** a **5** f **6** g **7** h **8** d

## British culture – an invitation to dinner I don't know what to say – I don't know what to do

**Situation** Your English colleague invites you to his house for dinner.
You don't know about British customs and habits.
You ask a friend to help you.

→ Look at the questions below and then the answers.
→ Write the correct question with the answer.

**a** What do I say if she offers me more food and I don't want it?
**b** What do I do if they speak very fast and I don't understand?
**c** Do I shake hands when I arrive?
**d** Do I take a present? And if so, what sort of present do I take?
**e** I don't know his wife's name? What do I call her? Do I call her 'madam'?
**f** What do I say if I want to use the bathroom?
**g** What do I say when I want to leave?

**Example:**

**1 You** _What do I wear?_
**Your friend** Informal clothes are fine.

**2 You** _____?
**Your friend** A box of chocolates or flowers is the most common type of present. Lots of visitors like to give a little present from their country. That's fine too.

**3 You** _____?
**Your friend** Punctuality's quite important here so it's best to get there within about 10 minutes of the time, but not before the time.

**4 You** _____?
**Your friend** Yes, the usual thing is to shake hands and say 'Pleased to meet you' or 'How do you do?' when you meet his wife. _How do you do_ is more formal than _Pleased to meet you_.

**5 You** _____?
**Your friend** No, we only use that word in shops and places like that. If you call her 'Mrs. Parker' to start with, she'll tell you her first name, I'm sure.

**6 You** _____?
**Your friend** You just ask them to speak more slowly.

**7 You** _____
**Your friend** You say, 'No thanks. I'm fine.'

**8 You** _____?
**Your friend** You just say, 'Is it alright if I use the toilet?'

**9 You** _____?
**Your friend** You can say, 'It's getting late. I'd better go now.'

**10 You** _____?
**Your friend** Between ten and eleven o'clock is normal.

_(Contd)_

**11 You** _____?

**Your friend** You shake hands again and say, 'Thank you for inviting me – it was a lovely evening.'

**12 You** _____?

**Your friend** You can say 'thank you' again to your colleague at work if you like but it's not necessary to write a letter. Some people write a short note or card. This is a formal thank you.

**Check your answers**
**1** i **2** d **3** h **4** c **5** e **6** b **7** a **8** f **9** g **10** l **11** k **12** j

→ Answer these questions about the meaning and form of the verbs in questions **a–l** on pages 262–3.

**Meaning**

In the exercise, the dinner is **a** in the past.

**b** in the present.

**c** in the future.

**Form**

The tense in the questions is **a** present simple.

**b** present progressive.

**c** future simple.

**Check your answers and Insight**
Meaning c. Form a

## Insight 95

★ We use the **present simple** to ask for and give instructions/help with systems. In the exercise above you are asking for help with the cultural systems, in other words, the habits and customs.

*Q What's the difference between, for example, 'What shall I wear?' (Topic 7) and 'What do I wear?'?*

*A What shall I (+ verb)…?* asks for a suggestion.

*What do I (+ verb)…?* asks for help with a system. In other words, 'What is the right thing to do/say/wear, etc., in this situation?'

## About your country: Invitations

→ Read the questions below.
→ Either write your answers or prepare to tell a friend.

**Situation** A colleague invites me to dinner.
Answer my questions about customs and habits in your country.

**1** In England it's common to invite someone to the house.
Which is more common in your country, an invitation to
the house or to a restaurant?

_____

**2** What do I wear?

_____

**3** Do I take a present? If so, what sort of present do I take?

_____

**4** The invitation is for seven. Is that a usual time here for a
dinner invitation? What time do I arrive?

_____

**5** What do I do when I arrive? Do I shake hands with him, with
his wife?

_____

**6** I don't know his wife's name. What do I call her?

_____

**7** What time do I leave?

_____

**8** Do I do or say anything the next day?

_____

*Our story continues...*
*Oliver is walking towards*
*the A1 Airbus. A man*
*talks to him*

## Understanding the important information

→ Cover the text of Recording 6 below.
→ Read the question below.
→ Listen and choose the correct answer.

What's the time?  **a** 8.00
                      **b** 7.55
                      **c** 7.52
                      **d** 5.28

### Recording 6 – The Story

◀) **CD2 TR 3, 06:34**

| | |
|---|---|
| **Man** | Excuse me, can you tell me the time, please? |
| **Oliver** | Yes, it's five to eight. |
| **Man** | Many thanks. |

**Check your answer**
b

## What do they say?

### The time

→ Cover the text of Recording 6 again.
→ Read the questions below.
→ Listen and complete the words.

1 The man asks Oliver the time. He says,
   'Excuse me, c _ _ / y _ _ / t _ _ _ / m _ / t _ _ t _ _ _ /, please?'
2 Oliver answers,
   'Yes, i _ ' _ / f _ _ _ / t _ / e _ _ _ t.'
3 The man thanks Oliver. He says 'M _ _ _ / t _ _ _ _ _ .'

## Check your answers

**1** Excuse me, can you tell me the time, please? **2** Yes, it's five to eight. **3** Many thanks.

---

# Grammar and communication 3

### Asking for and understanding travel information

**Saying the time**

→ Read 1–6 below and draw the hands on these watches.

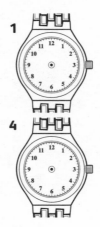 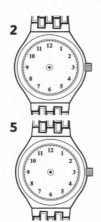 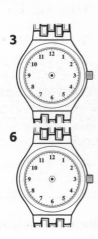

**1** Eleven o'clock      **4** A quarter to six
**2** Half past three      **5** Ten to nine
**3** A quarter past four      **6** Twenty-five past ten

## Check your answers

**1** 11:00   **2** 3:30   **3** 4:15   **4** 5:45   **5** 8:50   **6** 10:25

## Insight 96
### Timetables

★ There are two ways to say the time. The exercise above is the usual way in spoken English.

*(Contd)*

★ When we want to be very specific, for example, for a timetable:
  – we use the twenty-four hour clock
  – we say the exact number of minutes past the hour, even if it's more than 30. For example, '8.43' is 'eight forty-three' and '11.56' is 'eleven fifty-six'.
  – We say 'O' like the name of the letter for timetables.

## Timetables

Can you give me times of the trains to ..., please?

→ Cover the text of Recording 7.
→ Listen and write down the times you hear.

### Recording 7

◄)) **CD2 TR 3, 06:48**

| Times of the trains to go | To come back |
|---|---|
| 1 _____ | 1 _____ |
| 2 _____ | 2 _____ |
| 3 _____ | 3 _____ |
| 4 _____ | 4 _____ |

### Check your answers

| To go | To come back |
|---|---|
| **1** 6.22 (six twenty-two) | **1** 13.05 (thirteen 'o' five) |
| **2** 7.49 (seven forty-nine) | **2** 14.50 (fourteen-fifty) |
| **3** 8.13 (eight thirteen) | **3** 15.32 (fifteen thirty-two) |
| **4** 9.56 (nine fifty-six) | **4** 16.09 (sixteen 'o' nine) |

The first train in the morning leaves at 6.22, then there's another at 7.49, one at 8.13, and another at 9.56. To come back you can leave at 13.05, or 14.50, or there are later trains at 15.32 and 16.09.

## Frequency – how often do the trains go?

→ Read the expressions in the boxes below.
→ Read the timetables below.
→ Match each timetable (**a,b,c**) with one phrase from **Box 1** (**1,2,3**) and one phrase from **Box 2** (**A,B,C**).
→ Write the number and letter in the boxes after the timetables.

| Box 1 | Box 2 |
|---|---|
| **1** four times an hour<br>**2** twice an hour<br>**3** every hour | **A** on the hour<br>**B** at five past, twenty past, twenty-five to and ten to the hour<br>**C** at a quarter past and a quarter to the hour |

### The timetables

**a** 6.00, 7.00, 8.00, 9.00, 10.00, 11.00, 12.00 ☐ ☐
**b** 6.15, 6.45, 7.15, 7.45, 8.15, 8.45, 9.15, 9.45 ☐ ☐
**c** 6.05, 6.20, 6.35, 6.50, 7.05, 7.20, 7.35, 7.50 ☐ ☐

### Check your answers

**a** 3 A Every hour on the hour. **b** 2 C Twice an hour, at a quarter past and quarter to each hour. **c** 1 B Four times an hour, at five past, twenty past, twenty-five to and ten to the hour.

### How long from now?

**Example from *The Story*:** Oliver asks, 'When does the bus leave?' The employee answers 'In ten minutes'(time) at 8.05.'

*In ten minutes' time*

→ Make four mini-dialogues. Match the questions (1–4) with the correct response (**a**–**d**).

**1** When's the next train?

**a** In a week('s time). They're in Hong Kong at the moment.

**2** When's my Mummy coming?

**b** In two minutes(' time). Come on, let's run!

**3** When do they get to Australia?

**c** In 6 months(' time), at the end of my course.

**4** When are you going back to your country?

**d** In a few minutes (' time). She's on her way.

**Check your answers**
**1** b **2** d **3** a **4** c

**How long?**

**Example from *The Story*:**

Oliver wants to know the time the journey takes. He asks, 'How long does it take to get there?'

## Insight 97

★ To talk about length of time for an activity we use the verb *take*.

| It takes | my daughter | a long time | to get ready. |
|---|---|---|---|
| Or with the pronouns *me, you, him, her, us, them* | | | |
| It takes | her | a long time | to get ready. |

★ *It takes* (impersonal subject *it* + verb *take*) + verb with *to*.

→ Complete these mini-dialogues (1–4) with (a–d).

**1** How long does it take to get there?

**a** No, only a few minutes. It's easy.

**2** Does it take a long time to do that?

**b** I know. Mine's the same.

**3** It doesn't take long to walk there.

**c** About 10 minutes. It's not far.

**4** It takes my daughter a long time to get ready in the mornings.

**d** No, it's very near.

**Check your answers**
**1** c **2** a **3** d **4** b

## Insight 98

To talk about a specific person with the expression *it takes*, we say *it takes* + person + verb with *to*.

**For example:**

*How long does it take you?*

→ Tell me some things about you.

How long does it take you to have breakfast? _____

How long does it take you to get ready in the morning?_____

Does it take you a long time to get to work/school? Is it far?_____

How long does it take your best friend to get to your house from his/her house? _____

How long does it take you to get to the nearest supermarket from your house? _____

**Possible answers**

You can write short phrases – for example, 'Ten minutes.'
Or 'It takes me/him/her about (10) minutes.'

### Does it take you long?

→ Write questions for these answers.

**1** _____?
I don't eat much in the mornings, really – about 10 minutes,
I suppose.

**2** _____?
No time at all – I work from home

**3** _____?
I can walk there in about 5 minutes – I go shopping there
most days.

**4** _____?
School starts at 8.45 and they leave at 8.15 so it's about a
half-hour walk.

**Check your answers**

**1** How long does it take you to have breakfast? **2** How long does it
take you to get to work? **3** How long does it take you to get to the
nearest supermarket? **4** How long does it take the children to walk
to school?

### Asking and giving the time

→ Look at the clocks below.
→ Cover the text of Recording 8.
→ Listen to the six mini-dialogues asking and giving the time.
→ Write numbers 1–6 below the correct clock(s).

**a**          **b**          **c**

| 12.58 |    | 13.00 |    | 13.04 |

**Example:**  1_____      _____      _____

**Check your answers**

**a** 1, 3, 5, 6. **b** 2, 5. **c** 4, 5.

## Recording 8

◀))) **CD2 TR 3, 07:25**

> **1 A** Dad, what's the time?
> **B** It's a few minutes to one.
> **2 A** Excuse me, could you tell me the time, please?
> **B** Of course. Er, actually, it's exactly one o'clock.
> **3 A** John, have you got the time?
> **B** Yeah, it's just before one.
> **4 A** Could you tell me what the time is, please?
> **B** Yes, it's just after one.
> **5 A** Excuse me, can you tell me what time it is, please?
> **B** Sorry, I haven't got a watch but I think it's around one.
> **6 A** Do you know what the time is, Sharon?
> **B** Let me see, it's almost one.

## Asking the time

On Recording 8 there are five different expressions for asking the time.

→ Cover the text of Recording 8.

→ Listen again and, this time, complete the questions below.

**1** Dad, /_____'_/____ time?

**2** Excuse me,/ c_____/_____/____/____/___/time, please?

**3** John, / _____ /____ /_____/_____ time?

**4** Could/_____/____/____/what/_____/_____/____, please?

**5** Excuse me, /____/____/_____/_____/____/_____/ time/ ____/___,
please?

**6** ____/ you/____/_____/the time/_____, Sharon?

**Check your answers**

**1** Dad, what's the time? **2** Excuse me, could you tell me the time, please? **3** John, have you got the time? **4** Could you tell me what the time is, please? **5** Excuse me, can you tell me what time it is, please? **6** Do you know what the time is?

## Insight 99

There are lots of ways of asking this simple question in English. Look at the summary below.

★ All the questions are correct and appropriate and common in most situations.

★ The questions in the first group are the most direct.

★ 'Could you tell me ⎫ *what time it is?*' can be formal.
'Do you know    ⎭

| Summary – Asking the time | | | |
|---|---|---|---|
| What's<br>Have you got<br>Do you know | | the time (please)? | |
| Could you<br>Can you | tell me | the time (please)? | |
| | tell me what | the time | is (please)? |
| | | time | it is (please)? |
| Do you know | what | the time<br>time | is (please)?<br>it is (please)? |

**Timetables and itineraries**

**Situation** You are in London. You want to go to Cambridge for the day. You want to leave London between 9.00 and 10.00 a.m. You phone National Rail Enquiries for some information.

→ Cover the text of Recording 9 on page 275.
→ Look at the timetable below.
→ Listen and complete the timetable.

| London<br>King's Cross | d | 08:24 | 08:45 | | | | 10:00 | 10:25 |
|---|---|---|---|---|---|---|---|---|
| Cambridge | a | 09:28 | 09:42 | | | | 11:09 | 11:16 |

## Check your answers

| London<br>King's Cross | d | 08:24 | 08:45 | **09:00** | **09:24** | **09:54** | 10:00 | 10:25 |
|---|---|---|---|---|---|---|---|---|
| Cambridge | a | 09:28 | 09:42 | **10:12** | **10:16** | **10:46** | 11:09 | 11:16 |

### Recording 9

◀ CD2 TR 3, 08:20

| Information officer | National Rail Enquiries – Can I help you? |
|---|---|
| **You** | Yes, I'd like some information about the times of trains from London to Cambridge please. |
| **Information officer** | Which day are you thinking of travelling? |
| **You** | It's for tomorrow. |
| **Information officer** | And what time of day would you like to travel? |
| **You** | We'd like to leave London between nine and ten in the morning. |
| **Information officer** | *Right. There's one that **leaves** at exactly nine o'clock. |
| **You** | What time does that get to Cambridge? |
| **Information Officer** | The nine o'clock **gets** in at twelve minutes past ten. Then there's the nine twenty-four, which **arrives** at ten sixteen, and also a nine fifty-four, which **gets** to Cambridge at ten forty-six. |
| **You** | Let me just repeat that to make sure I've got it right. There are three trains. The nine o'clock **arrives** at twelve minutes past ten, the nine twenty-four **gets** there at sixteen minutes past ten and the nine fifty-four **arrives** in Cambridge at ten forty-six.* |
| | *(Contd)* |

| Information Officer | That's correct. |
| You | Thank you very much. |
| Both | Goodbye. |

d – Departure time  a – Arrival time

→ Verb *get*

In the exercise above *get* means **a** take  **b** arrive

## Check your answer
b

→ Answer these questions about meaning and form of the verbs in bold (* to *) in the text of Recording 9 on page 275.

## Meaning
In the exercise above, the journey to Cambridge is **a** in the past.
                                                **b** in the present.
                                                **c** in the future.

## Form
The tense of the verbs is **a** Present Simple.
                          **b** Present Progressive.
                          **c** Future Simple

## Check your answers
Meaning **c**.
Form **a**

## Insight 100

*Q Tomorrow is in the future. Why are these verbs in the present simple?*
*A* Because we are talking about a **timetable**.

★ When we talk about organized future activities and they are part of a timetable or like a timetable, we use the **present simple**.

276

→ Let's look at another example.

**Situation** Monica is going on a business trip to Scotland next week. Her secretary, Angie, is telling her the itinerary.

> **Angie**  **You leave** on the 10.30 flight on Monday and **you arrive** in Edinburgh at 11.10. **You have** a lunch meeting with Mr Jones at 12.30 and then at 3.30 **you take** the train to Glasgow.

All these verbs are in the **present simple** because they are Monica's itinerary or schedule.

→ Now look at the next part of the conversation.

> **Monica**  Where **am I staying** in Glasgow?
> **Angie**  I've got you a room at the King's Hotel. **You're staying** there for two nights.

## Insight 101

*Q Why are these verbs in the present progressive?*
*A* These are personal future arrangements (see Topic 5).

### Summary

To talk about fixed future events we use:

**a** Present progressive if it's a personal arrangement.
**b** Present simple if it's a timetable or like a timetable.

★ Sometimes both the present simple and present progressive are correct. The focus is a little different.

For example: 'I go home next week' – more factual, more focus on the itinerary.
'**I'm going** next week' – more personal.

## Insight 102

> *Q In this situation, can I also say, for example, 'I will go home next week'? (future simple)*
>
> *A No, not in this situation.* ☹
>
> ★ 'I will go home' is grammatically correct.
> ★ It has a different meaning.

→ Answer these questions about 'I'm going home next week' and 'I go home next week.'

**1** In both sentences, the decision is **a** in the past?
                                         **b** in the present?
                                           **c** in the future ?

**2** Actions to organize the trip home are **a** in the past?
                                                **b** in the present?
                                                **c** in the future?

**Check your answers**
**1 a** in the past. **2 a** in the past. For example, you've got your ticket.

'I'll go home next week' is only correct at the moment of making the decision. For example,

278

## Itineraries – present simple

**Situation** Simon is at a travel agent's, collecting his tickets for a short trip to Italy. The assistant talks about his itinerary.

→ Write the verbs in the correct tense.

**Travel agent** Here are the tickets for your trip to Italy. You (fly)_____(1) to Naples with Alitalia on the 12th of next month. The flight (leave) _____ (2) Heathrow at 10.15. When you get to Naples a coach (pick you up) _____(3) from the airport and they (drive)_____ (4) you direct to your hotel. The next morning the coach (take)_____(5) you on an excursion to the ruins of Pompeii. In the afternoon you (get) _____ (6) the Eurostar train to Rome.

**Simon** What (happen) _____ (7) when we arrive in Rome? How (get) _____(8) to the hotel?

**Travel agent** A bilingual guide (meet) _____ (9) the train and (take) _____(10) you on a city tour. They (show)_____(11) you all the important sights such as the Coliseum and the Vatican and then the coach (leave)_____(12) you at your hotel. On the Sunday you (be)_____(13) free in Rome and you (come) _____(14) back to London on the evening flight.

**Simon** What time (get)_____ (15) back?

**Travel Agent** I think it's twenty-past nine. Just let me check – yes, nine twenty-five.

**Simon** That all sounds wonderful. I'm looking forward to it.

### Check your answers

**1** fly **2** leaves **3** picks you up **4** drive **5** takes **6** get **7** happens **8** do we get? **9** meets **10** takes **11** show **12** leaves **13** are **14** come **15** do we get?

All these verbs are in the present simple because it is an itinerary.

## Insight 103

*Q In the mini-dialogue below, are the verbs in 'B' in the present simple?*
**A** Can you tell me how I get to Waterloo, please?
**B** <u>Go</u> to Oxford Street and <u>take</u> the Bakerloo Line.

*A* No. These verbs are in the imperative (verb without *to*).

★ People who work in transport often use the imperative to give instructions.
★ Here the imperative is impersonal and short.

(For more information and practice on the imperative, see Topic 9.)

### Summary of travel questions

There are a lot of different questions in this topic. How many can you use now?

→ Read the questions below.
→ Write the correct question for each answer on page 281.

**Example:** You *How can I get to Windsor?* (j)
'Take the train at Platform 5 and change at Egham.'

**a** Could you tell me how to get to London from here, please?
**b** How often do the trains run to Waterloo?
**c** When's the next coach to Glasgow, please?
**d** How long does it take to get to Cambridge from London?
**e** Is this the right train for Birmingham?
**f** Which platform is it for Brighton, please?
**g** I want to go to Cardiff. Where do I change?
**h** Do you know if this train stops in Reading?
**i** How much is a single to Hull, please?
**j** How can I get to Windsor?

**1** You *Excuse me, how can I get to Windsor?*
Take the train at Platform 5 and change at Egham.

**2** You _____?
No, this is a non-stop to Paddington.

**3** You _____?
Number 7, sir.

**4** You _____?
£22.

**5** You _____?
Every half an hour – at ten to and twenty past the hour.

**6** You _____?
No, this is the Liverpool train.

**7** You _____?
It's not necessary, this bus goes all the way there.

**8** You _____?
In ten minutes at half past.

**9** You _____?
Yes, take the next train from Platform 10.

**10** You _____?
On a fast train? – just under an hour.

**Check your answers**
**1** j **2** h **3** f **4** i **5** b **6** e **7** g **8** c **9** a **10** d

*Asking for information – transport*

→ Listen to Recording 10 and ask the questions from the exercise above in the spaces.

**Recording 10**

◀) **CD2 TR 3, 09:26**

| | | |
|---|---|---|
| **1** | You | Excuse me, how can I get to Windsor? |
| | | Take the train at Platform 5 and change at Egham. |
| **2** | You | Do you know if this train stops at Reading? |
| | | No, this is a non-stop to Paddington. |

*(Contd)*

| **3** **You** | Which platform is it for Brighton, please? |
|---|---|
| | Number 7, sir. |
| **4** **You** | How much is a single to Hull, please? |
| | £22. |
| **5** **You** | How often do the trains run to Waterloo? |
| | Every half an hour – at ten to and twenty past the hour. |
| **6** **You** | Is this the right train for Birmingham? |
| | No, this is the Liverpool train. |
| **7** **You** | I want to go to Cardiff. Where do I change? |
| | It's not necessary, this bus goes all the way there. |
| **8** **You** | When's the next coach to Glasgow, please? |
| | In ten minutes, at half past. |
| **9** **You** | Could you tell me how to get to London from here, please? |
| | Yes, take the next train from Platform 10. |
| **10** **You** | How long does it take to get to Cambridge from London? On a fast train? – just under an hour. |

*About your country: public transport*

→ Write answers to these questions or prepare to tell a friend.

**1** How do you go to work and/or the shops?

**2** How do people travel long distances without a car?

**3** What are the names of the big train and bus companies in your country?

**4** Is public transport cheap or expensive?

**5** Is there an underground in your town or capital?

**6** On the buses does the fare depend on distance?

**7** **a** When do you pay if you want to travel by bus?

**b**  Can you buy a return ticket?

**c**  If you need to take two buses, can you use one ticket?

_____

_____

### *What would you say?*

**1**  You are a tourist in London. You are at a station. Someone asks you, 'Excuse me can you tell me how to get to Wimbledon, please?'

_____

**2**  It's late at night. You want to get a train ticket from the machine – the ticket office is closed. You've only got a £20 note. The machine takes only coins and £5 and £10 notes.

_____

### Possible answers

**1** I'm sorry but I'm not from here. **2** Excuse me, have you got change for a £20 note, please? I need to buy a ticket from the machine.

_____

## Revision

### How do you say it in your language?

→ Here are some examples of the important points in this topic.
→ Translate the sentences below into your language in the spaces.
→ Remember – translate the idea, not the words.

**1 a**  Excuse me, can you tell me how to get to the centre of town, please?

_____

  **b**  Yes, you can go by bus, by train or by taxi.

_____

**2**  Which part of the town are you going to?

_____

**3 a** Where do I pay? **b** Over there, please, at the cash desk.

**4** Where do I go to get a ticket?

**5** Who are you talking to?

**6** Which excursions would you like to go on?

**7** You get a ticket before you get on the bus.

**8 a** Excuse me, have you got the time, please?

**b** Yes, it's just after ten.

**9** How often do the buses go to the station?

**10** How long does it take to get to the centre?

**11** Take the train at platform 6 and change at the next stop.

### Join the conversation

→ Look at Recording 1 (page 240) again.
→ Listen to Recording 11.

**◄) CD2 TR 3, 11:37**

→ Read Oliver's words in the spaces.

## Test yourself 8

### Which one is right?

→ Choose **a** or **b**.

**1** I go to work    **a** with     car.
                     **b** by

**2** The bus      **a** leaves    every hour.
               **b** is leaving

**3 a** Do you know what is the time?
   **b** Do you know what the time is?

**4 a** How long does it take to get to the park?
   **b** How long takes it for go to the park?

**5 A a** How often go the trains to London?
     **b** How often do the trains go to London?
   **B a** Three times in an hour.
     **b** Three times an hour.

**6 a** How much is it for go and come back?
   **b** How much is a return ticket?

**7 a** What do I do now?
   **b** What I do now?

**8 a** Take that train and change at Broad Street.
   **b** You will take that train and then you are changing at Broad Street.

**9 a** West Road, 24.
   **b** 24, West Road.

**10**    My English friend has got a new baby.
   **b** What am I writing in this card?
   **a** What do I write in this card?

## Write a dialogue

**Situation** You are at the ticket office at Waterloo Station.

You want two tickets to Hampton Court, a famous palace near London.

**1** Travel clerk

Next, please. Can I help you?

**You**
**2**

**3** Single or return?

**4** You want returns

**5** That's £9.80, please

**6**

**7** In 10 minutes, at twenty to eleven

**8** Return times – how often?

**9**

From Hampton Court to Waterloo, there are two trains an hour, at ten past and twenty to the hour.

**10**

Travelling time?

**11** About half an hour

**12**

*Thank you*

**13** You are near the platform. You want to know which platform to go to.

**14** You are on the train. You want to check this is the right train.

**Check your answers**
**1** b **2** a **3** b **4** a **5** A b B b **6** b **7** a **8** a **9** b **10** b

## Dialogue: model answers

| | | |
|---|---|---|
| **2** | **You** | Two tickets to Hampton Court, please. |
| **3** | **Clerk** | Single or return? |
| **4** | **You** | Return, please. |
| **5** | **Clerk** | That's nine pounds eighty please. |
| **6** | **You** | When's the next train? OR At what time does the next train leave? |
| **7** | **Clerk** | In 10 minutes, at twenty to eleven. |
| **8** | **You** | And to come back, how often do the trains run? |
| **9** | **Clerk** | There are two trains an hour, at ten past and twenty to the hour. |
| **10** | **You** | How long does the journey take? |
| **11** | **Clerk** | About half an hour. |
| **12** | **You** | Thank you. |
| **13** | **You** | Excuse me. Which platform is it for Hampton Court, please? |
| **14** | **You** | Excuse me. Is this the right train for Hampton Court, please? |
| | | **OR** |
| | | Excuse me. Does this train go to Hampton Court, please? |

# 9

# Meeting friends

Grammar and communication
- **Impersonal** *it*
- **Asking for opinions** – *how was?*
- **Adjectives** + *-ed* **or** *-ing*
- **Saying thank you**
- **Obligation and necessity** – *have to*
- **The imperative**
- **Offering, rejecting, insisting, accepting**
- **Introducing something negative politely**

Vocabulary
- **Public signs**
- **Large numbers**

Pronunciation
- **Intonation** – *expressing strong feelings*

*Tasha leaves customs. Who's there to meet her? What happens next?*

FLIGHT AA421 FROM MONTEVIDEO
VIA BUENOS AIRES, LANDED 7:15
...............LUGGAGE IN HALL...............

## Understanding the important information

→ Cover the text of Recording 1, *The Story*.
→ Read the sentences below. Only one is correct.
→ Listen to the recording and choose the correct answer.

**a** Tasha gets the bus with Oliver.
**b** Tasha's friend, Helen, is at the airport to meet her.
**c** Helen is at the airport with her husband and children.
**d** Tasha goes to Helen's house by taxi.

### Recording 1 – The Story

◀) **CD2 TR 4, 00:16**

| Helen | Tasha, Hi, how are you? It's lovely to see you again! |
|---|---|
| Tasha | Hello, Helen! It's great to see you too. How are things? |
| Helen | I'm fine. We're all fine. How was your flight? |
| Tasha | It was alright – 13 hours is a bit long and tiring, but I'm here now. Thanks for picking me up, by the way. |
| Helen | That's OK We're glad you could come. The car's in the car park, this way. David and the children are at home, waiting for you. |

**Check your answer**
b

## Understanding more

→ Read the sentences below.
→ Listen to Recording 1 again and answer *True/False/We don't know*.

**1** Tasha's flight was terrible.  True/False/We don't know
**2** David is at home with the  True/False/We don't know
children.

**3** Tasha knows David and the       True/False/We don't know
children.
**4** Helen meets Oliver.       True/False/We don't know
**5** Tasha tells Helen about Oliver.       True/False/We don't know
**6** Helen can't drive.       True/False/We don't know

**Check your answers**
**1** False **2** True **3** We don't know **4** False **5** False **6** False

---

## What do they say?

→ Read the sentences below.
→ Listen to the recording again and try to complete the words.
→ Then read the text of the recording if necessary.

**1** Helen says, 'Hello' but Tasha says 'H _ !'

**2 a** Helen is happy to see Tasha.
   She says, ' I _ ' _ / l _ _ _ _ y / t _ / s _ _ you again.'
   **b** Tasha is happy to see Helen.
   She says, ' _ t's / g _ _ _ t / _ _ / _ _ _ / you / t _ _.'

**3** Helen asks, 'How are you?' but Tasha asks 'H _ _ / a _ _ /t _ _
   _ _ s?'

**4 a** Helen asks Tasha about her journey.
   She says, 'H _ _ / w _ _ / y _ _ r / flight?'
   **b** Tasha responds, ' I _ / w _ _ / a _ _ _ _ _ t.'
   **c** Tasha talks about the flight.
   She says ' 13 hours is a b _ _ / l _ _ _ / and /t _ _ _ _ _ but I'm
   here now.'

**5 a** Tasha is happy Helen is at the airport to meet her. During
   the conversation Tasha decides to thank her friend.
   She says: 'Thanks / f _ _ / p _ _ _ _ _ g / m _ / u _ , b _ /
   t _ _ / w _ _.'

**b** When Tasha says, 'Thanks', Helen responds,
'T _ _ _'_ OK W_'_ _ / g _ _ _ / you / c _ _ _ d / c _ _ e.'

## Check your answers

**1** Hi. (informal) **2 a** It's lovely to see you again. **b** It's great to see
you too. **3** How are things ('things' is informal) **4 a** How was your
flight? **b** It was alright. **c** 13 hours is a bit long and tiring but I'm
here now. **5 a** Thanks for picking me up by the way **b** That's OK
We're glad you could come.

---

## Insight 104

### Common mistake – impersonal *it*

Example from *The Story*:
Helen is happy to see Tasha again.
She says, 'It's lovely to see you again.'
Tasha says, 'It's great to see you too.'

(Not: ~~Is lovely~~ to see you again.
OR ~~Is great~~ to see you too.)

*Q Why do we say 'it' here?*
*A* All verbs need a subject in English (except imperatives).
'It' is the impersonal subject.

*Q What's the negative? Can I say, 'It's nice <u>to not work</u> at the weekend?'* ☹
*A* No – *not* is before *to*. 'It's nice **not to** work at the weekend.'

---

| Grammar summary – impersonal *it* | | | |
|---|---|---|---|
| **Impersonal subject** | **Verb** *be* | **Adjective** | **Verb + *to/not to*** |
| It | is<br>'s | lovely<br>frustrating | to see you again<br>not to understand |

292

→ Complete the sentences below with – one adjective from **Box 1**
  and – one verb from **Box 2**.

→ Use your dictionary if necessary.

| Box 1 |
| --- |
| difficult   wonderful |
| expensive   frustrating |
| useful   hard   correct |
| ~~cheap~~   interesting   tiring |
| boring   kind   important |

| Box 2 |
| --- |
| go   know   ask   work   eat |
| understand   arrive   ~~travel~~ |
| get   invite   see   visit |

**Example:**

It doesn't cost much – in fact it's quite *cheap* to *travel* by coach.

**1**   It's too＿＿＿＿＿＿ to ＿＿＿＿ by plane. Let's go by
        train.

**2  A**  Is it ＿＿＿＿＿to ＿＿＿＿'Where are you live?' or
          'Where do you live?'
     **B**  'Where do you live.'

**3**   At first it's ＿＿＿＿＿＿ to ＿＿＿＿＿＿a foreign language
        because people speak fast.

**4**   For some people it's very ＿＿＿＿＿ to ＿＿＿＿ museums –
        they really enjoy it.
        For others it's the opposite. They find it really ＿＿＿＿＿

**5**   I've got an invitation to stay with my friend abroad.
        It's very ＿＿＿＿ of him to ＿＿＿＿＿＿ me.

**6**   When you travel abroad, it's always ＿＿＿＿＿ to
        ＿＿＿＿＿＿ a few words of the language.

**7**   It's ＿＿＿＿＿not to ＿＿＿＿ late for an exam.

**8**   It's ＿＿＿＿＿ to ＿＿＿＿＿ long hours.

**9** It's _____ to see old friends after a long time.

**10** Every time I try to telephone him there's no reply It's really _____ not to _____ an answer.

**11** If you are on a diet, it's _____ not to _____sweet things!

## Check your answers
**1** expensive to go. **2** correct to ask. **3** difficult/hard to understand. **4** interesting to visit/boring. **5** kind of him to invite. **6** useful to know. **7** important not to arrive. **8** tiring to work. **9** wonderful to see. **10** frustrating not to get. **11** difficult/hard not to eat.

*It's* **+ adjective + verb with** *to/not to*

→ Write these words in the correct order.

**1** _____

to/again/nice/talk/it's/you/to

**2** _____

better/not/it's/go/to

**3** _____

with/contact/easy/to/it's/people/e-mail

**4** _____

for/wait/it's/someone/time/for/long/boring/to/a

**5** _____

country/to/exciting/it's/visit/a/foreign

**6** _____

normal/language/understand/not/it's/in/foreign/to/everything/a

## Check your answers
**1** It's nice to talk to you again. **2** It's better not to go. **3** It's easy to contact people with e-mail. **4** It's boring to wait for someone for a long time **5** It's exciting to visit a foreign country. **6** It's normal not to understand everything in a foreign language.

# Grammar and communication 1

### Asking for opinions – how was...?

**Example from *The Story*:**
Helen asks Tasha about her journey.
She says: '**How** was your flight?'
Tasha answers: 'It was alright'.

→ Answer these questions about *How was...?*

## Meaning
**1** Is the flight **a** in the present?
              **b** in the future?
              **c** in the past?
**2** In 'How was your flight?' Helen is asking,
   **a** for a long description of the flight or
   **b** if the flight was OK or not for Tasha.

## Form
*Was* is the past of **a** verb *be*
                      **b** verb *do*?

## Check your answers
Meaning: **1** c **2** b
Form: a

| Grammar summary – Past of *be* | | | |
|---|---|---|---|
| **Affirmative** | | | |
| I<br>He/she/it } was | | You<br>We } were<br>They | |
| **Negative** | | | |
| I<br>He/she/it } wasn't | | You<br>We } weren't<br>They | |

| Question | | | | |
|---|---|---|---|---|
| Was { | I he/she/it? | Were { | you? we? they | |

→ Complete these mini-dialogues with *was* or *were* + *not* where necessary.

**1 A** How _____ your holiday?

**B** The hotel _____ bad but the food _____ terrible.

**2 A** _____ your parents alright last night?

**B** My mother _____ fine but my father _____ very well at all, actually.

**3 A** _____ that film boring!

**B** Yes, it _____ very good at all, _____ it?

**4 A** *[On Monday morning]* How _____ your weekend?

**B** Really relaxing and quiet thanks. And yours?

**A** It _____ nice, very nice.

**5 A** Why _____ you at school yesterday, David?

**B** I _____ ill, Miss.

**6 A** How many people _____ at the party?

**B** About 20, I suppose.

**7** Nobody _____ at home – the answer-machine _____ on.

**Check your answers**
**1 A** was **B** wasn't, was **2 A** were **B** was, wasn't **3 A** wasn't
**B** wasn't, was it? **4 A** was **A** was **5 A** weren't **B** was (Children call their teachers *Miss* or *Sir*). **6 A** were **7** was, was

# How do you pronounce it?

**Was**

## Insight 105

★ The vowel 'a' in *was* has two pronunciations.

– weak / ə / when *was* is with an adjective or noun
– strong / ɒ / when *was* is the important word.

**For example:** '*Was* your flight OK?' – weak / ə /.
'Yes, it *was*, thanks.' – strong / æ /.

★ The pronunciation of the 'a' in strong *was* / æ / and *wasn't* is the same.

→ Look at the text of Recording 2, with the stress.
→ What is the pronunciation of *was* in each one?
→ Choose 'strong' or 'weak'.

**Recording 2**

◄) **CD2 TR 4, 00:48**

| | |
|---|---|
| **1** How was your day? | strong/weak |
| **2** Your party – how was it? | strong/weak |
| **3** It was fantastic, thanks. | strong/weak |
| **4** Was your hotel comfortable? | strong/weak |
| **5** Yes it was, thanks. | strong/weak |

**Check your answers**
**1** weak **2** strong **3** weak **4** weak **5** strong

→ Now listen to Recording 2 and repeat the sentences.

### Intonation – big falls to express strong feelings

In Topic 4 we practise intonation to sound positive. In this topic we practise intonation to express strong feelings.

**Examples from *The Story*:**
Helen is happy to see Tasha.
She says, 'It's lovely to see you again.'
Tasha responds, 'It's great to see you, too.'

## Insight 106

★ Remember, with flat intonation you express that actually you are not very happy to see the person. ↘

★ To express strong feelings, the voice moves a lot on the ↘ syllable with stress.

→ Read the sentences below.
→ On Recording 3 you will hear each sentence twice.
→ Which expresses stronger feelings, **a** or **b**?

**Recording 3**

◄) **CD2 TR 4, 01:25**

| | |
|---|---|
| **1** It's **wonderful** to see you again. | **a** or **b** |
| **2** It's **great** to hear from you. | **a** or **b** |
| **3** I think it's a good **idea**. | **a** or **b** |
| **4** It's so **kind** of you to invite me. | **a** or **b** |
| **5** I don't know **what** to do. | **a** or **b** |
| **6** But I **can't**! | **a** or **b** |
| **7** I'm so sorry! | **a** or **b** |
| **8** Happy **Birth**day! | **a** or **b** |

**Check your answers**
**1** a **2** a **3** b **4** a **5** b **6** b **7** a **8** b

→ Listen to Recording 3 again and repeat the sentences. Pay special attention to the big falls in the sentences with strong feelings.

# Grammar and communication 2

**Feelings – adjectives + -ed or -ing**

**Example from *The Story*:**
Tasha talks about the flight. She says, 'It was a bit long and tiring…'
In other words, Tasha is tired because the flight was tiring.

## Insight 107
### Common mistake

Tasha: 'The flight was a bit long and tiring…'

NOT: ~~'The flight was a bit long and tired'~~…

BUT: 'Tasha was tired after her flight' is correct

**Meanings and forms – adjectives + -ed and -ing**
How is Tasha? She feels **tired**.
Why does Tasha feel tired?
What's the source of her tiredness?
The flight. The flight was **tiring**.

| *Adjectives with -ed/-ing* | | |
|---|---|---|
| **The feeling** **Reason or source of the feeling** | Tasha is tired The flight was tiring | adjective +-*ed* adjective +-*ing* |

**Here's another example:**

| How does John feel? | Interested | Internal Feeling + -ed |
| Why? | His book is interesting | Source of feeling + -ing |

→ Complete the dialogue opposite
→ Choose the correct form of the adjective in the brackets ( ).
→ Use your dictionary if necessary.

**A** I feel a bit _____1 (tired/tiring) actually – it was a very long journey. And the plane was completely full!

**B** Oh! That's _____2 (surprised/surprising) at this time of year. When I travel, I go to sleep if I'm _____3 (bored/boring) on a plane. But sometimes it's _____4 (interested/ interesting) to talk to the person next to you.

**A** Oh, the man next to me on this flight was really _____5 (bored/boring). The conversation was all about his business trips – I wasn't very _____6 (interested/interesting) at all, really.

**A** Yes, but it is _____7 (fascinating/fascinated) to travel and visit different countries, isn't it?

**B** Absolutely! I just find it _____8 (frustrated/frustrating) if I can't speak the language at all.

**A** Yes, I was a bit _____9 (disappointed/disappointing) with our last holiday because of that.

**Check your answers**
**1** tired **2** surprising **3** bored **4** interesting **5** boring **6** interested
**7** fascinating **8** frustrating **9** disappointed

→ Correct the *-ed/-ing* adjectives in these sentences, if necessary.

**1** The journey was very tired.
**2** I'm very exciting about my trip.
**3** I was really surprising about the new job.
**4** The film was bored.
**5** It's a fascinating story.

**Check your answers**
**1** tiring – source  **2** excited – feeling  **3** surprised – feeling
**4** boring – source  **5** *Correct*

---

## Grammar and communication 3

### Saying Thank you

**Example from *The Story*:**
Tasha is happy that Helen is at the airport to meet her.
She says, 'Thanks for picking me up.'

| Summary – Saying *Thank you* | | |
|---|---|---|
| | **Preposition** *'for'* | **Verb + *-ing* – gerund** |
| **Neutral** Thank you Thank you very much **Formal** Thank you very much indeed **Informal** Thanks Many thanks | for | picking me up |

## Insight 108

*Q Can I also say*

**a** *'Thank you to meet me?'* ×
**b** *'Thank you for meet me?'* × OR
**c** *'Thank you for to meet me?'* ×

*A* No, 'Thank you for meeting me'
   *Thank you + for + verb -ing.* } is the only correct expression.

→ Complete these sentences.

**1** Thanks _____/ _____ (help) me.
**2** Thanks ____ /_____(come) to pick us up.
**3** Thank you very much _____/_____ (wait) for me.
**4** Thank you _____/ _____ (meet) us.
**5** Thanks _____/ _____ (call). (on the telephone)

**Check your answers**
**1** Thanks for helping me. **2** Thanks for coming to pick us up.
**3** Thank you very much for waiting for me. **4** Thank you for
meeting us. **5** Thanks for calling.

### Saying Thank you

→ Use the verbs in the box to say *thank you* in the situations below.

> let me know   go   tell   come   help   call   invite   wait   ask

**Example:**

A friend tells you something very important.
You ***Thank you for telling me.***

**1** A friend in another country invites you for a holiday.
   You _____

**2** You arrange to meet a friend at 2 o'clock. You arrive at 2.20.

You _____

**3** Your colleague shows you how to use the new computer in the office.

You _____

**4** You've got an appointment for tomorrow – but something happens and you can't go. You telephone and tell them. The other person says,

_____

**5** Your colleague's partner was ill yesterday. Today you ask about her. Your friend says, 'She's much better today.'

_____

**6** Your friend goes to the doctor's. You go with her. Later, at home she says,

_____

**7** You call a business friend. At the end of the conversation he/she says,

_____

**8** You invite some friends to your house. When they leave you can say,

_____

**Check your answers**

**1** Thanks for inviting me. **2** Thanks for waiting for me. **3** Thank you for helping me. **4** Thanks for letting me know. **5** Thank you for asking. **6** Thanks for going with me. **7** Thanks for calling. **8** Thanks for coming.

**Responding to** *Thank you*

→ Read the formal, neutral and informal expressions in the box on page 304.

→ Choose an appropriate expression for the situations 1–6.

| Formal – You're welcome OR | Not at all |
|---|---|
| Neutral – That's OK OR | That's alright |
| Informal – No problem OR | Any time |

**1** Your friend says, 'Thank you for helping me with my English.'
You respond, _____

**2** On the bus, you give your seat to an old lady. She says 'Thank you so much. You're very kind!'
You respond, _____

**3** A young person talks to you in the street. He says 'Excuse me, where's the station, please?' You say, 'Just there.' He says, 'Thank you.'
You respond, _____

**4** The bus is at the bus stop. A woman is getting on the bus with three young children. You help her. She says, 'Thank you ever so much.'
You respond, _____

**5** In a class you lend your dictionary to a friend. S/he says, 'Thanks.'
You respond, _____

**6** You're in a shopping centre. You open the door for someone. The person says, 'Thank you.'
You respond, _____

### Check your answers
**1** Informal: Either *No problem* or *Any time* **2** Formal: Either, *You're welcome* or *Not at all* **3** Neutral: *That's OK* or *That's alright* **4** Neutral: *That's OK* or *That's alright* **5** Informal: *No problem* or *Any time* **6** Formal: *You're welcome* or *Not at all*

## British culture – meeting people at the end of a journey

▶ **Clothes**

In your country, do you wear formal clothes to meet a friend or family member at the end of a journey? In Britain, it is usual to wear everyday clothes.

▶ **Saying** *Hello*

When we meet a family member or friend, it is common to **kiss them on the cheek (1)** and sometimes **hug them (2)**

Men often **shake hands (3)** or just say *Hello*. Good friends or family members sometimes shake hands and **hold the other person's arm (4)**, or **pat each other on the back (5)**. When we meet a business friend, it is common to shake hands.

Adults often hug and/or kiss children.

▶ In Britain, some friends and families touch each other. Others don't. Touching isn't always the norm.

*About your country: meeting people you know*

→ Read the questions below.
→ Either write your answers or prepare to tell a friend.

What do you do when you meet someone after a journey?
  **a** a family member? _____
  **b** a friend? _____
  **c** business friend? _____
  **d** child? _____

## What's the right word?

### Saying large numbers – *and*

→ How do we say the numbers below? Choose the correct expression from the box.

| 10 | 100 | 1,000 | 10,000 |
|----|-----|-------|--------|
| 100,000 | 1,000,000 | 1,000,000,000 | |

> a million  a hundred  ten thousand  ten  a billion
> a hundred thousand  a thousand

### Check your answers

10 – ten
100 – a hundred
1,000 – a thousand
10,000 – ten thousand
100,000 – a hundred thousand
1,000,000 – a million
1,000,000,000 – a billion

→ Now look at the following numbers – where's the *and*?

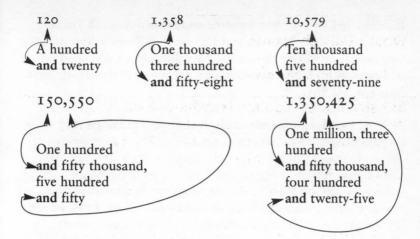

→ Read the sentence about *and* and choose True or False.

With big numbers we say *and* before the 'tens'.
('Tens' are twenty, thirty, forty, etc.) True/False

**Check your answer**
True

### Saying large numbers

→ Write these numbers in words – don't forget the *and*.

**1** 594,000 _____
**2** 611,420 _____
**3** 4,601 _____
**4** 827 _____
**5** 32,158 _____
**6** 24,250,000 _____
**7** 6,368 _____
**8** 923,750 _____

**Check your answers**
**1** Five hundred **and** ninety-four thousand. **2** Six hundred **and**
eleven thousand, four hundred **and** twenty. **3** Four thousand, six

hundred **and** one. **4** Eight hundred **and** twenty-seven. **5** Thirty-two thousand, one hundred **and** fifty-eight. **6** Twenty-four million, two hundred **and** fifty thousand. **7** Six thousand, three hundred **and** sixty-eight. **8** Nine hundred **and** twenty-three thousand, seven hundred **and** fifty.

→ Read aloud the numbers in the text about Heathrow Airport on page 306.

## Check your answers

sixty-three million passengers, one thousand two hundred and fifty-five flights, ninety airlines, one hundred and sixty destinations, sixty-eight thousand people, twenty-six thousand cups of tea, six thousand five hundred pints of beer, six thousand five hundred sandwiches.

### *About your country: large numbers*

→ Read the questions below.
→ Either write your answers or prepare to tell a friend.

**1** What is the population of your country / the capital / your town / village, etc.?

_____

**2** If you work, how much do you earn a year?

_____

**3** How much does a room/flat/house cost in your area? – to rent a month/to buy?

_____

**4** How much does a new car cost in your country?

_____

*Our story continues ... Helen and Tasha go to the airport car park to get Helen's car*

## Understanding the important information

→ Read the sentences below.
→ Listen to Recording 4, *The Story* and choose *True/False/We don't know*.

**1** Tasha pays for the car park.  True/False/We don't know
**2** They can't find the car.  True/False/We don't know
**3** They ask a man for help with the suitcase.  True/False/We don't know

### Recording 4 – The Story

🔊 **CD2 TR 4, 02:52**

| | |
|---|---|
| **Helen** | The car's on level 4. We can take the trolley in the lift. But first, I have to pay at the machine just here. Now, where's the ticket? Wait a minute…Oh, here it is, in my pocket. How much do I need? One hour –£2.60. Let me see if I've got the right money. |
| | *(Contd)* |

| Tasha | I'm afraid I haven't got any change. I've only got notes. |
| Helen | No, don't worry. I'm getting this. Look, the machine gives change. |
| | Right, let's find the car. The lift is this way. |
| Helen | Here we are – it's the green Ford. Now, let's get your luggage in the boot. Can I help you with your suitcase? |
| Tasha | No, really, it's alright thanks – I can manage. Could you just hold this bag for a minute while I get the suitcase in, then we can put the bag on top. |
| Helen | Come on! Let me help. Don't lift that suitcase on your own. |
| Tasha | OK – Thanks – it is quite heavy… Ready? One, two, three… |
| Helen | We can put our coats on the back seat. |
| Tasha | I think I'll keep mine on. I'm really cold. |
| Helen | I expect that's because you're tired after your long journey. Let's get home and you can have a rest. |

**Check your answers**
**a** False **b** False **c** False

---

## Understanding more

→ Cover the text of Recording 4.
→ Read the sentences below. Some are True, some are False.
→ Listen and tick ✓ the True sentences.

**1** The car is on level 2.
**2** First they pay, then they get the car.
**3** The car park costs £3.60.
**4** They take the lift.
**5** They leave the trolley on the ground floor.
**6** Helen's got a red Honda.
**7** Tasha's suitcase is heavy.

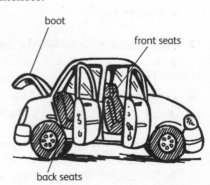

boot

front seats

back seats

**8** They put the luggage on the back seat.
**9** Helen helps Tasha with her luggage.
**10** They put their coats in the boot.
**11** They're going straight to Helen's house.

**Check your answers**
**1** False **2** True **3** False **4** True **5** False **6** False **7** True **8** False **9** True
**10** False **11** True

→ Now listen again and correct the wrong information in 1, 3, 5,
6, 8, 10.

**Check your answers**
**1** The car is on level 4. **3** The car park costs £2.60. **5** They take
the trolley in the lift. **6** Helen's got a green Ford. **8** They put the
suitcase in the boot. **10** Helen puts her coat in the back but Tasha
keeps her coat on.

---

## What do they say?

→ Read the sentences below
→ Listen to Recording 4 again and try to complete the words.
→ Then read the text of the recording to help you if necessary.

**1** The Car Park isn't free. Helen says, 'But first, I / h _ _ _ / t _ /
pay at the machine.'

**2** Helen needs time to find the car park ticket. She says, 'W _ _ _ /
a / m _ _ _ _ _.'

**3** Helen needs time to see if she's got £2.60 in change. She says,
'L _ _ / m _ / s _ _ / i _ / I've got the / r _ _ _ _ / m _ _ _ y.'

**4 a** Tasha is sorry she hasn't got change. She says,
'I' _ / a _ _ _ _ _ / I haven't got any change.'
  **b** Helen tells her it isn't a problem.
    She says, 'D _ _ ' t / w _ _ _ _ .'

**5** Helen tells Tasha she's paying. She says,
'I' _ / g _ _ _ _ _ g / t _ _ _.'

**6 a** Helen offers to help with Tasha's suitcase twice. The first time, she says,
'C _ _ / I / h _ _ _ / y _ _ with your suitcase?'

**b** Tasha says no. She says,
'No, / r _ _ _ _ _, / it's / a _ _ _ _ _ t / thanks./ I / c _ _ / m _ _ _ _ e.'

**c** Helen insists. She offers Tasha help again. She says,
'C _ _ _ / _ n! / L _ _ / m _ / help. D _ _' _ / l _ _ t / that big suitcase...'

**d** Tasha accepts. She says,
'O _ / T _ _ _ _ _ /. It / _ _ / q _ _ _ _ / h _ _ _ y.'

**Check your answers**
**1** But first, I have to pay at the machine. **2** Wait a minute. **3** Let me see if I've got the right money. **4 a** I'm afraid I haven't got any change. **b** Don't worry. **5** I'm getting this. **6 a** Can I help you with your suitcase? **b** No, really, it's alright, thanks. I can manage. **c** Come on! Let me help. Don't lift that big suitcase. **d** OK Thanks. It <u>is</u> quite heavy.

---

## Find the words and phrases

→ Read the sentences below.
→ Read the text of Recording 4 on page 309 and complete the words and phrases.

**1** Helen finds the car park ticket.
She says, 'H _ _ _ / i _ / i _/, in my p _ _ _ _ _.'

**2** It's not necessary to pay the exact money because the machine gives / c _ _ _ _ _ /. You can pay with /n _ _ _ _ .

**3** Tasha needs help with the bag. She says,
'C _ _ _ _ / you / j _ _ _/ h _ _ _ / this bag for a minute?'

**4** Helen holds the bag /w _ _ _ _ / Tasha puts the suitcase in.

**5** They put the suitcase in the boot first.
Then they put the bag / o _ / t _ _ / t _ _

**6** Helen wants to help Tasha with the suitcase. She says,
'Don't lift it / o _ / y _ _ _ / o _ _ .'

**7** Is the suitcase very heavy? No, but it's q _ _ _ _ heavy.

**8** Tasha decides not to take her coat off. She's cold.
She says, 'I / think / I ' _ _ / k _ _ _ / m _ _ _ / o _.'

**9** Tasha's tired. When they get to the house she can go to her
room and relax – she can h _ _ _ / a / r _ _ t.

**10** Verb *get*. In the sentences below *get* means    **a** go/ arrive

                                                   **b** put – with
                                                      difficulty
                                                      **c** pay

  **i** Let's get your luggage in the car.
 **ii** Don't worry! I'm getting this.
**iii** Let's get home.

## Check your answers

**1** Here it is, *in* my pocket. (preposition!) **2** change/notes
**3** Could you just hold this bag for a minute? **4** while. **5** *on* the top
(preposition!). **6** on your own. **7** quite. **8** I think I'll keep mine *on*.
(preposition!) **9** have a rest. **10** Get **i** b **ii** c **iii** a.

---

## Using these words and phrases

→ Match the following 1–10 with a–j.

| | | | |
|---|---|---|---|
| **1** | Why don't you take your jacket off? | **a** | Yes, it's quite interesting, actually. |
| **2** | Where's John? | **b** | I can give you two ten pound notes. |
| **3** | Don't go on your own. | | |
| **4** | The boot is full. | **c** | with chocolate sauce on the top. |
| **5** | I'll pay for the drinks. | **d** | Oliver is going to the centre by bus. |
| **6** | I love vanilla ice cream | **e** | I'll go with you. |
| **7** | Have you got change for £20? | **f** | I'll put the bag on the back seat then. |
| **8** | Is that a good TV programme? | **g** | No, thanks, it's alright. I can manage. |
| **9** | While Tasha is going to Helen's, | **h** | He's upstairs, having a rest. |
| **10** | Do you need help with that? | **i** | I prefer to keep it on, thanks. I'm a bit cold. |
| | | **j** | No, it's my turn. I'll get them. |

**Check your answers**
**1** i **2** h **3** e **4** f **5** j **6** c **7** b **8** a **9** d **10** g

---

## Insight 109

*Q What's the difference between 'car park' and 'parking'?*
*A Car park is* a noun. It's a public place to leave a car.

For example: 'When I go to London, I leave the car in the car park at the station.'

Not: 'I leave the car in the parking'.

*Park* is a verb, for example, 'You can't park here'.

The phrase *No parking* means 'You can't park here'. This is a **verbal noun** (a verb used as a noun).

# Grammar and communication 4

### Obligation and necessity – have to

**Example from *The Story*:**
The car park isn't free. Helen says,
'But first, **I have to** pay at the machine just here.'

### Meaning
Is it necessary to pay?     Yes, it is a regulation of the car park.
And if Helen doesn't pay? She'll have a problem – she is obliged
to pay.

| Grammar summary – *have to* – obligation and necessity | | | | | | | |
|---|---|---|---|---|---|---|---|
| **Affirmative** | | | **Negative** | | | **Questions** | |
| I | have | to + verb | I don't | have to + verb | | Do I | have to + verb |
| S/he | has | | S/he doesn't | | | Does s/he | |

Look at these examples:

**1**  **I don't have to** go now. I can stay until 1.00.
**Meaning** It's not necessary for me to go now.

**2**  **Do I have to** enrol before the next course or can I just come on
the first day?
**Meaning** Is it an obligation to enrol before the next course or
is it possible to just go to the class on the first day?

## Insight 110
Learners of English often say, *Is it necessary for me to...?*
★ This isn't wrong but *Do I have to...?* is more common.

*Q What's the difference between 'Where <u>do I have to go</u> now?'*
*and 'Where <u>do I go</u> now?'? (Topic 8)*

*A* The difference is small:

**a** asks more about obligation – rules and regulations

**b** asks more about systems – what is the custom/norm?

★ In some situations both are appropriate.

**Examples:**

**1** You are filling in a form:
'Where do I sign?' and
'Where do I have to sign?' are both correct and appropriate.

**2** You are using a new photocopier:
'Which way do I put the paper?' and
'Which way do I have to put the paper?' are both correct and
appropriate.

**Obligation and necessity –** *have to*

→ Complete these sentences with the correct form of *have to*.

**1** My husband _____ travel a lot for his job. He's always
away.

**2** How many times a day _____ take this medicine,
doctor?

**3** We _____ go if you don't want to. I really don't
mind.

**4** **Mother** Come on Tommy – it's time for bed. **Tommy** Oh,
Mum _____? I'm not tired.

**5** You _____ say 'yes' or 'no' now. You can tell me later.

**6** I _____ come back again tomorrow, do I? Can't we finish all the work today?

**7 A** What time _____ be at the airport for your flight?
**B** Half past ten.

**8** I'm sorry but I really _____ go now, or I'll miss my train.

**9 A** Could you please tell me why I _____ fill this form in?
**B** I'm sorry, sir. It's a company regulation.

**10** Which number _____ phone to confirm my return flight?

### Check your answers
**1** has to. **2** do I have to. **3** We don't have to. **4** Do I have to?
**5** you don't have to. **6** I don't have to. **7** do you have to. **8** have to.
**9** have to. **10** do I have to.

---

## Grammar and communication 5

### The imperative

**Examples from *The Story*:**

**1** Helen needs time to find the car park ticket.
She says, '**Wait** a minute.'
**2** Tasha wants to help with the money. Helen says it isn't a problem.
She says, '**Don't worry**.'

**Meanings**

**1** '*Wait.*' Helen is telling Tasha to do something.
**2** '*Don't worry.*' Helen is telling Tasha not to do something.

'*Wait*' is the imperative. '*Don't worry*' is the negative imperative.

| Grammar summary – The imperative | | |
|---|---|---|
| | | *Examples* |
| Positive imperative | Verb without *to* | Stop! |
| Negative imperative | *Don't* + verb without *to* | Don't forget! |

### The negative imperative – prohibition – *don't*

→ Use the correct form of the verbs in the box below to complete the sentences.

> write   wait   forget   worry

**1** _____ for me. I'll be home late tonight.
**2** _____ it's Mum's birthday tomorrow.
**3** _____! Everything will be alright.
**4** _____to me. It takes too long. Can't you e-mail me instead?

**Check your answers**
**1** Don't wait. **2** Don't forget. **3** Don't worry! **4** Don't write.

## Insight 112
### The positive imperative

★ Be careful! The imperative is a **danger zone** for communication in English. In many languages it is very common to use the imperative in many situations.

★ In English we use the imperative in some situations.
In other situations it is impolite.

**When do we use the positive imperative?**

→ Look at the examples 1–6 and match with **a–f** from the box below.
→ Use your dictionary if necessary.

**1** **A doctor** 'Stay in bed for two days.' _____
**2** 'Come in!' _____
**3** 'Have a good weekend!' _____
**4** 'Be careful!' _____
**5** 'Stay in touch.' _____
**6** 'Go to the end of the road and turn right.'

---

**a** invitations and offers
**b** instructions – telling someone to do something
**c** giving street directions
**d** asking for contact
**e** hopes and wishes
**f** warnings

---

**Check your answers**
**1** b **2** a **3** e **4** f **5** d **6** c

What are they saying? What are they communicating?

→ Match the situations (**A–F**) on pages 320–1 with the correct imperative phrase from **Box 1** and the correct communication from **Box 2**.

**Example: 'Have a good holiday'**
     **Hopes and wishes**

Situation A

Situation B

Situation C

Situation D

Situation E

Situation F

---

**Check your answers**

| Situation A | **2** 'Go ahead. Help yourself! | **c** Offers and invitations |
|---|---|---|
| Situation B | **6** 'Look out!' | **e** Warning |
| Situation C | **4** 'Please write to me.' | **f** Asking for contact |
| Situation D | **5** 'Enjoy yourselves!' | **d** Hopes and wishes |

| Situation E | **3** | 'Put the cup here and press that button.' | **a** | Instructions |
| Situation F | **1** | 'Take the second on the left.' | **b** | Street directions |

## Insight 113

★ For instructions and street directions, you can also use *you* + verb (the present simple, Topic 8).

This form is also very common.

**Examples:**
**A Instructions**
  **1** You put your cup here then you press that button.
  **2** First you fill this form in, then you pay over there.
**B Street Directions:**
  **1** You take the second on the left.
  **2** You go as far as the station and then you turn right.

## Insight 114
### Be careful with the positive imperative

*Q When is the positive imperative impolite?*
*A* When we ask people to do things.

→ Look at these examples.

**Situation** You are eating with friends or colleagues. A person at the table says,
  **a** 'Give me some bread.' ☹
    'Can you give me some bread, please?' ☺
  **b** 'Put this on the table.' ☹
    'Could you put this on the table, please?' ☺

(See Topic 7 for more practice with *Can you…?*, *Could you…?* for asking people to do things.)

# Insight 115
## Telling people to do things – The imperative

★ The positive imperative is appropriate in some situations.

→ Match sentences (1–4) below with situations a–d.

1 Do your homework first.
2 Empty your pockets onto the table.
3 Sit, Jack, sit.
4 Don't go home yet! Stay a bit longer.

a with a close friend
b an adult to a child
c a policeman
d to an animal

**Check your answers**
1 b 2 c 3 d 4 a

★ To make an imperative more polite, add *please*.
For example, 'Please tell me' or 'Tell me please'.

### Summary – the use of the imperative – spoken English

→ Read these sentences about the use of the imperative.
→ Choose true or false.

1 The negative imperative is appropriate in many situations,
e.g. 'Don't say that!' True/False
2 The positive imperative can be impolite, e.g. 'Sit here.' True/False
3 We use the positive imperative for wishes, e.g. 'Have a good
journey!' True/False
4 We use the positive imperative for invitations and offers,
e.g. 'Come and join us.' True/False
5 We use the imperative with good friends and children. True/False

**Check your answers**
1–5 are all True.

# What's the right word?

## Public signs – the imperative

---
### Insight 116
#### The positive imperative
★ The positive imperative is common in written instructions and warnings.

---

→ Look at the pictures below and the imperative phrases in the box on page 325.

→ Write the correct imperative phrase for each picture.

→ Use your dictionary if necessary.

**Example:**

## Check your answers

**1** Mind your head **2** Insert your card here **3** Queue here **4** Look right **5** Please drive slowly **6** Cut along the dotted line **7** Beware of the dog **8** Book your tickets here **9** Stop **10** Give way

**Verb** *mind*

---

## Insight 117

★ In the exercise above, *mind* means 'be careful of...' This verb is common for warning people.

You can use the verb 'mind' with both
  **a** the person or thing in danger:
    For example, 'Mind your head'.
  **b** the dangerous thing:
    For example, 'Mind the door'.

---

→ Write an expression with the verb *mind* for the following situations.

**1** You are crossing the road. A bus is coming. Warn your friend.
**2** There's a step. Warn your friend.
**3** A child is sitting in a car, his legs outside the car. You want to shut the car door.
**4** Your friend is in the car with the door open. Another car is coming.

## Check your answers

**1** Mind the bus! **2** Mind the step! **3** Mind your legs! **4** Mind your door! or Mind the car!

# Find the right word

## Public signs – Negative imperative

→ Label the signs below with the correct expression from the box.
→ Use your dictionary if necessary.

No entry      No parking      No photography      No left turn
No bathing    No smoking

**Check your answers**
**1** No smoking **2** No parking **3** No bathing **4** No entry **5** No left turn **6** No photography

326

# Grammar and communication 6

## Offering, rejecting, insisting, accepting

**Examples from *The Story*:**

**a** Helen offers to help Tasha with her suitcase.
   She says, 'I'll help you with that suitcase.'
**b** Tasha says no.
   She says, 'No, really, it's alright thanks. I can manage.'
**c** Helen insists. She offers Tasha help again.
   She says, 'Come on! Let me help.'
**d** Tasha accepts.
   She says, 'OK Thanks. It is quite heavy.'

### a Offers
For more practice with *I'll*, see Topic 6.

### b Rejecting an offer
Example from *The Story*: 'No really, it's alright. I can manage.'

## Insight 119
★ We use *manage* when the action is difficult but possible.
  *Manage* is about effort and success.

In the sentence above, 'manage' means 'It's difficult to lift the suitcase because it's heavy, but I can lift it with effort.'

→ Listen to these mini-dialogues on Recording 5.
→ Repeat B's responses in the spaces.

### Recording 5

◀» CD2 TR 4, 04:27

| 1 | A | Can I help you with that? |
|---|---|---|
| | B | Thanks very much, but I think I can manage it on my own. |
| 2 | A | Let me do that. |
| | B | No, honestly, I can manage thanks. |
| 3 | A | I'll take that if you like. |
| | B | No, really, I'm fine thanks. I can manage. |
| 4 | A | Shall I do that? |
| | B | It's OK I can manage, thanks. |
| 5 | A | Would you like me to carry that for you? |
| | B | Thanks for the offer but I think I can manage it. |

**Verb** *manage*

→ Complete the mini-dialogues below with the correct sentence from the box.

**Example:** How often do you go home to see your parents?
B *I usually manage to go about once a month.*

| 1 | A | The meeting is now at three o'clock and not four. Can you manage to get here one hour earlier? |
|---|---|---|
| | B | _____ |
| 2 | A | That's a big box! Mind your back! |
| | B | _____ |
| 3 | A | I'm sorry I can't help. |
| | B | _____ |
| 4 | A | I've got no idea how to do this. |
| | B | _____ |
| 5 | A | Tom worries so much about exams. |
| | B | _____ |
| 6 | A | How much do you understand when you watch a film in English now? |
| | B | _____ |
| 7 | A | Do you do any sport? |
| | B | _____ |
| 8 | A | Do you see your children in the evenings? |
| | B | _____ |

**a** I try to get to the gym twice a week but I don't always manage it.

**b** Don't worry! I'll manage on my own.

**c** It's alright. I think I can manage it. Where shall I put it?

**d** If we work together, we'll manage something.

**e** Yes, I usually manage to spend an hour or so with them before they go to bed

**f** ~~I usually manage to go about once a month.~~

**g** I can try.

**h** Yes, but he always manages to get good marks.

**i** I manage to understand quite a lot, actually.

**Check your answers**
**1** g **2** c **3** b **4** d **5** h **6** i **7** a **8** e

**c Offering again – insisting**
Example from *The Story:*

Helen insists. She offers Tasha help again.
She says, 'Come on! Let me help.'

> **Verb** *let*

**Form:** Verb *let*, imperative form    person    verb.

## Insight 120

★ The expressions 'Come on!' and 'Go on!' make the phrase stronger.

→ Look at the situations 1–7 opposite. You are the person
→ Complete the dialogues with sentences from the box.

Let me call an ambulance.
No, it's heavy. Let me take it!
Wait a second. Let me open the door for you.
Come on! It's my turn. Let me pay this time.
Come on! Let me have a look at it.
No, really. Let me do something to help.
Come on, its late! Let me take you.

**1**  **A**  Can I carry that for you?

    **B**  I'm alright thanks.

    **A**  _____

    **B**  Thank you. It is very heavy, actually.

**2**  **A**  I'll get this.

    **B**  _____

    **A**  OK Thanks.

**3**  **A**  Can I take some of those for you?

    **B**  No, it's alright. I can manage.

    **A**  _____

    **B**  Thanks.

**4**

    **A**  Can I just sit down for a minute?

    **B**  Of course. Would you like me to get you anything?

    **A**  No, I'm… oh, the baby…

    **B**  _____

**5**  **A**  Do you know where the nearest bus stop is?

    **B**  It's OK I've got the car. I can drive you home.

    **A**  No, I can get the bus. It's no problem.

    **B**  _____

    **A**  Thanks. It's really nice of you to offer but I can get the bus.

| 6 | A | Can I do anything? |
|---|---|---|
| | B | No, you go and sit down. |
| | A | _____ |
| | B | Thanks, could you peel the vegetables? |

7 A Oh! My eye!
B What's the matter?
A I think I've got something
B in it.

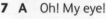

### Check your answers

**1** No, it's heavy. Let me take it! **2** Come on! It's my turn. Let me pay this time. **3** Wait a second. Let me open the door for you. **4** Let me call an ambulance. **5** Come on, it's late! Let me take you. **6** No really. Let me do something to help. **7** Come on! Let me have a look at it.

---

## Grammar and communication 7

### Introducing something negative in a polite way – *I'm afraid*

**Example from *The Story*:**
Tasha is sorry she hasn't got change. She says,
**'I'm afraid** I haven't got any change.'

## Insight 121

★ Use *I'm afraid* to introduce something negative in a polite way.

→ Match 1–8 on page 332 with the correct response **a–h**.

| | |
|---|---|
| **1** Excuse me, are you the manager? | **a** I'm afraid I can't. I'm driving. |
| **2** Could you tell me the time please? | **b** I'm afraid I don't know. I'm not from here. |
| **3** Excuse me, where I can get a taxi? | **c** I'm afraid I've got some bad news. |
| **4** Could I borrow your dictionary? | **d** I'm afraid we can't. We're going to my mother's. |
| **5** Come on! Have another glass of wine. | **e** No, actually I'm not. I'm afraid he's not here at the moment. |
| **6** Would you like to come to dinner on Saturday? | **f** I'm afraid I can't eat another thing! |
| **7** Do have some more cake. | **g** I'm afraid I haven't got a watch. |
| **8** What's the matter? | **h** I'm afraid I haven't got one. |

**Check your answers**
**1** e **2** g **3** b **4** h **5** a **6** d **7** f **8** c

## Insight 122
**Short answers –** *I'm afraid so, I'm afraid not*

★ To respond to questions with *Yes* or *No* alone can sound rude.
★ To express that you are sorry about a situation, use *I'm afraid so* and *I'm afraid not*.

**I'm afraid so**
Meaning
I'm sorry but yes.
Examples:

He's drunk, isn't he?
He isn't ill, is he?
It's a big problem, isn't it?
It's too expensive, isn't it?

**Response:** I'm afraid so.

**I'm afraid not**
**Meaning**
I'm sorry but no.
**Examples:**

Is he here?
You haven't got a car, have you? | **Response:** I'm afraid not.
Have you got any change?
Can you help me?

→ Respond with *I'm afraid so* or *I'm afraid not*.

**1  A**  It's a bad accident, isn't it?        **B** _____
**2  A**  This isn't right, is it?             **B** _____
**3  A**  Do you know where he lives?          **B** _____
**4  A**  You don't like this, do you?         **B** _____
**5  A**  You can't swim, can you?             **B** _____
**6  A**  Do we have to pay?                   **B** _____

**Check your answers**
**1** I'm afraid so. **2** I'm afraid not. **3** I'm afraid not. **4** I'm afraid not.
**5** I'm afraid not. **6** I'm afraid so.

## Using these words and phrases

**Get** for *pay* or *buy*

**Example from *The Story:***
Helen tells Tasha she's paying. She says,
'I'm **getting** this.'

## Insight 123
★ *Get* is an indirect verb for *pay*.

→ Put the words in the right order to make sentences.

**1** _____ this/get/I'll

**2** No, I insist!_____ getting/I'm/these

**3** _____ It was your turn last week.
     me/ice creams/the/get/today/let

**4** _____
     card/get/I'll/on/credit/this/my

## Check your answers

**1** I'll get this. **2** I'm getting these. **3** Let me get the ice creams today.
**4** I'll get this on my credit card.

## Insight 124

*Q What's the difference between 'I'll get this' and 'I'm getting this'?*

*A I'll get this is an offer*
*I'm getting this insists more.*

### What would you say?

**1** You come to England to stay with an English family. You don't know whether to use their first names or their surnames. You ask.

_____

**2** Your friend hasn't got any change for the car park. You have.

_____

## Possible answers

**1** What shall I call you? Advanced alternative: What would you like me to call you? **2** I've got some change. Here you are.

_____

## Revision

### How do you say it in your language?

Here are some examples of the important points in this topic.

→ Translate the sentences below into your language in the spaces.
→ Remember – translate the idea, not the words.

**1** It's lovely to see you again.

_____

**2** How was your journey?

_____

**3** I'm tired! My job is very tiring!

_____

**4** Thank you for inviting me.

_____

**5** Don't wait for me. I have to finish this.

_____

**6** **A** Shall I do that?
**B** Thanks but I think I can manage.

_____

**C** Come on! Let me help you.

_____

**7** I'm afraid the manager's not here.

_____

**8** Have a good weekend!

_____

### Join the conversation

→ Look at Recording 1 (page 290) again.
→ Listen to Recording 6.

◆) **CD2 TR 4, 05:21**

→ Read Tasha's words in the spaces.

# Test yourself 9

## Which one is right?

→ Choose **a** or **b**.

**1**  **a**  It's nice to have a holiday.
   **b**  Is nice to have a holiday.
**2**  **a**  How was your day?
   **b**  How were your day?
**3**  **a**  I'm very interesting in football.
   **b**  I'm very interested in football.
**4**  **a**  Thank you for to ask me to go with you.
   **b**  Thank you for asking me to go with you.
**5**  **a**  I'm have to leave now.
   **b**  I have to leave now.
**6**  **a**  I'll pay this.
   **b**  I'll get this.
**7**  **a**  Please come with us today.
   **b**  Please to come with us today.
**8**  **a**  Let me to do that.
   **b**  Let me do that.
**9**  Can you come with us?
   **a**  I afraid no.
   **b**  I'm afraid not.
**10**  Can I help with that?
   **a**  Thanks but I can manage.
   **b**  Thanks but I manage.

## Write a dialogue

Meeting someone after a journey

**Situation** You travel to visit a friend. Your friend is at the station to meet you.

**1 Your friend**
greets you. She is happy to see you.

**2 You**
greet your friend. You are happy to see her.

**3 Your friend asks about your journey**

**4 Say something positive**
You ask about her life in general

**5 Your friend replies and shows you the way to the taxis**

**6 You thank your friend for meeting you**

**7 Your friend responds and then says**

_____Look, here's a taxi. Go on! You get in first.

**8 You arrive. Your friend asks the driver how much it is.**

**9 You decide to pay**

**10** Your friend says <u>she's</u> paying

## Check your answers
1 a 2 a 3 b 4 b 5 b 6 b 7 a 8 b 9 b 10 a

## Dialogue: model answers

| | | |
|---|---|---|
| 1 | **Your friend** | Hello, X. It's great to see you again. |
| 2 | **You** | Hi, X. It's lovely to see you too. |
| 3 | **Your friend** | How was your journey? |
| 4 | **You** | It was good thanks. How are things with you? |
| 5 | **Your friend** | I'm fine. The taxis are this way. |
| 6 | **You** | Thank you for picking me up, by the way. |
| 7 | **Your friend** | That's OK Look, here's a taxi. Go on! You get in first. |
| 8 | **Your friend** | How much is it, please? |
| 9 | **You** | Let me pay. |
| 10 | **Your friend** | No, I'm getting this. |

# 10

# Finding accommodation

Grammar and communication
- **Asking** *who?* **+ short answers**
- **Talking about the number of people**
- **Talking about the same thing** – *one, ones*
- **Asking for an alternative**
- **Negative comparisons**
- **Decisions – buying things**
- **Verb** *hope*
- **Talking about the past – past simple**
- **Past experience – present perfect**

Vocabulary
- **Hotel language**
- **Ordinal numbers**

Pronunciation
- **Schwa / ə /**

*Oliver is at the hotel reservations desk in the tourist information centre at Victoria station in central London. He needs a room.*

## Understanding the important information

→ Cover the text of Recording 1 below.
→ Read the sentences below.
→ Listen to Recording 1 *The Story* and answer *Yes* or *No* to the sentences.

| | | |
|---|---|---|
| **1** | Oliver books a hotel room. | Yes/No |
| **2** | They talk about | |
| | – type of room | Yes/No |
| | – hotel facilities | Yes/No |
| | – prices | Yes/No |
| | – one particular hotel | Yes/No |

**Recording 1 (and 9) –** *The Story*

◀) **CD2 TR 5, 00:18**

| | |
|---|---|
| **Assistant** | Who's next, please? |
| **Oliver** | I think I am. I'd like to book a room, please. |
| **Assistant** | Yes, how many of you are there? |
| **Oliver** | It's just for me. |
| **Assistant** | And how long is it for? |
| **Oliver** | I need a room from tonight until the end of next week. |
| **Assistant** | OK. So that's a single room for 14 nights altogether. |
| **Oliver** | Yes, that's right. |
| **Assistant** | In any specific area? |
| **Oliver** | I don't mind, as long as it's central. |
| **Assistant** | What sort of price are you looking to pay? |
| **Oliver** | Between £50 and £60 a night. |
| **Assistant** | There's the Trafalgar Hotel. It's very near here. |
| **Oliver** | How much is that one? |
| **Assistant** | £55 a night. |
| **Oliver** | That would be fine. |
| **Assistant** | I'll just see if they have any vacancies. Would you like to take a seat for a moment? |
| **Oliver** | Thanks. |

## Check your answers

**1** No  **2 a** Type of room      Yes
         **b** Hotel facilities     No
         **c** Prices             Yes
         **d** One particular hotel    Yes

---

## Understanding more

### Finding a room

→ Cover the text of Recording 1 again.
→ Read the table below.
→ Listen to the recording and complete the table.

| Number of nights | Oliver's price range | Location (where?) | Name of hotel | Price |
|---|---|---|---|---|
| | £..... –£..... | | | |

## Check your answers
Number of nights: 14; Price range: £50 – £60 a night; Location: central; Name of hotel: Trafalgar; Price: £55

---

## What do they say?

→ Read the sentences below.
→ Listen to Recording 1 again and try to complete the words.
→ Then read the text to help you if necessary.

**1 A** The assistant starts the conversation.
     She asks, 'W _ _ 's / n _ _ _?'
   **B** Oliver responds, 'I think _ / _ m.'
**2 A** The assistant asks about the number of people.
     She says, 'H _ _ / m _ _ y / o _ / y _ _ / a _ e / t _ _ r _?'
   **B** Oliver responds, 'J _ _ _ / m _ .'

**3 A** The assistant suggests the Trafalgar and Oliver asks the price.
He says, 'How much is /t _ _ _ / o _ _?'
**B** The assistant responds, '£55 / _ / n _ _ _ t.'

## Check your answers

**1 a** Who's next? **b** I think I am.
**2 a** How many of you are there? **b** Just me.
**3 a** How much is that one? **b** £55 a night.

---

## Find the words and phrases

→ Read the sentences below.
→ Read the text of Recording 1 and complete the words and phrases.

**1** Oliver is looking for a room.
He says, 'I'd like to / b _ _ k / a room, please.'

**2 a** The assistant asks about the number of nights.
She says, 'H _ _ / l _ _ g / _ s / i _ / f _ r?'
**b** Oliver responds, 'F _ _ _ / tonight / u _ _ _ _ / the end of the week.'

**3** Oliver needs a room for one person. He needs a /s _ _ _ _ _ / room.

**4** The location of the hotel isn't very important to Oliver, but he wants to be in the centre. He says, 'I don't mind, / a _ /l _ _ _ / a _ / it's central.'

**5 a** The assistant asks how much Oliver wants to pay. She says, 'W _ _ _ / s _ _ _ / o _ / price / are / you /l _ _ _ _ _ g / t _ / p _ _ ?'
**b** Oliver's minimum is £50 and his maximum £60. He says, 'B _ _ _ _ _ n / £50 and £60 / _ / n _ _ _ t.'

**6** When you need a room, you can say,
'Have you got any rooms free?' or
'Have you got any v _ _ _ _ _ _ _?'

**7** The assistant asks Oliver to sit down.
She says, 'Would you like to t _ _ _ / a / s _ _ _ / for a moment?'

**Check your answers**
**1** I'd like to book a room, please. **2 a** How long is it for? **b** From tonight until the end of next week. **3** He needs a single room.
**4** I don't mind, as long as it's central. **5 a** What sort of price are you looking to pay? **b** Between £50 and £60 a night. **6** Have you got any vacancies? **7** Would you like to take a seat for a moment?

---

## Using these words and phrases

### 1 Questions with *for* at the end

**Example from *The Story*:**
The assistant asks about the number of nights.
She says, '**How long is it for?**'

**Insight 125**
\**How long* asks about the number of days.
It refers to 'the room'.
\*She can also say, *How long for?* but this is more direct. It can sound abrupt.

**Summary – Questions with *for* at the end**

| How many | is | it/this/that | |
|---|---|---|---|
| How long<br>When<br>Who | are | they/these/those | for? |

→ Complete these dialogues. Make questions from the words in the table above.

**1** A Good evening, sir.

_____?

B There are four of us.

A If you would like to follow me, I'll show you to your table.

**2** A Here are our tickets to New York.

B _____?

A Next Wednesday.

**3** A Here's the bill.

B Let's pay half each.

_____?

A £20.50.

**4** A They're beautiful.

_____?

B Oh, that's my little secret.

**5** A If you want to go out on the lake you can hire a boat. It costs £10.

B _____?

A One hour.

**Check your answers**
**1** How many is it for? ('it' refers to 'table') **2** When are they for?
**3** How much is it for? **4** Who are they for? **5** How long is that for?

**2** As long as

The location of the hotel isn't very important to Oliver, but he wants to be in the centre.

The assistant asks, 'In any specific area?'

Oliver says, 'I don't mind, as long as it's central.'

→ Complete the mini-dialogues below.
→ Use *as long as* + the correct phrase from the box.
→ Change the verb if necessary.

| | |
|---|---|
| as long as… | be in a non-smoking area |
| | get there by twenty past |
| | be back before 11 o'clock |
| | go to London |
| | find me a room |
| | rain |
| | take me home afterwards |
| | ~~be careful~~ |

**Example:**
A  Dad, can I borrow the car?
B  Yes, **as long as you're careful**.

**1**  A  Can we go on a trip to England?
    B  Why not, _____ we _____

**2**  A  Could you baby-sit for us on Saturday evening?
    B  Of course, _____ you _____

**3**  A  We're going to the open-air theatre this evening.
    B  That can be really good, _____ it _____

**4**  A  The train leaves at half past three.
    B  So, _____ we _____ we'll be OK

**5**  A  Would you like a table by the window, sir?
    B  I don't mind, _____ it _____

**6**  A  Mum, can I go out?
    B  Yes, _____ you _____

**7 A** I'm sorry sir, but the hotel is full. I understand you've got a booking but...

**B** I don't mind how long I have to wait, _____ you

_____

**Check your answers**

| | | |
|---|---|---|
| **1** | | we go to London. |
| **2** | | you take me home afterwards. |
| **3** | | it doesn't rain. |
| **4** | as long as | we get there by twenty past. |
| **5** | | it is in a non-smoking area. |
| **6** | | you are back by 11 o'clock. |
| **7** | | you find me a room. |

### 3 Talking about how much you want to spend

Example from *The Story*:
The assistant asks Oliver how much he wants to pay.
She says, 'What sort of price are you looking to pay?'

## Insight 127

*Q What's the difference between*

**a** *'How much do you want to pay?'*
and
**b** *'What sort of price are you looking to pay?'*

*A* The grammar is correct in both questions. The meaning is the same.

**a** 'How much do you want to pay?' is more direct.
**b** 'What sort of price are you looking to pay?' is indirect.

Question b is common in shops and when you are buying a service.

*Q Can I say, 'What kind of price...?' instead of 'sort'.*
*A* Yes, What kind of...? and What sort of...? are the same.

## Responses – the price

Oliver's minimum is £50 and his maximum is £60.
He says, 'Between £50 and £60.'

Other possible responses:

| | |
|---|---|
| Anything up to £20 is alright <br> Anything under £20 is OK <br> As long as it's less than £20 } | These expressions mean <br> £20 is your maximum |
| About £20 <br> Around £20 } | It can be a little more or a little <br> less than £20 |

## Prices, quantities and time

How much is a room at the Trafalgar? '£55 a night.'

## Insight 128

★ We use *a/an* for measurements of time, units of quantity etc.
For example, 50p a packet.

→ Complete the mini-dialogues below. Use one picture from
page 348 and one word from the box under the pictures.
→ Use your dictionary if necessary.

**Example: A** He's very good at his job. How much does he charge?
**B** *£25 an hour*

**1 A** How much does it cost to have a car?
**B** About_____. Expensive, isn't it?
**2 A** Can you tell me how much those flowers cost, please?
**B** Yes,_____
**3 A** How much are these bananas, please?
**B** Yes,_____
**4 A** Those strawberries look nice. How much are they, please?
**B** _____
**5 A** Can you tell me the price of these biscuits, please?
**B** _____
**6 A** Let's get some more of that wine, shall we? How much is it?
**B** _____

| month | kilo | bunch | packet | bottle | box | hour |

### Check your answers

**1** £90 a month. **2** £3 a bunch. **3** 90p a kilo. **4** £1.49 a box.
**5** 65p a packet. **6** £3.99 a bottle.

### Insight 129

*Q Can I also say 'per', for example, '£20 per hour'?*

*A A/an* is normal in spoken English.

*Per* is formal. It is more common in written English.

## How do you pronounce it?

**Schwa / ə /**

### Insight 130

★ This is the most common sound in English.

★ Why? The vowel in unstressed syllables is often
pronounced *schwa*.

★ In the words and phrases below, all the letters with the
*schwa* symbol / ə / on the top have the same sound *schwa*.

→ Listen to Recording 2 and repeat the words and phrases.
The stress is underlined in each phrase.
→ Pay special attention to the pronunciation of the *schwa* / ə /.

**Recording 2**

◀) **CD2 TR 5, 01:05**

/ə/ /ə/ /ə/ /ə/ /ə/ /ə/
**1** to, to <u>book</u>, a, a <u>room</u>, to book a <u>room</u>,

/ə/ /ə/
I'd <u>like</u> to book a <u>room</u>

/ə/ /ə/ /ə/
**2** for, for <u>me</u>, it's just for <u>me</u>

/ə/ /ə/ /ə/ /ə/
**3** to<u>night</u>, from, from to<u>night</u>

/ə/ /ə/ /ə/
**4** of, the <u>end</u> of, the <u>end</u> of next <u>week</u>

/ə/ /ə/ /ə/ /ə/ /ə/ /ə/
**5** as, as <u>long</u> as, as <u>long</u> as it's <u>central</u>

/ə/ /ə/ /ə/ /ə/ /ə/
**6** <u>sort</u> of, sort of <u>price</u>, what sort of <u>price</u> are you, to <u>pay</u>,

/ə/ /ə/ /ə/
What sort of <u>price</u> are you <u>look</u>ing to <u>pay</u>?

/ə/ /ə/
**7** a <u>night</u>, £55 a <u>night</u>

/ə/
**8** <u>vacancies</u>

/ə/ /ə/ /ə/ /ə/ /ə/ /ə/
**9** to <u>take</u>, to take a <u>seat</u>, for a <u>moment</u>,

/ə/ /ə/ /ə/ /ə/ /ə/
Would you like to take a <u>seat</u> for a <u>moment</u>?

# What's the right word?

## In a hotel

→ Complete these mini-dialogues with the correct response from the box below.

→ Use your dictionary if necessary.

**1** **A** There are two of us.
　　**B** _____

**2** **A** Does the room have a private bathroom?
　　**B** _____

**3** **A** Is it half board?
　　**B** _____

**4** **A** Do you do full board?
　　**B** _____

**5** **A** I see B & B signs everywhere. What does B & B mean?
　　**B** _____

**6** **A** What does 'No vacancies' mean?
　　**B** _____

**7** **A** I'm very sorry but the lift isn't working.
　　**B** _____

**8** **A** Don't I need a key to open the door of my room?
　　**B** _____

**9** **A** Where could I have a business meeting, please?
　　**B** _____

**10** **A** We're really thirsty and I'd like something to eat, too.
　　**B** _____

**a** No, sir. Just put this card in the machine on the door.
**b** Yes, the price includes dinner.
**c** Do you prefer a double or twin room?
**d** Yes, all our rooms have ensuite facilities, madam.
**e** It means there are no rooms free. The hotel is fully booked.
**f** The lounge is always open to visitors, madam.

**g** Yes, that price includes a light lunch and a 3-course dinner.
**h** It stands for 'bed and breakfast'. It's very common in Britain.
**i** The bar is open all day for refreshments, sir.
**j** Oh, dear ! We'll have to go up the stairs.

**Check your answers**
1 c 2 d 3 b 4 g 5 h 6 e 7 j 8 a 9 f 10 i

---

# Grammar and communication 1

### Asking *Who?* + short answers

**Example from *The Story*:**

The assistant asks, 'Who's next?' Oliver responds, 'I think I am.'

★ Short answers are very common in English.

→ Look at the examples below.

| | | |
|---|---|---|
| Who works in this office? | → | I do |
| Who likes coffee? | → | Peter does |
| Who can drive? | → | David and Sally can |
| Who hasn't got a sister? | → | Tom hasn't |
| Who's hungry? | → | We are |
| Who's going to Italy? | → | I am |

→ Complete the short answers in these mini-dialogues.
→ Choose from

| | | |
|---|---|---|
| *am/am not* | *is/isn't* | *are/aren't* |
| *do/don't* | *does/doesn't* | |
| *have/haven't* | *has/hasn't* | |
| *can/can't* | *could/couldn't* | |

**1 A** Who lives at No. 12?

 **B** John and Sheila _____. You don't remember them, do you?

**2 A** Who's coming to the cinema with us tonight?

 **B** I _____. Have you got my ticket?

**3 A** Who's not here yet?

 **B** Sue _____ – she's always late.

**4 A** Who's got a watch?

 **B** I _____. It's six o'clock.

**5 A** Who can cook tonight?

 **B** We _____, if you like.

**6 A** Do you all like pizza?

 I'm afraid Mike _____. He can't eat cheese.

**7 A** Who has to go to work tomorrow?

 **B** I _____ but my partner _____ Isn't she lucky?

**8 A** Who's using the computer?

 **B** Robert _____, as usual.

**9 A** Who thinks it's a good idea?

 **B** I _____ – I think it's great!

**10 A** Who understands her?

 **B** No-one _____ . She talks so fast.

**11 A** Who's got a car?

 **B** Kate _____

 **A** Good! Perhaps she can take us there.

**12 A** Who watches TV in your house?

 **B** We all _____

**Check your answers**

**1** John and Sheila do. **2** I am. **3** Sue isn't. **4** I have. **5** We can.
**6** I'm afraid Mike doesn't. **7** I do but my partner doesn't.
**8** Robert is. **9** I do. **10** No-one does. **11** Kate has. **12** We all do.

---

## Grammar and communication 2

**Talking about the number of people –** *how many?*

**Example from *The Story*:**
The assistant asks about the number of people.

She says, 'How many of you are there?'
Oliver responds 'Just me.'

**How many of you are there?**

→ Answer the following questions about you.

**1** How many of you are there in your family?
*There are _____ of us.*
**2** How many of you are there in the room at this moment?
T_____/ are / _____/ o _/ u _
or
J_____/ m_____
**3** If you are a student – how many of you are there in your class?
_____
**4** If you work – how many of you are there in the company?
_____

**Check your answers**
All answers: 'There are XXX of us.' If you're alone, the answer to
question 2 is: 'Just me.'

_____

## Grammar and communication 3

**Talking about the same thing –** *one/ones*

**Example from** *The Story*:
The assistant suggests the Trafalgar Hotel and Oliver asks
the price.
He says 'How much is that one?'

.................................................................................
# Insight 131
★ Don't repeat the noun. Use 'one' or 'ones' instead.
.................................................................................

→ Complete the speech bubbles on page 354.
→ Choose from the sentences in the box.

**Check your answers**
**1** e **2** d **3** c **4** a **5** b

**Common mistake – *one/ones***

→ Look at these examples.

**1** A Would you like a large Coke? B No, can I have a small one?

**2** I like the green car but I prefer the white one.

**3** This bag is too big. Can I see that one, please?

**4** A Peter's out on his new bike. B A new bike? Who's got his old one?

**5** A I like green apples. B Do you? I prefer red ones.

| Example sentence | Grammar summary –One/Ones | | |
|---|---|---|---|
| 1 | a | adjective | one |
| 2 | the | adjective | one or ones |
| 3 | my etc. | | |
| 4 | this/that | adjective | one |
| 5 | these/those | adjective | ones |
| | no article | | |

Let's look at sentence 4 above, about the bike.

→ Complete the mini-dialogues below. Use *a*, *the*, *my* etc. + *one*, *ones*.

---

**1** **A** Would you like a hot or a cold drink?
   **B** Could I have /_____/ cold_____, please?

**2** **A** Which umbrella is yours?
   **B** _____black_____

**3** **A** Do you like your new computer?
   **B** Not really, I prefer _____/ old /_____

**4** **A** Do you like that blue hat?
   **B** It's too expensive. How about _____ red _____?

**5** **A** Are you going on a long trip?
   **B** No, it's just _____ short _____ this time.

**6** **A** Which shoes shall I wear?
   **B** Why don't you wear _____new _____?

**7** **A** Can I borrow a pen?
   **B** I've only got _____ red _____

**8** **A** Where do I put the clean plates?
   **B** Here.
   **A** And _____ dirty _____?
   **B** They go over there.

**9** **A** How many children have you got?
   **B** Two. They're both girls. The oldest one's called Marie and _____ other ____'s name's Danielle.

---

**Check your answers**
**1** a cold one. **2** the black one. **3** the/my old one. **4** the/this/that red one. **5** a short one. **6** the/your new ones. **7** a red one. **8** the dirty ones. **9** the/my other one's.

---

## Insight 134

*Q* **Where's the stress in the sentences above?**

*A* Stress is always on the important or new information.

---

So, in these sentences, the stress is on the adjectives, for example, *cold*, *black*, *old*, etc. A *cold* one, the *black* one, my *old* one etc.

*Our story continues… the assistant telephones the Trafalgar Hotel and talks to Oliver again*

## Understanding the important information

→ Cover the text of Recording 3.
→ Read the sentences below.
→ Listen to the recording and answer the questions.

**1** Oliver books a room at the Trafalgar Hotel? Yes/No.
**2** They talk about two, three, four or five hotels?

**Recording 3 –** *The Story*

◀) **CD2 TR 5, 02:47**

| | |
|---|---|
| **Assistant** | Sorry to keep you waiting sir. I'm afraid the Trafalgar is fully booked. There are no vacancies until next week. |
| **Oliver** | Have you got anything else? |
| **Assistant** | How about these two? The Park Hotel is in the Holland Park area and the Royal is very central, near Oxford Street. |
| **Oliver** | Are they about the same price? |
| **Assistant** | Let me see. The Royal is £60 a night and the Park is a bit cheaper, £55. They're both 3-*** (3-star) hotels so the facilities are about the same. Breakfast is included, of course, and both have ensuite bathrooms, television, direct-dial telephones and tea and coffee facilities in the room. |
| **Oliver** | Which one is more central? |
| **Assistant** | The Royal, but the Park is smaller, it's in a quieter street and is perhaps a little more comfortable. It's more traditional, a family-run hotel. Breakfast at the Royal is Continental, buffet style, where you help yourself but at the Park they also do a full, traditional English breakfast. |
| **Oliver** | I think I'll take the room at the Park. I prefer smaller, quieter hotels and it's better for me because it's nearer the office where I'm working for the next two weeks. |

## Understanding more

→ Cover the text of Recording 3 again.
→ Read the grid below.
→ Listen to Recording 3 again and complete the grid.

| Name of Hotel | The Park Hotel | The Royal Hotel |
|---|---|---|
| Price per night | £ | £ |
| Ensuite bathrooms | | |
| Direct-dial telephones | | |
| Tea and coffee facilities | | |
| Breakfast included | Yes/No | Yes/No |
| Type of breakfast | Continental/ English | Continental/ English |
| Oliver chooses | | |

**Check your answers**

| Name of Hotel | The Park Hotel | The Royal Hotel |
|---|---|---|
| Price per night | £55 | £60 |
| Ensuite bathrooms | ✓ | ✓ |
| Direct-dial telephones | ✓ | ✓ |
| Tea and coffee facilities | ✓ | ✓ |
| Breakfast included | Yes | Yes |
| Type of breakfast | Continental/English | Continental |
| Oliver chooses | ✓ | |

# What's the right word?

**Hotels**

→ Choose words from the box below to complete these sentences.
→ Use your dictionary if necessary.

**1** My hotel is very _____ because it's ___ a park. There's not much traffic.

**2** **A** How much is that hotel?
**B** I don't know but it's in the centre of town. That means it's _____

**A** I prefer to pay a bit more and be _____ so I can walk to the museums, shops and all the other places I want to visit. I also need a hotel that is _____ – being a tourist is tiring.

**3** I really like my hotel. Everything looks so _____ and the staff are very _____ – they always talk to me.

**Check your answers**
**1** quiet... near **2** expensive... central... comfortable **3** clean... friendly

# What do they say?

→ Read the sentences below.
→ Listen to Recording 3 again and try to complete the words.
→ Then read the text of the recording to help you if necessary.

**1** Oliver waits and the assistant comes back. She starts the conversation. She says, 'S _ _ _ y / t _ / k _ _ p / y _ _ / w _ _ _ _ _ g.'

**2** When she says the Trafalgar is full Oliver asks about other possibilities.

He says, 'H _ _ _ / y _ _ / g _ t / a _ _ t h _ _ g / e _ s _?'

**3** The assistant compares the Royal and the Park. What does she say about the Park Hotel? She says, 'The Park is s _ _ _ _ _ r, it's in a q _ _ _ _ street and is perhaps a little m _ _ _ /c _ _ _ _ _ _ _ _ _ e./ It's m_ _ _ / t r _ _ _ _ _ _ _ _ l/'.

**4** Oliver decides on the Park.
He says ' I ' _ _ / t _ _ _ / the room at the Park.'

---

## How do they pronounce it?

*Schwa* **(Part 2)**

→ Listen to Recording 4 and repeat these words and phrases from the conversation above.
→ Remember *schwa* / ə / is common in unstressed syllables.
→ Pay special attention to the letters with the *schwa* symbol / ə / on the top. The pronunciation is always *schwa* / ə / – they are unstressed.
→ Stressed syllables are <u>underlined</u>.

**Recording 4**

◀) **CD2 TR 5, 04:15**

| | | | |
|---|---|---|---|
| /ə/<br>**1** <u>Roy</u>al | | /ə/<br>**4** fa<u>ci</u>lities | |
| /ə/<br>**2** Holland <u>Park</u> | | /ə//ə/ /ə/<br>**5** tra<u>di</u>tional | |
| /ə/<br>**3** <u>Ox</u>ford Street | | /ə/<br>**6** <u>break</u>fast | |

7 conti**nen**tal /ə/

8 **chea**per /ə/

9 **small**er /ə/

10 **qui**eter /ə/ /ə/

11 **near**er /ə/

12 **bet**ter /ə/

## Grammar and communication 4

### Asking for an alternative

**1 A general alternative**

**Example from** *The Story*:
The Trafalgar Hotel is full. Oliver asks about other possibilities.
He says, 'Have you got **anything else?**'

## Insight 135
★ This question is very general.
★ You can use it to ask about everything.

**2 A more specific alternative**
→ Look at this example.

Receptionist: I've got one room at £100 a night.
Client: Have you got **anything cheaper?**

## Insight 136
★ We can use the **comparative** with this question.

→ Ask questions in these situations. Use the comparative.

**1** In a shop
   You _____?

**2** In a shop
You _____?

**3** Your travel agent suggests a flight at 22.00. It's too late.
You _____?

**4** You book a hotel room in London. Your friend tells you it's far from the centre. You phone your travel agent.
You _____?

**Check your answers**
**1** Have you got anything smaller? **2** Have you got anything longer?
**3** Have you got anything earlier? **4** Have you got anything nearer the centre? / more central?

---

## Grammar and communication 5

### Negative comparisons

Oliver chooses The Park because it's **smaller, quieter, more comfortable**, it is more **traditional** and it's **nearer** the office than the Royal.

Why doesn't Oliver choose the Royal?

The Royal's **not as quiet** (as The Park) or
The Royal **isn't as quiet** (as The Park).

**Insight 137**
The pronunciation of 'as' is also with *schwa* / ə /.

→ Complete the sentences below. Use adjectives from the box.

> quiet   comfortable   big   traditional
> good   near   expensive

1 The Royal's not___/_____. It's in a really busy street.
2 The Royal's _____as_____/___ the Park. The beds
are hard.
3 The Royal's ____/____ traditional. The style is more modern.
4 The Royal's ___/___ good ____ the Park for Oliver because it
isn't /____/n_____his office.

**Check your answers**
**1** not as quiet. **2** not as comfortable as. **3** not as traditional. **4** not
as good as, as near.

## British culture – accommodation for visitors

### Where to stay

▶ In Britain you can stay in a hotel, a guest house or a 'bed and
breakfast'.
   – Hotels have 1* (star), to 5*****. It depends on the
     facilities.
   – A guest house is a small hotel. It can be part of a private
     house. Visitors have breakfast and sometimes an evening
     meal in a guest house. Guest houses are cheaper than big
     hotels.
   – A Bed and Breakfast is also a private house. Sometimes it
     is just one or two rooms in a family home.
▶ Tax (VAT – Value Added Tax – currently 17.5%): It is
common to include VAT in hotel prices.

→ Read the text and label the pictures on the next page.
→ Use your dictionary to help you if necessary.

### Breakfast

Breakfast is usually included in the price of hotels in the UK.

▶ Continental breakfast can include cereals, yoghurt, rolls,
croissants, toast, butter, cheese, jam, coffee, tea and hot
chocolate.

*(Contd)*

▶ English breakfast includes fruit juice, cereals, eggs, bacon (sometimes tomatoes, sausages, mushrooms), toast, butter, marmalade, tea and coffee.

– Nowadays not many people in Britain eat a traditional full English breakfast at home. Sometimes it's a treat (something special) for weekends.

## Continental breakfast

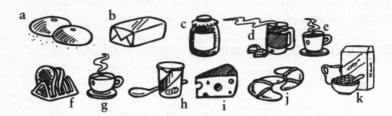

## English breakfast

## Check your answers

**a** rolls **b** butter **c** jam **d** hot chocolate **e** coffee **f** toast **g** tea **h** yoghurt **i** cheese **j** croissants **k** cereal **l** coffee **m** cereal **n** eggs **o** bacon **p** tomatoes **q** mushrooms **r** sausages **s** marmalade **t** fruit juice **u** toast **v** butter **w** tea

→ Now read about this London hotel.

## The Royal Scot Hotel, London

→ Look at the map opposite. Where is the Royal Scot Hotel?

→ Read the text from a London Tourist brochure and choose **A**, **B**, **C**, **D**, or **E**.

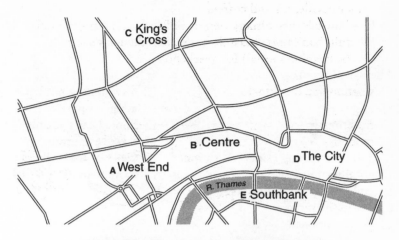

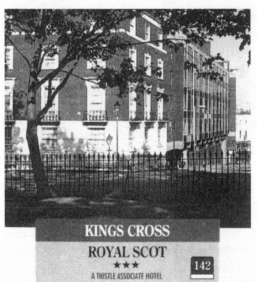

*Situated between the West End and the City of London, close to Kings Cross station, this modern hotel with 211 comfortable rooms, provides the ideal base for a shopping and sightseeing visit to the capital. London Zoo and Madame Tussaud's famous waxworks are within easy reach and local attractions include the British Museum and Sadler's Wells.*

**Check your answer**
C – Close to (near) King's Cross Station.

→ Read the questions below.
→ Read the text again and tick ✓ all the right answers.

The Royal Scot is:
☐ small
☐ large
☐ traditional
☐ modern
☐ good for visiting London's shops
☐ good for tourists
☐ good for sports enthusiasts
☐ hot in the summer
☐ air-conditioned

It has got:
☐ a swimming pool
☐ a big car park
☐ limited car parking
☐ three restaurants
☐ views of the park
☐ more than 200 rooms

**Check your answers**
The Royal Scot is:
large
modern
good for visiting London's shops
good for tourists (sightseeing)

It has got:
more than 200 rooms

## Grammar and communication 6

### Decisions – buying things

**Example from *The Story*:** Oliver decides on The Park Hotel.
He says, 'I'll take the Park.'

## Insight 138
★ Say *I'll take* when you decide to buy.

**Situation** You are in a shop and you decide to buy.

**1** You look at two boxes of chocolates, a big one and a small one.
You decide to buy the small one.
**You** _____

**2** You look at two pictures – one in black and white, one in colour.
You decide to buy the one in black and white.
**You** _____

**3** You look at two watches – a more expensive one and a cheaper one.
You decide to buy the more expensive one.
**You** _____

**Check your answers**
**1** I'll take the small one, please. **2** I'll take the black and white one please. **3** I'll take the more expensive one, please.

*Our story continues. Oliver arrives at the Park Hotel.*
*He checks in*

_____

## Understanding the important information

→ Read (a–f) below.
→ Listen to the recording 5 and choose *Yes* or *No*.

They talk about

| | | |
|---|---|---|
| **a** | Oliver's passport | Yes/No |
| **b** | his room number | Yes/No |
| **c** | the restaurant | Yes/No |
| **d** | the breakfast room | Yes/No |
| **e** | the cost of the room | Yes/No |
| **f** | Oliver's luggage? | Yes/No |

🔊 **CD2 TR 5, 05:30**

| | |
|---|---|
| **Receptionist** | Good afternoon. Can I help you? |
| **Oliver** | Yes, I've got a room booked. |
| **Receptionist** | In what name, sir? |
| **Oliver** | Rees, R – double E – S, Oliver. |
| **Receptionist** | Yes, here it is, a single room for 14 nights. |
| **Oliver** | That's right. |
| **Receptionist** | Could you sign this registration card, please? |
| [*Oliver signs*] | |
| **Oliver** | There you are. |
| **Receptionist** | Thank you. Here's your key. Room 508's on the fifth floor. Breakfast is served in the breakfast room downstairs from 7 to 10 o'clock and the lift is round the corner to your right. Do you need help with your luggage? |
| **Oliver** | No thanks, I'm fine. |
| **Receptionist** | I hope you enjoy your stay with us, Mr Rees. |
| **Oliver** | Thank you. |

**Check your answers**
**a** passport – no **b** room number – yes **c** restaurant – no **d** breakfast room – yes **e** cost – no **f** luggage – yes

---

## Understanding more

→ Cover the text of Recording 5 again.
→ Read the questions below.
→ Listen to the recording and write short answers.

**1** What does Oliver sign?  _____

**2** What's his room number?  _____

**3** Where's the breakfast room? _____

**4** What time's breakfast? _____

**5** How much luggage has Oliver got? _____

**Check your answers**
**1** the registration card. **2** 508. **3** downstairs. **4** 7.00 – 10.00.
**5** Not much.

---

## What do they say?

→ Read the sentences below.
→ Listen to Recording 5 again and try to complete the words.
→ Then read the text of the recording to help you if necessary.

**1** Oliver says he has a reservation.
He says: 'I've / g _ _ / a / _ _ _ _ / b _ _ _ _ d.'
**2** The receptionist asks his name.
She says, ' I _ / w _ _ _ / n _ _ e / sir?'
**3** Where is room 508?
'.../ _ n / the / f _ _ t _ / floor.'
**4** Where can Oliver have breakfast?
She says, ' Breakfast / i _ / s _ _ _ _ d / in the
breakfast room.'
**5** Where's the breakfast room? 'D _ _ _ _ _ _ _ s.'
**6** Where's the lift?
'R _ _ _ _ / the / c _ _ _ _ _ / t _/ y _ _ _ / r _ _ _ t.'
**7** The receptionist wants Oliver to enjoy his stay.
She says: 'I / h _ _ _ / you enjoy your stay with us, Mr Rees.'

**Check your answers**
**1** I've got a room booked. **2** In what name? **3** ... on the fifth floor.
**4** Breakfast is served in the breakfast room. **5** Downstairs. **6** Round
the corner to your right. **7** I hope you enjoy your stay.

---

## What's the right word?

### Ordinal numbers

**Example from *The Story*:**

'Room 508 is on the fifth floor.'

→ Look at this lift notice and complete the words on the right.

| | |
|---|---|
| ▶ 12th | twelfth |
| ▶ 11th | eleventh |
| ▶ 10th | _ _ _ th |
| ▶ 9th | _ _ _ _ h |
| ▶ 8th | e _ g _ _ _ |
| ▶ 7th | _ _ _ _ _ _ _ |
| ▶ 6th | _ _ _ t _ |
| ▶ 5th | _ _ f _ _ |
| ▶ 4th | _ o _ _ _ h |
| ▶ 3rd | third |
| ▶ 2nd – Restaurant | second |
| ▶ 1st – Bar/Lounge | first |
| ▶ G – Reception | ground floor |
| ▶ LG – Breakfast room | lower ground |

**Check your answers**
**10**th – tenth; **9**th – ninth; **8**th – eighth; **7**th – seventh; **6**th – sixth;
**5**th – fifth; **4**th – fourth

370

→ Look at the lift notice above and complete these mini-dialogues.

**Example:** ◁▭ 617 ▭ Where's your room? *I'm on the sixth floor*.

**1 A** Excuse me, where's reception?
**B** It's / _ _ / t _ _/ g _ _ _ _ _/ f _ _ _ _ .

**2 A** Can you tell me where the restaurant is, please?
**B** Yes, / i _ ' _/ o_ / t _ _ / s _ _ _ _ _ / floor.

**3 A** Where do we go for breakfast?
**B** Downstairs. The breakfast room's /_ n / t _ _ /l _ _ _ _ /g _ _ _ _ _/ floor.

**4 A** Excuse me, where can I get a drink?
**B** The bar's / on / t _ _ /f _ _ _ _ / f _ _ _ _.

**Check your answers**
**1** It's on the ground floor. **2** Yes, it's on the second floor.
**3** Downstairs, the breakfast room's on the lower ground floor.
**4** The bar's on the first floor.

→ Complete the rule below.

For ordinal numbers in English, add the letters _ _ to the number.

The ordinals f _ _ _ _, s _ _ _ _ _ and _ _ _ _ d are irregular.

**Check your answer**
For ordinal numbers, add the letter 'th' to the number. The ordinals *first*, *second*, and *third* are irregular.

*On which floor?*

→ Answer these questions.

**1** If you live in a flat – where is your flat? On which floor?
You _____

**2** If you live in a house – where is your bedroom? On which floor?
You _____

**3** Where do you work or study – on which floor?
You _____

**4** Where are you now?
You _____

_____

## Grammar and communication 7

**Verb** *Hope*

**Example from *The Story*:**

The receptionist wants Oliver to enjoy his stay.

She says, 'I hope you enjoy your stay.'

→ Write sentences for these situations. Use the verb *hope*...

**1** It's the end of the week.
What do you say to your colleagues when you leave work?
*I hope* _____

**2** Your friend is going out for the evening.
You _____

**3** Your friend is going on holiday.
You _____

**4** Your friend is going on a journey.
You _____

**5** Your friend is taking an exam/having a baby/taking a driving test etc.
You _____

**Check your answers**

**1** I hope you have a good weekend. **2** I hope you have a nice evening. **3** I hope you enjoy your holiday. **4** I hope you have a good journey. **5** I hope everything goes well.

## Insight 140

*Q* **What's the difference between 'I hope you have a good weekend' and 'Have a good weekend'? (Topic 9)**

*A* They are very similar. Both are appropriate in most situations. *I hope* can be more formal.

## How do you pronounce it?

*Schwa* **(Part 3)**

→ Listen to Recording 6 and repeat the words and phrases from Oliver's conversation in the hotel.

→ Pay special attention to the letters with the *schwa* symbol / ə / on the top. The pronunciation is always *schwa* / ə /. Stressed syllables are <u>underlined</u>.

**Recording 6**

◀))**CD2 TR 5, 06:21**

| | |
|---|---|
| /ə/<br>**1** Can I <u>help</u> you? | /ə/<br>**6** <u>sig</u>nature |
| /ə/<br>**2** Oliver | /ə/<br>**7** just <u>here</u> |
| /ə/<br>**3** <u>sin</u>gle | /ə/<br>**8** to your <u>right</u> |
| /ə/<br>**4** regis<u>tra</u>tion | /ə/  /ə/<br>**9** round the <u>cor</u>ner |
| /ə/<br>**5** of <u>course</u> | /ə/<br>**10** Do you need <u>help</u>? |

*Our story continues... Oliver is in his hotel room in London.*
*He phones his mother in Edinburgh.*

_____

## Understanding the important information

→ Cover the text of Recording 7.
→ Read the sentences below.
→ Listen to the recording and choose *Yes* or *No*.

Oliver and his mother talk about

| | | |
|---|---|---|
| **a** | the weather | Yes/No |
| **b** | Oliver's hotel | Yes/No |
| **c** | his trip | Yes/No |
| **d** | his work in London | Yes/No |
| **e** | Tasha | Yes/No |
| **f** | Oliver's father | Yes/No |
| **g** | a message | Yes/No |

**Recording 7 –** *The Story*

🔊 **CD2 TR 5, 07:10**

| | |
|---|---|
| **Oliver** | Hi→ Mum, it's Oliver. How are you? |
| **Mother** | Hello, dear. Where are you? |
| **Oliver** | I'm in a hotel in London, the Park. I haven't stayed here before. It's quite nice – small but comfortable and quiet. I've just got here from the airport. |
| **Mother** | How was your trip? |
| **Oliver** | It went quite well, actually. First, I visited our new representative in Chile, and then on Tuesday, Wednesday and Thursday I went to the Computer Fair in Buenos Aires. I talked to a lot of people there and had lots of meetings. And then on the flight on the way back I met a very interesting girl. |

| | |
|---|---|
| **Mother** | Oh, did you? |
| **Oliver** | Yes, she's an English teacher in South America. She's on holiday here, staying with friends, just outside London. I've got her number there so I can contact her again. I'm going to call her one day next week. We might have dinner together, or something. Anyway, how are you? |
| **Mother** | Did you get my message? |
| **Oliver** | What message? |
| **Mother** | I left a message at your hotel in Argentina two days ago. |
| **Oliver** | What was it about, Mum? Come on→ What's happened? |

**Check your answers**

**a** No **b** Yes **c** Yes **d** No **e** Yes **f** No **g** Yes

---

## Understanding more

→ Read the sentences below.
→ Listen to Recording 7 and choose the correct answer.

**1** The name of Oliver's hotel is
   **a** the Palmer.
   **b** the Park.
   **c** the Plaza.
   **d** the Spa.
**2 a** This is Oliver's first visit to this hotel.
   **b** This isn't Oliver's first visit to this hotel.
   **c** Oliver always stays at this hotel.
**3** Oliver thinks the hotel is
   **a** excellent.
   **b** good.
   **c** poor.
**4** Oliver's business trip was
   **d** good.
   **e** not very good.
   **f** terrible.

**5** Oliver is thinking about inviting Tasha

    **a** for lunch.

    **b** for a drink.

    **c** for dinner.

    **d** to the cinema.

**6** Oliver doesn't know about...

    **a** a letter.

    **b** a problem.

    **c** a ticket.

    **d** an invitation.

**Check your answers**

**1** b **2** a **3** b **4** d **5** c **6** b

---

## What do they say?

→ Read the sentences below.

→ Listen to Recording 7 again and try to complete the words.

→ Read the text to help you, if necessary.

**1** This is Oliver's first visit to the Park Hotel.
He says, '/ I / h _ _ _ n ' _ / s _ _ _ _ d / here before.'

**2** Oliver talks about this trip.

    **a** He says, 'First / I / v _ _ _ _ _ d / our new representative...'

    **b** ... then on Tuesday, Wednesday and Thursday I / w _ _ _ /
to the Computer Fair...'

    **c** He talks about his activities there.
He says, 'I / t _ _ _ _ d / t _ / a / l _ _ / o _ people there and
h _ _ / l _ _ _ / o _ / meetings.'

**3 a** Oliver tells his mother about Tasha.
He says, 'On the flight on the way back / I / m _ _ / a very
interesting girl.'

    **b** His mother is interested. She says, 'Oh, d _ _ / y _ _?'

**4** Oliver plans to phone Tasha next week.
He says, 'I ' _ / g _ _ _ _ / t _ / call her one day next week.'

**5** Oliver talks about the possibility of dinner with Tasha.
He says, 'We / m _ _ _ _ / h _ _ _ / dinner together.'

**6 a** Verb *get*: Oliver's mother asks him about her message.
She says, 'Did you get my message?
Here, 'get' means *find, buy, receive*?
  **b** Oliver says no. His mother gives more information about the message. She says, 'I / l _ _ _ / a message at your hotel two days / a _ _ /.
  **c** Oliver asks about the message.
He says, 'W _ _ _ / w _ _ / _ _ / a _ _ _ _?'

**7** He wants to know what the situation is.
He says, 'W _ _ _ ' _ / h _ _ p _ _ e _ ?'

**Check your answers**
**1** I haven't stayed here before. **2 a** First I visited our new representative... **b** then on Tuesday, Wednesday and Thursday I went to the Computer Fair. **c** I talked to a lot of people there and had lots of meetings **3 a** On the flight on the way back I met a very interesting girl. **b** Oh, did you? **4** I'm going to call her one day next week. **5** We might have dinner together. **6 a** Here, *get* means *receive* **b** I left a message at your hotel two days ago. **c** What was it about? (preposition!) **7** What's happened?

## Find the words and phrases

→ Read the sentences below.
→ Read the text of Recording 7 again and complete the words and phrases.

**1** When Oliver's mother starts the conversation, she says, 'Hello, / d _ _ _ /' to her son.

**2 a** What's the hotel like? It's q _ _ _ _ / n _ _ _ .
 **b** Is there a lot of traffic noise? No it's a /q _ _ _ _ / hotel.

**Check your answers**
 **1** Hello dear. (Older people often say *dear* to be friendly.)
 **2 a** quite nice **b** No, it's a quiet hotel.

> ## Insight 141
> *Q What's the difference in pronunciation between 'quite' and 'quiet'?*
> A *Quite* has one syllable / kwaɪt /.
>   *Quiet* has two. (qui-et) / kwaɪət /

## Grammar and communication 8

### Talking about the past – past simple

**Example from *The Story*:**
Oliver talks about his trip.
He says, 'First I **visited** our new representative.
Then on Tuesday, Wednesday and Thursday I **went** to the
Computer Fair. I **talked** to a lot of people there and I **had** a lot of
meetings.
On the flight on the way back, I **met** a very interesting girl.'
All the verbs in **bold** are in the **past simple tense**.

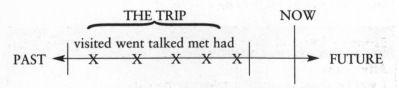

→ Read these questions and answers about the past simple.

**Meaning**
*Q* Is the trip **a** in the past?
  **b** in the present?
  **c** in the future?

*A* In the past.

*Q* Oliver **visited** the new representative. Do we know when?
*A* Yes, during his trip. His trip is in the past.

*Q* Oliver **went** to the Computer Fair. Do we know when?
*A* Yes, on Tuesday, Wednesday and Thursday.

*Q* Oliver **talked** to lots of people and **had** lots of meetings. When?
*A* During the Computer Fair. The Computer Fair is in the past.

*Q* Oliver **met** Tasha. When?
*A* On the way back to England.

## Insight 142

★ All these activities were during his trip. His trip is in the past.

Are we saying anything about the present? No.

## Form – past simple

| Regular verbs – verb + -ed | Irregular verbs |
|---|---|
| visit – **visited** | go – **went** |
| talk – **talked** | have – **had** |
| | meet – **met** |

Note: The verbs in **bold** are the past simple.

| Summary – Past simple | | |
|---|---|---|
| **Affirmative**<br>I, you, he, she, it we, they | talked (verb + -ed or irregular verb) | |
| **Negative**<br>I, you, he, she, it we, they | didn't | talk (verb) |

*(Contd)*

**Past simple**

→ Complete the dialogue below.

**Situation** It's Monday morning. Two colleagues, Natalie and Dan are talking about the weekend.

Is the weekend in the past? Yes
Is it finished? Yes
So, the verbs are in the past
simple.

**Natalie**  Hi, Dan, _____ you _____(have/had) a good weekend?

**Dan**  Yes, I _____ thanks. It _____ (be/was) really nice, actually. On Saturday, I _____ (wash) the car. Then in the afternoon I _____(take/took) the children to the park. Yesterday I _____ (play) tennis in the morning and for lunch we _____ (have/had) a barbecue in the garden.

**Natalie**  Great!

**Dan**  How about you? What _____ you _____ ? (do/did)

**Natalie**  I _____ (be/was) so tired after last week. I really _____ / _____ (do/did) much at all. I _____ (see/saw) a good film on the TV on Saturday night and yesterday I just _____ (relax) at home. My husband's sister _____ (come/came) to see us. We _____/ ___ (want) to cook so we _____ (get/got/got) an Indian takeaway. Later, in the evening we _____ (go/went) out for a drink and then we _____ (drive/drove) her home.

380

**Check your answers**

| | |
|---|---|
| **Natalie** | Hi, Dan, did you have a good weekend? |
| **Dan** | Yes, I did thanks. It **was** really nice, actually. On Saturday, I **washed** the car. Then in the afternoon I **took** the children to the park. Yesterday I played tennis in the morning and for lunch we **had** a barbecue in the garden. |
| **Natalie** | Great! |
| **Dan** | How about you? What **did** you **do**? |
| **Natalie** | I **was** so tired after last week. I really **didn't do** much at all. I **saw** a good film on the TV on Saturday night and yesterday I just **relaxed** at home. My husband's sister **came** to see us. We **didn't want** to cook so we got an Indian takeaway. Later, in the evening we **went** out for a drink and then we **drove** her home. |

# Grammar and communication 9

## Experiences up to now – present perfect

**Examples from *The Story*:**

**1** This is Oliver's first visit to the Park Hotel.
  He says, 'I **haven't stayed** here before.'
**2** Oliver asks what was in the message.
  He says, 'What's **happened**?'
                **has**

**Now look at this example:**
'I've stayed in this hotel three times.'

**Meaning**
→ Read these questions and answers about '*I have stayed*.'

**1** Is the action in the past? Yes.
**2** Do we know when? No. When is not the focus.

We use the present perfect to connect past actions with the present.

**3** Is there a connection between staying in the hotel and now?
Yes. I know the hotel now because of my three visits in the past.

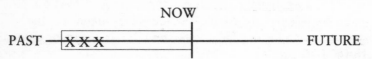

---

## Insight 143

The name of this tense is present perfect.

*Q Why is it called the present perfect?*
*A* Let's look at another example.

| I | **have** | **lived** | **in France** |
|---|---|---|---|
| subject | *have* in present | past participle | |

Half the verb is present (*have*) and half is the past participle (*lived*).
\*This tense connects the past and the present.
My time in France is in the past, but the experience is with me today. In other words, the past action of living in France has present importance.

---

| Grammar summary – Present perfect | | |
|---|---|---|
| I/you/we/they | + have ('ve) | + past participle |
| He/she/it | has ('s) | (regular verb + 'ed') or irregular |
| **Negative** | | |
| I/you/we/they | + haven't | + past participle |
| He/she/it | hasn't | |
| **Question** Have Has | I/you/we/they he/she/it | + past participle |

| Tag questions, echo questions and short answers | |
|---|---|
| Have(n't) | I/you/we/they? |
| Has(n't) | He/she/it? |

The past and the present are connected = present perfect.

## Insight 144

★ Asking questions with the present perfect:
The **present perfect** is the same as all other two-word verbs in English. To make questions you change the word order.

For example: (1) He → (2) has → (3) visited
For questions, say (2) Has → (1) he → (3) visited?
(2) auxiliary, *Has* (1) the subject, *he*
(3) the past participle, *visited*.

## Insight 145

★ The past participle is the third in a list of irregular verbs.
For example: see – saw – **seen**
write – wrote – **written**

'I have **seen** this film before.'
'She has **written** three books.'

→ Put the words in the right order to make sentences about Oliver.

**1** _____ at his hotel.
arrived/Oliver/has/

**2** _____ to his mother.
spoken/has/he

**3** _____ Tasha? No, not yet. He's going to call her next week.
called/he/has

**4** _____ the office. He's going there later.
contacted/hasn't/he

**5** How many times _____ to South America? About six
times.
he/been/has

## Check your answers
**1** Oliver has arrived. **2** He has spoken. **3** Has he called. **4** He
hasn't contacted. **5** has he been.

→ Use the verbs in brackets in the present perfect to complete these
mini-dialogues.

**1** A ____ you _____(see/saw/seen) the film 'Titanic'?
   B Yes I ___.
**2** A How many times ____ you _____ (go/went/been) to
    France?
   B I '__ / ___ lots of times.
**3** A How many countries ____ you _____ (visit)?
   B Me? I' ___/_____ to the States but I ____/_____ anywhere
    else.
**4** A How many jobs ____ your brother ____(have/had/had)?
   B He _____n't / ____ many, actually.
**5** A How many English books ___ you _____ (read/read/read)?
   B I' ___ / _____ hundreds!
**6** A ____ they _____ (finish)?
   B No, not yet.
**7** A You ____ _____ (forget/forgot/forgotten), have you?
   B No, of course not.
**8** A My sister '__ / _____ (buy/bought/bought) a new house.
   B Oh! _____ she? Whereabouts?

## Check your answers
  **1** A Have you seen the film 'Titanic'?
    B Yes, I have.
  **2** A How many times have you been to France?
    B I've been lots of times.
  **3** A How many countries have you visited?
    B Me? I've been to the States but I haven't been anywhere
    else.

**4** **A** How many jobs has your brother had?

   **B** He hasn't had many actually.

**5** **A** How many English books have you read?

   **B** I've read hundreds.

**6** **A** Have you finished?

   **B** No, not yet.

**7** **A** You haven't forgotten, have you?

   **B** No, of course not.

**8** **A** My sister's (has) bought a new house.

   **B** Oh! Has she? Whereabouts?

---

## Insight 146

Use the present perfect for past actions with present results or importance.

---

## Goodbye!

### Leaving the hotel

→ Put this conversation in the right order. Use the letters.

_____ **A** Certainly. What room number is it, please?

_____ **B** Good morning. Can I help you?

_____ **C** Room 201.

_____ **D** Of course. If you wait at the front door, one will be here in a few moments. Goodbye. I hope you have a good flight.

_____ **E** Let me see... Here's your bill. How would you like to pay?

_____ **F** Thanks. Goodbye.

_____ **G** Morning. Yes, I'd like to check out, please.

_____ **H** There you are. Could you possibly call me a taxi to go to the airport?

_____ **I** If I could ask you to just sign here then, please.

_____ **J** By card, if that's OK

→ Listen to Recording 8 and check your answers.

**Check your answers** (*Recording 8*)
🔊 **CD2 TR5, 08:35**

| Receptionist | B | Good morning. Can I help you? |
|---|---|---|
| Guest | G | Morning. Yes, I'd like to check out, please. |
| Receptionist | A | Certainly. What room number is it, please? |
| Guest | C | Room 201. |
| Receptionist | E | Let me see… Here's your bill. How would you like to pay? |
| Guest | J | By card, if that's OK |
| Receptionist | I | If I could ask you to just sign here then, please. |
| Guest | H | There you are. Could you possibly call me a taxi to go to the airport? |
| Receptionist | D | Of course. If you wait at the front door, one will be here in a few moments. Goodbye. I hope you have a good flight. |
| Guest | F | Thanks. Goodbye. |

*About your country: hotels*

→ Write answers to these questions or prepare to tell a friend.

**1** When was the last time you stayed in a hotel?

_____

**2** Talk or write about **a** the place.
                  **b** how long you stayed.
                  **c** who you went with.
                  **d** why you went there.

_____
_____
_____

**3** What was the hotel like? Describe it and talk or write about the facilities.

_____
_____

**4** How much did you enjoy your stay there?

_____

### *What would you say?*

**1** You are in a hotel. You would like to watch TV. You turn the TV on and nothing happens. You call reception.

_____

**2** You can't find your hotel key. You look everywhere but you can't find it. You're at reception.

_____

### Possible answers

**1** The television in my room doesn't work. **2** I'm very sorry but I can't find my key. Advanced alternative: I'm terribly sorry but I think I've lost my key.

_____

## Revision

### How do you say it in your language?

Here are some examples of the important points in this topic.

→ Translate the sentences below into your language.
→ Remember – translate the idea, not the words.

**1** **A** Who's next? **B** I think I am.

_____

**2** **A** How many of you are there? **B** There are four of us.

_____

**3** **A** How much is this one?

_____

**4** £3 a packet.

_____

**5** I don't mind where we go as long as you come too.

_____

**6** Have you got anything cheaper?

_____

**7** On the 6th floor.

_____

**8** I haven't been to Singapore.

_____

**9** He telephoned last week.

_____

**10** I got the letter yesterday.

_____

### Join the conversation

→ Look at the text of Recording 1 (page 340) again.
→ Listen to Recording 9 and say Oliver's words in the spaces.

◀) **CD2 TR5: 09:16**

_____

## Test yourself 10

### Which one is right?

→ Choose **a** or **b**.

**1** I've seen that film on DVD.
   **a** Did you? What's it like?
   **b** Have you? What's it like?

**2**  **a** My room is in the 1st floor.
   **b** My room is on the 1st floor.

**3**  **a** This ice cream costs £3 a box.
   **b** This ice cream costs £3 the box.

**4**  **a** Could I see the red one, please?
   **b** Could I see the red, please?

**5**  **a** I hope you to enjoy your trip.
   **b** I hope you enjoy your trip.

**6**  **a** Yesterday I went to the cinema.
   **b** Yesterday I was to the cinema.

**7**  **a** Where you met my brother?
   **b** Where did you meet my brother?

**8**  **a** How would you like to pay?
   **b** How would you like to paying?

**9**  **a** With card, please.
   **b** By card, please.

**10**  **a** The bar is in the downstairs.
   **b** The bar is downstairs.

**11**  **a** What did you at the weekend?
   **b** What did you do at the weekend?

**12**  **a** When have you arrived?
   **b** When did you arrive?

**13**  **a** I'll take this one, please.
   **b** I buy this one, please.

**14**  **a** In which floor is the restaurant, please?
   **b** What floor is the restaurant on, please?

**Write two dialogues**

**1** **A In the travel agency**
The travel agent asks about
the type of hotel you want.

**You**

**2** The only thing you don't
like is noise

**3** She asks about the number
of people

**4** You and your partner

**5** She asks you about the
price you want to pay

**6** Your maximum is £70

**7** She suggests the
Plaza Hotel – £65

**8** You say yes

**9** She asks about method of
payment

**10** In cash, please

**B** You pay and then you go to the shop next door to buy a suitcase. You are looking at a small suitcase:

**1** Shop assistant

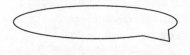

**2** You want the same suitcase but bigger

**3** The shop assistant says yes and shows it to you

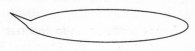

**4** You decide to buy it

### Check your answers
**1** b **2** b **3** a **4** a **5** b **6** a **7** b **8** a **9** b **10** b **11** b **12** b **13** a **14** b

### Dialogues: model answers

| **A 1** | **Travel agent** | What sort of hotel are you looking for? |
| **2** | **You** | I don't mind, as long as it's quiet. |
| **3** | **Travel agent** | How many of you are there? |
| **4** | **You** | There are two of us. |
| **5** | **Travel agent** | What sort of price are you looking to pay? |
| **6** | **You** | Anything up to £70. |
| **7** | **Travel agent** | How about the Plaza Hotel? It's £65 a night. |
| **8** | **You** | OK |
| **9** | **Travel agent** | How would you like to pay? |
| **10** | **You** | In cash, please. |
| **B 1** | **Shop assistant** | Can I help you? |
| **2** | **You** | Yes, have you got a bigger one like this? |
| **3** | **Shop assistant** | Yes, I have – this one. |
| **4** | **You** | I'll take that one, please. |

## To the learner

We hope you have enjoyed learning with *Complete Teach Yourself English as a Foreign Language* and that you are happy with the progress you have made. We enjoyed finding a method to help you learn English in English, without a teacher, and writing this course for you.

We wonder what will happen to Oliver and
Tasha in the future?
Will Tasha enjoy her holiday?
Will Oliver and Tasha meet again?
What do you think?
We'll see!
With best wishes

Sandra Stevens

# Glossary

**Auxiliary (verb)** A verb used with another verb. The auxiliary (verb) shows tense etc. For example:

| | |
|---|---|
| *She is reading* | Present progressive |
| *He can drive* | Modal auxiliary/ability |
| *I have finished* | Present perfect |

*Reading, drive* and *finished* are the main verbs – they give the meaning. *Is, can't, have* are the auxiliaries.

▶ The auxiliary for the present simple is *do/does*
▶ The auxiliary for the past simple is *did*
▶ Auxiliaries are always part of the verb in all other tenses

We use auxiliaries to make questions. We change the word order: the auxiliary goes *before* the person. For example:

*She is reading*
*Is she reading?*
*She likes Coke*
*Does she like Coke?*

To make the verb negative, we add '*n't*' (*not*) to the auxiliary. For example:

*He can't drive*
*She doesn't like Coke*

Some auxiliaries have a short form or contraction (see **Contraction**), for example *he's, they're, we've*. Contractions are common in spoken English and informal written English.

Auxiliaries are very important in English because we use them a lot to make conversation: **Question tags** and **short answers** both use **auxiliaries**.

Some examples of **auxiliaries** in **question tags** are:
*He's working, **isn't** he?*
*They're married, **aren't** they?*
*She's got a cat, **hasn't** she?*

And here are some examples of **auxiliaries** in **short answers**:
**A** *He's here*          **B** *Oh, **is** he?*
**A** *They can't come*    **B** ***Can't** they? Why not?*
**A** *She's had the baby* **B** ***Has** she? Is it a boy or a girl?*

. . . . . . . . . . . . . . . . . . . . . . . . . . . . . . . . . . . . . . . . . . . . . . . . . . . . . . . . . . . .

**Comparative** Comparing two things. For example:

*Peter is older **than** his brother.* Short adjective *old + er* (*than*)

*A house is **more** expensive **than** a flat.* Longer adjective, *more + adjective (+ than)*

. . . . . . . . . . . . . . . . . . . . . . . . . . . . . . . . . . . . . . . . . . . . . . . . . . . . . . . . . . . .

**Contraction** A short form of verbs *be* and *have*, some auxiliary verbs and *us* in *let's*. We write an apostrophe (') in the place of the missing letters. For example:

*I am = **I'm***
*It is and it has = **it's***
*He would not = **He wouldn't***

Contractions are very common in spoken and informal written English.

. . . . . . . . . . . . . . . . . . . . . . . . . . . . . . . . . . . . . . . . . . . . . . . . . . . . . . . . . . . .

**Direct language** can be impolite in English. For example: *Give me a glass of water* is often impolite. It is more polite to use indirect language, for example, *Could you give me a glass of water, please?*

**Echo questions** help conversation. They show you are interested and want to continue the conversation. Echo questions have two words: the auxiliary + subject. For example:

A *I live in Paris*  B *Do you?*
A *He hasn't got a car*  B *Hasn't he?*

**Formal language** is appropriate with people you don't know, people in authority and official situations and documents. (see **Informal language** and **Neutral language**). For example: *Thanks* is informal language. *Thank you very much indeed* is formal.

**Gerund** The verb + *ing*, used like a noun. For example: *I enjoy **travelling***.

**Imperative** The verb without *to*, for example, ***Wait** a minute.*

Remember the imperative is a danger zone for learners of English. We often use other forms of the verb to ask/tell someone to do something.

The imperative is common for:

| | |
|---|---|
| **Wishes:** | *Have a nice day!* |
| **Instructions:** | *Take this train* |
| **Directions:** | *Turn left at the end of the road* |
| **Warnings:** | *Be careful!* |

**Informal language** Appropriate with family, friends and children. For example, *Hi!* is informal, *Hello* is neutral/formal.

**Intonation** is the music or movement of the voice on the syllable with stress. English expresses different meanings through intonation. For example:

*Yes* →
Flat intonation. The person isn't interested.
*Yes* ↘
A big movement in the pitch of the voice. The person is interested.

**Less direct language** English uses indirect language a lot. It helps conversation and communication. Direct language with flat intonation can sound rude. For example:

| Dialogue 1 – direct | Dialogue 2 – less direct |
|---|---|
| A *Where's John?* | *Do you know where John is?* |
| B *I've got no idea* | *I'm afraid I've got no idea* |

The words in Dialogue 1, with flat intonation, can sound rude. The words in Dialogue 2 are less direct.

**Neutral language** Appropriate in most situations. For example, *Hello* is appropriate with people you know, people you don't know, people in authority and children (see **Formal language** and **Informal language**).

**Past participle** The verb + *ed*. The third part of an irregular verb, for example *see/saw/seen – seen*, is the past participle. We use the verb *have* + past participle to form the perfect tenses. For example, *I have eaten* – present perfect.

**Plural** More than one. For example, *sandwiches*, *grapes*.

**Preposition** Little words that connect nouns, etc., with other words. For **example**, *to the station* (direction), *at the restaurant* (place), *before two o'clock* (time).

The preposition is sometimes part of a phrase. For example, *interested in*, *I'm interested in sport* or *to be married to*, *She's married to a Frenchman*.

There are lots of prepositions in English. They are a problem zone for learners because it's often difficult to know which preposition to use. To help you:

▶ Try to learn the meanings of the prepositions (for example direction = *to*)
▶ When you learn a phrase with a preposition, remember to learn the preposition, too!

**Question tag** A short question form at the end of a sentence. This question form with falling intonation isn't really a question. It *is* a way of starting or making conversation. For example:

> **A** *Terrible weather, isn't it?* **B** *Yes. It's not very good, is it?*

The speakers know that the weather is terrible. They are not really asking questions. They are using question tags to start/continue the conversation.

**Schwa** The vowel sound / ə /, as in *a* book. It is the only sound in English with a name!

**Short answers** *Yes* and *No* alone can often sound rude in English. Short answers are: *Yes/No* + person + auxiliary. For example:

| | |
|---|---|
| **A** *Is Sue here?* | **B** *Yes, she is.* |
| **A** *Can you drive?* | **B** *No, I can't.* |

**Singular** One only, for example, a *bus*, a *biscuit*.

**Stress** Emphasis or force on a syllable or word. In all words with two syllables or more in English, one syllable has stress. Example, *Eng* - lish, fan – *tas* – tic.

In sentences, the stress is on the important words, the words with a lot of meaning. For example, *I've bought some **bread**, some **cheese** and some **fruit**.*

In English we also use stress to give a particular meaning or emphasis: *Could I have a **cold** drink?* (meaning not a *hot* one).

We also use it to correct people. For example, *The books **on** the desk, not **under** it.*

**Syllable** Part of a word with a vowel sound. For example, the word *question* has two syllables, *ques – tion*. And the word *popular* has three, *pop – u – lar*.

**Uncountable** Nouns that you can't count – mass nouns. For example, *rice* and *money* are uncountable nouns. You can't say one, two, three + noun.

**Weak form** In some short, common words (for example *but, for, from, to, was, does*), the vowel has two pronunciations: one strong (when the word has stress), for example, *who is it for?*; and one weak (when the word doesn't have stress), for example, *it's for you, but not **now**, from **Tom**, to **Paris**, Was it good? Does she **know**?* In all these words, the pronunciation of the vowel is *schwa* – it is very short and weak. *Schwa* is the most common weak form vowel sound.

# Quick reference: communicative functions

The figure in brackets ( ) is the topic number.

**Ability (3)**
    Questions:        *Can you + verb?*
                      *Do you + verb?*
    Responses:        *No, not at all*
                      *Yes, but not very well*
                      *Yes, not too badly*

**Asking about the same topic (3)**
    *And you?*
    *How about you?*

**Asking for an alternative – general (10)**
    *Have you got anything else?*

**Asking for an alternative – specific**
    *Can I / Could I have X instead,*
    *please? (2)*
    *Have you got anything...*
    (+ short adjective +er?)
    *Example: Have you got anything*
    *cheaper? (10)*
    (+ more + long adjective)
    Example: *Have you got anything more suitable?*

**Asking for help – indirect questions (7)**
    *Can you tell me where X is, please?*
    *Do you know how much X costs, please?*
    *Could you tell me if...*

**Asking for help, systems – present simple (8)**
*What/Where/When/How do I... + verb?*
Example: *Where do I sign?*

**Asking for information (6)**
*Could you tell me...? I'd like (to know)... What's the...?*

Could you tell me
I'd like (to know) } *the time of the next train, please?*
What's

**Asking for opinions (9)**
*How is/was...?*
Example: *How was your meal?*

**Asking for things (2)**
*Could I have...?*
Example: *Could I have a glass of water, please?*

**Asking someone to do something**
*Can you..., Could you..., Would you mind + verb + -ing (7)*
Examples: *Can you*
         *Could you* } *wait a moment, please?*
         *Would you mind waiting a moment?*
*If you would like to...* (very indirect) (7)
Example: *If you would like to call again tomorrow...*

**Attracting attention (1)**
*Excuse me...*
Example: *Excuse me, could I have the bill, please?*

**Buying things, decisions (10)**
*I'll take...*
Example: *I'll take this one*

**Choosing – responding to offers (2)**
*X, please*
*X for me, please*
*I'd like X, please*

*Could I have X, please?*
*I'll have X, please*

**Decisions (2)**
*I'll...*
*Negative decisions – I don't think I will (2)*

**Decisions, buying (10)**
*I'll take...*
Negative decision – *I think I'll leave it*

**Insisting, offering help (9)**
*Come on! Let me... + verb*
Example: *Come on. Let me do that!*
Response: Yes: *Thank you / Thanks*
No: *No thank you / thanks. I can manage*

**Invitations and offers**
Question: *Would you like a...?* (1)
Example: *Would you like an ice cream?*
Responses: Yes: *Yes, please. That would be nice*
*Yes, please. I'd love one/some*
No: *No, thank you*
*No, thanks. I'm fine*
Question: *Would you like to...?* (7)
Response: Yes: *Yes, that would be nice*
No: *I'm sorry, I'm...* (reason)
Question: *If you would like to...* (a very indirect way of asking someone to do something)
Responses: Yes: *Thank you*
*Yes, of course*
*Yes, that's fine*
*Yes, I'll...*
No: *I'm sorry but I can't*

**Likes and dislikes –** *like, enjoy, mind, be keen on* (4)
Question: *Do you like/enjoy X/verb + ing?*
*Do you like your job?*
*Do you enjoy being a mother/father?*

Responses: Very positive: *Yes, I really enjoy it*
           Yes: *Yes, I quite like it*
           Neutral: *I don't mind it*
           No: *I'm not very keen on it, actually*
           Very negative: *Actually, I don't like it at all*

## Making conversation
*actually* (3)         *Actually, I+ verb or I+ verb, actually*
Example: *I live in London, actually*
echo questions (3)
auxiliary + person
   *Do you? / Have you? / Can she? / Aren't they?* etc.

## Number of people, talking about the (10)
Question: *How many of you are there?*
Response: *There are X of us*

## Offers (see Invitations and offers)
### Offering help (6)

Offers:    *I can...*
          *I could...*
          *I'll...*
          *Shall I...?*
          *Would you like me to...?*
Example:  *I can*
         *I could* } *do that for you, (if you like)*
         *I'll*
Example:  *Shall I*
         *Would you like me to* | *do that for you?*
Responses: Yes: *Thanks*
               *Thank you*
               *That's very kind of you*
               *Can you? Could you? Would you?*
         No: *Thanks for the offer but it's alright*
              *Thanks but I can manage*

## Offering more

*(some) more, another* (1)

Question: *Would you like some more coffee?*

*Would you like another sandwich?*

Responses: (see **Invitations**)

## Permission, asking for (2)

Questions: *Is it alright if I...?*

*Could I...?*

*Can I...?*

Example: *Is it alright if I* ⎫

*Could I* ⎬ *use your phone?*

*Can I* ⎭

Responses: Yes: *Of course*

*Go ahead*

No: *I'm sorry but...*+ reason

## Possibilities and suggestions (6)

*We could...*

Example: *We could go to the cinema*

*You can...*

Example: *You can tell me tomorrow*

## Possibilities, suggestions and offers (see Offering help)

## Price, talking about the (10)

Question: *What sort of price are you looking to pay?*

Response: Maximum: *Anything up to XXX*

*Anything under XXX*

*As long as it's less than XXX*

Approximately: *About XXX*

*Around XXX*

## Rejecting an offer of help (9)

*No, really. It's alright thanks*

*No, really. I can manage*

**Requests (see Asking for things/Asking people to do things)**

**Same, asking for the (2)**
*The same for me, please*
*I'll have X, too, please*

**Starting a conversation – question tags (1)**
Adjective,+ *isn't it?*
Example: *Nice, isn't it?*
*Not very* + adjective, + *is it?*
Example: *Not very interesting, is it?*
Sentence + question tag
Example: *He isn't playing very well, is he?*
*It was a good film, wasn't it?*

**Suggesting doing something together (7)**
*Let's ... +* verb
Example: *Let's go to the cinema*
Responses:  Yes:  *OK*
*Alright*
*Yes, why not?*
*That's a good idea*
*Yes, why don't we?*
No:  *Do you really want to?*
*I'm not too sure*
*Perhaps not*
*Actually, I'm not too keen*
Negative suggestion: *Let's not...*
Example: *Let's not go to the party. I'm too tired*

**Suggestions, possibilities and offers (see Offering help)**
**Thanking (9)**

| | | |
|---|---|---|
| Neutral: | *Thank you* | *for+ verb + -ing* |
| | *Thank you very much* | *e.g. for inviting* |
| Formal: | *Thank you very much indeed* | *me* |
| Informal: | *Thanks* | |
| | *Many thanks* | |
| | *Thanks a lot* | |

| Responses: | |
|---|---|
| Neutral: | *That's OK* |
| | *That's alright* |
| Formal: | *You're welcome* |
| | *Not at all* |
| Informal: | *No problem* |
| | *Any time* |

**Why, saying (5)**

| | |
|---|---|
| Question: | *Why are you...?* |
| Responses: | *to...+ verb* |
| | *because I want to...* |
| | *because I need to...* |
| | *because I like to...* |
| | *so (that) (I can)* |
| | *because...* |
| | *because of...+ noun* |
| Example: A | *Why are you going to Italy?* |
| B | *To* |

*Because I want to*
*Because I need to*          *visit my Italian*
*Because I like to*          *friends*
*So (that) (I can)*

*Because of my friends – they're Italian*
*Because I'm going to visit my Italian friends*

# Quick reference: English grammar

**Grammar** is about the job of each word or phrase in a sentence. Let's look at eight of the main parts of speech.

**1 Nouns:** e.g. table, John, happiness – are people, things, animals, places and abstract concepts.

**1.1 Nouns can be common or proper,** e.g. *'bus'* is a common noun and *'July'* is a proper noun, i.e. it starts with a capital letter

**1.2 Nouns can be singular or plural,** e.g. **a dictionary** (singular = one), **three clocks** (plural = more than one). We usually add 's' or 'es' to make a noun plural but there are some exceptions, e.g. one **child**, two **children.**

Some nouns are singular in English and plural in some other languages, e.g. *news, information, advice, furniture.*

**1.3 Nouns can be countable** (= you can count the things) **or uncountable** (= you can't count it), e.g. *one brother, two brothers* but *water, rice, happiness.*

TIPS

**1** Some nouns can be both. 'Coffee' is uncountable but we often say *'Three coffees'* as a short way of saying 'Three cups of coffee'.

**2** We often use unit words with uncountables, e.g. *a loaf of bread.*

**1.4 Genitive or possessive's** is about possession, e.g. *the manager's office* means the office belonging to the manager. Apostrophe 's' is also used with some expressions of time e.g. *yesterday's newspaper, in two years' time* and for buildings, e.g. *St. Paul's* (cathedral), *the optician's* (shop).

TIP: 's or s'?

*My brother's teacher* = 1 brother but *My brothers' teacher* =
2 + brothers.

Similarly.... in a **year's** time (singular) – but ........in a few **years'**
time (plural).

**1.5** Compound nouns are two nouns together that make one,
e.g. *car key, wine-glass, river bank.*

PRONUNCIATION TIP: The stress falls on the first part,
e.g. *finger nail, rain hat.*

**1.6** Gerunds are verbs used as nouns, e.g. *Eating fruit and*
vegetables is good *for you* (subject) or *I like swimming.* (object)

**2 Pronouns, (pro-noun = instead of a noun) are words used in
the place of a noun.**

**2.1** Personal pronouns can be the subject or object of a verb,
e.g. **She** (subject) *sings. I like **her*** (object). Object pronouns can be
direct or indirect, e.g. *Eat **it!*** (direct), *Give **me*** (indirect) *a call.*

TIP: Verbs need a subject in English. If there isn't one, use '***it***' or
'***there***' e.g. ***It's*** *raining again.* ***It's*** *difficult to say.* ***There's*** *a meeting
at 3.30.*

**2.2** Possessive pronouns, e.g. mine, yours, his, etc., are 'owners',
e.g. A: *Whose glasses are these*? B: They're ***mine***. Possessive
pronouns replace the noun.

**2.3** Reflexive pronouns are used when the subject and the object of
the verb are the same person or thing, e.g. *Oh no! I've cut **myself**.
The washing machine turns **itself** off automatically.*

**2.4** Pronouns 'one'/'ones' are used to avoid repeating a countable
noun e.g. A: *Which cake?* B: *The big **one**, please...* or *I'd like some
trousers like the **ones** in the window.*

**2.5 Relative pronouns.** These 'relate' or link two parts of a sentence, e.g. (i) A lady called. She's here. To join these two sentences together we say, *The lady who/that called is here* ... Lady is subject – must use 'who/that'

## 3 Quantifiers tell us about the quantity or number.

**3.1 Articles** – look at the three types of article in the table below.

| Zero article | Indefinite article 'a'/'an' | Definite article 'the' |
|---|---|---|
| With plural and uncountable nouns | With singular nouns | With singulars, plurals and uncountable nouns |
| Meaning: unspecific/ general | Meaning: unspecific – new information/ first mention | Meaning: particular, common knowledge/old information |
| e.g. **I like peas and cheese (in general)** | e.g. **I've bought a car.** (We don't know which car) | e.g. **The car's here** (We know which car – the car you've bought) |

TIP: Some languages don't have articles so this can be a completely new area. Remember that a singular noun always needs something in front of it, e.g. the word 'hat' can be *a hat (general,) **the hat** (particular), **this hat** (demonstrative) or **her hat** (possessive)*, but there must be something in front of the noun.

**3.2** Other expressions of quantity, e.g.. **some/any/a little/anyone/ nobody.**

*Some people were late for the meeting because of the transport strike* (quantifier + noun). **Others** walked and got there on time (quantifier as pronoun + verb).

Tip: Remember to use a singular verb with *everyone/everybody and no-one/nobody.*

# 4 Adjectives – these words give information about a noun

**4.1 Ordinary adjectives** go in front of the noun, e.g. *a young girl*.

They don't change in English, i.e. We don't add 's' to the adjective with a plural noun, e.g. *Two expensive rings*.

## 4.2 The order of adjectives

Look at the categories below with the three examples.

|      | Personal evaluation | size | Shape/ | Quality/ colour | Origin | Material |   |
|------|---------------------|------|--------|-----------------|--------|----------|---|
| A    | beautiful | large | oval |  | French | beech | dining table |
| Some | amazing | small |  | brown | forest |  | mushrooms |
| The  |  | King size |  | white | Egyptian | cotton | sheets |

## 4.3 Comparative and superlative adjectives

### Comparative adjectives

e.g. *1. She's younger than Paul* (short adjective = adj + '*er*' + *than*). *2. This restaurant is more expensive than the other one* (long adjective = **more** + adjective + **than**).

### Superlative adjectives

e.g. *La Paz is the highest capital in the world* (short adjectives = 'the' + adj. with 'est').

*This is the most frightening film I've ever seen* (long adjectives = **the** + **most** + adjective).

**Form – two syllable adjectives.** Some use -er/est for the comparative and superlative, e.g. *lovely, lovelier, the loveliest*. Others use more/most + adjective, e.g. *famous, more famous, the most famous*.

TIP: If in doubt, use the long form.

Some comparatives and superlatives are irregular: e.g. *good, better, best and bad, worse, worst.*

TIPS: **1** To compare three or more things, use the superlative.

> **2** The pronunciation of the 'a' in 'than' is the same as the second 'a' in the word 'Africa'.

**5 Verbs** are the spine of the English language. They tell us about action or situation and time.

### 5.1 Verb tenses

There are 12 tenses in English, 4 present tenses, 4 past tenses and 4 future tenses. Each of these groups has a simple tense:

Present simple: I **swim** a lot.

Past simple: I **went** to Africa last year.

Future simple: **I'll** see you tomorrow.

To these 3 base tenses we can add one or two extra pieces of information about the action or situation

### 5.1.1 Continuous/progressive tenses

One piece of extra information we can show in the verb is that the action or situation continues over time. To do this we use **a continuous/progressive tense.**

e.g. **Present continuous**, e.g. *Daniel's (= is) **using** the computer.* This action is happening 'now' or 'around now'.

**Past continuous**, e.g. *At 10:00 last night Barbara **was watching** television.* This action continued over time in the past.

**Future Continuous**, e.g. *At this time tomorrow **I'll be taking** my driving test.* This action will continue over time in the future

Form of the 6 Progressive Tenses: verb 'be' in the appropriate tense + verb – ing

## 5.1.2 Perfect tenses

The other piece of information we can show in the verb is that with a perfect tense, we make a connection between two points in time e.g. I've cut the grass, i.e. the speaker is looking for a reaction in the present about his/her past action of cutting the grass. e.g. **present perfect** – *I've (have) made* some cakes (past action/present result) The next sentence may be about the cakes e.g. *'Would you like one?'*

**Past Perfect** – e.g. *When we got to the cinema the film **had started**.* This is like a double past – an action before another action in the past, used for looking back from the second action to the first. We're looking back from 'getting to the cinema' to the film starting, which happened before we arrived.

**Future Perfect** – e.g. *By the time I get home, everyone **will have gone** to bed.* This tense looks back from a point in the future (getting home) to a connected action before it (everyone going to bed).

Form of the 6 perfect tenses: verb 'have' in the appropriate tense + Past Participle.

## 5.1.3 Perfect continuous progressive tenses

Lastly we can combine both the 'continuous' form for 'happening over time' and the perfect form for showing a connection between two points in time. These are the three 'perfect continuous tenses'.

**Present perfect progressive**, e.g. *I've (=have) been working in the garden for three hours* – an action that started in the past and has continued up to now.

**Past Perfect Progressive**, e.g. *I was tired because I'd been studying* – looking back from a situation in the past (I was tired) to the action before that caused it (I'd been studying).

**Future Perfect Progressive, e.g.** *When we arrive in Australia next Wednesday, we'll have been travelling for 24 hours* – Looking back from the time of arriving in Australia, which is in the future, to the action of 'travelling' which will continue up to that time.

TIP: As languages vary greatly in the number of tenses and their meanings, learning to use English tenses correctly can take time. To help you decide which tense to use, ask yourself these questions about the action or situation:

**a** when? – use a past, present, or future.
**b** over time? No = use a simple tense. Yes = use a continuous tense.
**c** Showing a connection/between two points in time Yes = use a perfect tense.
**d** both over time and Yes – use a perfect continuous tense.

### 5.2 Modal auxiliary verbs

Showing a connection between two points in time Modal auxiliary (helping) verbs go between the subject and main verb. They tell us about:

ability –  My son **can** play the guitar.
probability – We **might** go on holiday next month.
requests  – **Could** you open the door for me please?
obligation – You **have to** turn left here.
prohibition – You **mustn't** say that!
advice – You **should** give her a call
condition – If we won the lottery, **we'd (would)** go round the world.

TIP

Don't put 'to' after a modal e.g. *I should go* – I should to go X.

We also use modals to deduce from evidence or knowledge.

e.g. *The two people in the photo* **might be** *brother and sister. They look alike.*
*They* **must be going** *on holiday tomorrow – their car is fully loaded.*
*I* **must have left** *my glasses at home. They're not in my pocket.*
Past = modal + *have* + past participle.

## 5.3 The passive

We use the passive when the 'receiver' of the action has more importance than the person doing the action.

e.g. *Shopping* **is delivered** *free of charge.*

*Food and medical supplies* **are being sent** *to the disaster area.*

Form: '**Be**' in the appropriate tense + **Past participle** of the main verb.

The passive is common in formal written English such as formal letters, reports, books and technical documents.

A reduced passive is used in headlines e.g. *Election* **won** *by the Democrats.*

To include (the 'doer'),  use the preposition 'by' e.g. *The President was* **attacked** *by a tall man in his thirties.*

## 5.4 Multi-word verbs (also known as phrasal verbs)

Multi-word verbs are a verb + particle that changes the meaning of the verb.

There's a large number of phrasal verbs in English. They are informal and therefore common in spoken English.

There are 4 types:

**1** *My car's* **broken down**. – intransitive, i.e. no object.
**2** Can you *turn* the TV *on, please?*

Or

*Can you **turn on** the TV please?* This is a little more formal.
With pronoun = *Can you **turn it on**.* Can you turn on it? X

3  *I'll look **after the children*** – no change of order with pronoun = *I'll look **after them**.* I'll look them after X

4  *I can't **put up with** her shouting any more* – 2 particles. With pronoun, no change of word order – *I can't put **up with** it any more.*

TIPS

1  The particle can sometimes give an indication of the meaning, e.g (i) *In* = a movement in – *Join **in** when you're ready.*

2  Pronunciation: The stress is usually on the particle e.g. *Turn it **off**.*

With 2 particles, stress the first one. e.g. *I can't put **up** with this any more!*

**6 Adverbs** describe or add to the meaning of a verb or adjective. They tell us the manner, place or time of the action or how often it happens.

**6.1** Adverbs can be one word e.g. *She sings **beautifully*** (i.e. adjective + ly) or a phrase, e.g. *They come to the club **every week**.*

**6.2** Adverbs with adjectives

Adverbs give extra meaning to adjectives:

e.g. *This book is **really interesting**.*

*Paul's **unbelievably fluent** in French.*

**7 Prepositions**, e.g. *at the bank, before 1.00, to the supermarket, it's for you* – are words that tell us about place, time, directions and purpose, etc.

**7.1** Many verbs are followed by a particular preposition, e.g. *to believe in something, to suffer from an illness, to congratulate someone on something.*

**7.2** Prepositions are also used in many fixed expressions, e.g. *at home, in hospital, for example.*

**7.3** When a verb follows a preposition, add -ing to the verb e.g. *Please lock the door before leaving.*

TIP

Prepositions are known for giving learners problems. If a verb takes a preposition, try to learn both together.

**8 Conjunctions** – (Con+ junction) These words and phrases link two parts of a sentence, one sentence to another or one paragraph to another.

**8.1** Conjunctions signal addition, contrast, result, an opposing view. etc.,

e.g. (i) Addition  *He opened the door **and** saw that the window was open.*
(ii) Contrast: *My sisters went to the party **but/whereas** I stayed at home.*
(iii)  Result: *She had a free day **so** she went to the beach.*

TIP

Learning to use conjunctions is an important part of writing well in English.

# Index